Paul Foster Case
His Life
and Works

Dr. Paul A. Clark

First Published in 2013 by
The Fraternity of the Hidden Light
P.O. Box 5094
Covina, CA 91723
U.S.A.

Library of Congress Cataloging-in-Publication Data

ISBN 978-0-9710469-4-8

Printed in the United States of America

Cover Art: Joseph Sherman
Photo of Jesse Burns Park courtesy of Charles Lee McLaughlin

ACKNOWLEDGEMENTS

This work is dedicated to Ron Ferrara, that gentle soul whose dedication, research, and friendship made this book possible.

I would like to express my appreciation also to Dee and J.B. Morgan for their friendship and support, to my sons Richard and Michael (I'm so proud of you guys!) And, finally to the other six Stewards of the Work; Patti, Joanne, Ken, Linda, Melvin, and Tom. It's been a long journey, but perhaps we did, in our small way, change the world for the better. S.U.A.T.

Finally, I would like to thank my mate (and editor) Cindy, for her love, support, and encouragement. She is the most dedicated and selfless initiate I know.

CONTENTS

CONTENTS

A Personal Perspective

In the spring of 1975, I received an early morning phone call from my much-beloved mentor, Eugene Emard. He was, at the time, serving as the Grand Cancellarius or Secretary/Archivist for the Grand Chapter of the Builders of the Adytum. He had taken me "under his wing" more than a decade before, when I had been selected as a group leader for B.O.T.A. in Tulsa, Oklahoma. He stated that William Chesterman, the Prolocutor-General (Executive/Teaching Head) of the Order, wanted to see me if I was available later that morning.

I was both excited and apprehensive. Since the passing of Ann Davies and subsequent resignation of Jacob Fuss, her successor, I had been working with the next Prolocutor-General, Reverend Chesterman very closely. We had been looking through the Order's archives, cataloging and preserving them for the future. He had appointed me as the General Manager of the organization just months before.

In this position I organized, expanded, and combined the libraries of Paul Case, Ann Davies and the Headquarters, and had installed it in the upstairs of the B.O.T.A. Temple, where it was to be accessible as a research resource for serious students.

Here I met Ron Ferrara, who was one of our employees. As general manager, I appointed Ron to the position of librarian. I tasked him with the job of organizing the materials and preparing for us to write a history of the Order. Much of this book is a result of Ron's tireless research.

He would regularly submit to me results on this project with the end that I would provide the "writing" and when completed we would release this material to the public. But not everyone at B.O.T.A, however, was enthusiastic about having an accurate re-telling of the life of Paul Case. Some looked on Paul as their own private domain and wanted to limit his fame to the organization. Others, to be honest, really thought it would lead to the formation of a Personality Cult. And still others thought an accurate biography would reveal the foibles of their founder.

Following the resignation of Ann's widower Jacob Fuss, and the ratification of the Second Order, Will Chesterman (previously Grand Prolocutor) assumed the role of Prolocutor General. But his succession was far from secure. A group of chapter members, along with a faction of non-initiates, were simultaneously promoting their own agendas. All of these issues were on my mind as I drove to the meeting, which is described under the heading, "The Secret Meeting." I communicate them only now because I pledged to Chesterman and Emard to wait until after their deaths to do so. To ensure privacy, it was decided to the hold the meeting at Ann's little house rather than at the headquarters on Figueroa Street.

I want to emphasize the debt we owe Ron Ferrara. Without his dedicated assistance and research this work could not have been completed.

Who was Paul Case?

Adepts come into incarnation to assist humanity in their evolutionary destiny to achieve full potential of divine co-creatorship. They are rare, but they also have to deal with the many restrictions and limitations of being human. This narrative summary of Paul Case's life and work, punctuated with letters and words of people who knew him, is an attempt to paint a portrait of this great soul. His contributions to the esoteric, mystical tradition of the twentieth century are incalculable.

His dedication to the mission was the highest. The motivation for this dedication was always clear—service; service to humanity, service to the tradition, and service to the aspirant who came to him and to Truth. Through his writings he has directed students along the Path of Awakening, guided them to Initiation and Self-fulfillment (I am personally in his debt more than I could hope to communicate).

Yet, as was mentioned previously, he was a human being, with faults, frustrations and trials. One of the purposes of this work is to afford the reader a realistic glimpse of the man; to unveil the illusion that Adepts are perfect and have risen above the tests of the Path. Paul was human, but filled with inspiration. An inspiration of how one (using dedication) may achieve greatness through unselfish service.

Here truly is the life of an Initiate. One who desired to know in order to serve.

Sub Umbra Alarum Tuarum...

Paul A. Clark
Vernal Equinox, 2013.

The Secret Meeting

There have been many questions and assertions about how I came upon the source material for this book, as well as the other materials that form the foundation of the initiated section of The Fraternity of the Hidden Light. I hope this narrative will fully explain that mystery.

After the passing of Dr. Paul Case in 1954, Ann Davies assumed the role of Prolocutor General of the Builders of the Adytum, one of the foremost esoteric teaching organizations in the world. After her passing in 1975, the position was again open.

Although Ann named her husband, Jacob Fuss, to succeed her, he only stayed in the position for about six months. Jacob was pressed by several factions to step down, and eventually he did just that. At that same time, various individuals in the organization were determined to influence the decision as to who would ultimately fill the open position of Head of the Order. The movement was led by B.O.T.A.'s attorney, whose wife had ambitions to be the new Ann Davies. An office worker at the Los Angeles headquarters also coveted the position. Jacob resigned because of health issues, and because of the pressure being exerted by these individuals.

B.O.T.A.'s senior initiates unanimously elected William Chesterman to assume the office of Prolocutor General, but this did not stop the lawyer and the clerk from continuing to maneuver for the position. The Grand Chiefs began to fear that, for the first time since its founding, if Chesterman was forced out, the Order could be controlled by "non-initiates" who had not received the training of the grade systems, persons that had not been selected by the Inner School, in other words.

During this same period of turmoil I was appointed to the position of General Manager of the B.O.T.A. office. Previously, I had been named by Ann as one of the Seven Stewards, a group she trained as future successors (none of the individuals are now members of B.O.T.A.).

In the summer of 1976, in the midst of these events, I received a phone call one Saturday morning from Eugene Emard, the Grand Cancellarius or Secretary of the Grand Lodge. He informed me that the Prolocutor General, Will Chesterman, wanted to see me as soon as possible up at the "little house," a reference to the house Ann Davies had lived in. I drove there directly.

When I arrived, I was met by both Emard and Chesterman. They explained to me that there was a very real possibility that B.O.T.A. was going to be taken over by non-initiates. They pointed to three very large boxes and explained that they each contained reproductions of all the archival material and initiated material of the Order. The original, they explained was located in a bank vault in downtown Los Angeles. One of the copied sets was going to the library at B.O.T.A. headquarters while another was destined to be shipped to the Headquarters in New Zealand.

I asked, "What about the third set?"

I was informed that it was to go to me. I was then told that, if in my opinion, circumstances occurred whereby I thought it was best, I had dispensation to found the Order anew, using the material. This I pledged to do. Aware of the great responsibility and confidence they were placing in me, I vowed that I would to the best of my ability perform the duty if necessary.

In the years that followed, I became a target for these same disruptive individuals. Accusations were made, most of them false. But I was young and arrogant and I did nothing to try to "douse the flames." Instead I fed the fire with my own self-righteousness. The result was my expulsion from Builders of the Adytum. In 1982, I founded the Fraternity of the Hidden Light using my experience and the materials entrusted to me by the Head of the Order.

Ironically, five years later, those same divisive members at B.O.T.A were themselves expelled. For a time, I considered reapplying to B.O.T.A., but by then the Fraternity of the Hidden Light had several operating groups for whom I was responsible. We also had successfully established a link with the Third Order.

As it turned out, Will Chesterman continued as Prolocutor General until his death. This book is based on archival material found in that box, given to me by Chesterman and Emard, acting under the dispensation I received those decades ago. I am making this material available now to those sincere students who, I hope, will benefit.

Paul A. Clark
Steward of the Fraternity of the Hidden Light

Editor's Note

A variety of sources were used to complete this work, including but not limited to: summaries from Paul Case's notebooks, letters and correspondence between Case and other members of the Alpha et Omega and B.O.T.A., and Ann Davies' lectures. Much of the information contained in this book is recorded in various B.O.T.A. or F.L.O. publications. Many of the stories are interpretations based on Dr. Paul Clark's memory of the words of Ann Davies. Wherever possible direct sources have been quoted. This book focuses on Dr. Case's mystical life and achievements. It is meant to be a compilation of other published works, recorded in one place, for the first time.

Chapter 1
The Child Prodigy

Paul Foster Case's life is a tale of magical, mystical moments, and profound insights. He is one of the most accomplished, erudite and still down to earth and understandable esoteric teachers of the twentieth century.

Paul Foster Case was one of the primary figures in the American section of the Rosicrucian Order of the Alpha et Omega (the branch of the Hermetic Order of the Golden Dawn that remained loyal to S.L. MacGregor-Mathers) yet his name rarely appears in the many histories of this famous mystical Order. Why?

Perhaps a clue to his "invisibility" is revealed in a letter written to Case by the famous mystic, Freemason, and fellow initiate, Arthur Edward Waite. In the early 1930's, Waite asked, "What books have you written?" By this time Case had composed volumes of material on subjects ranging from Occult Psychology, Tarot, Qabalah, Esoteric Healing, Alchemy, and the Rosicrucian Order. Indeed, he rivaled and surpassed most of his better known English brethren. But, as he explained to Waite, "Most of my writing has been in the form of lessons."

In fact, over a thirty-year period (approximately 1920–1950), Case wrote dozens of courses directly for the affiliates of the organization, The Builders of the Adytum. While in the opinion of this author they comprise absolutely the best, most well-rounded course of instruction of these esoteric subjects, their distribution has been limited to the members of this organization. For this reason, much of Case's writings have remained in this limited audience (these courses are still available to the interested student through B.O.T.A., Los Angeles. See appendix).

Recently some of Paul Case's earlier writings, now in the public domain, have been published creating a renewed interest in this great soul. It is hoped that this account of his life and works will yield insight into the story of this fascinating Adept.

*   *   *   *   *

Dolores Ashcroft Norwicki, the Director of Studies of The Servants of the Light, has commented that some individuals come into embodiment with an insatiable hunger for the knowledge of the hidden meanings of life. This was certainly true of Paul Foster Case.

Dr. Case was born on October 3, 1884, in Perendor (now known as Fairport) New York, just outside of Rochester. His father, Charles Case, was himself a New York native. His mother, Ella Foster, born in Wisconsin, was a descendant of gypsies and an ancestor of the famous puritan pilgrim Miles Standish.

Charles Case served as the curator and librarian of a large private library. Ella was a local school teacher. Together they provided a stable and loving environment for young Paul, rich in education and guidance. As a matter of fact, it has often been said that Dr. Case was literally, "born among books."

According to oral tradition, Paul began to read somewhere between the ages of 2 and 3. As a preschooler he could often be found curled up in the attic of his father's library, closely examining "forbidden books" of esoteric lore. At that young age he most likely didn't understand much of their content, but as his zealous studies continued throughout his childhood, he gained a great deal of knowledge.

Ella Case was widely read and highly educated. She tutored young Paul to the end that he, at a very early age, developed an extraordinary command, not only of English, but also of Latin and Greek. A child prodigy musically, he also had an exceptionally gifted musical talent. By the age of nine, he was the regular organist for the congregational church in which his father was Deacon.

This early exposure to the workings of the church provided a "behind the scene" look at organized religion and influenced Case's views on the "church" for the rest of his life. Young Case had little patience for the hypocrisy he felt he frequently observed. According to his successor Ann Davies, if it hadn't been for his early spiritual endeavors, he might have become an atheist.

Paul's father was a steadfast, fundamentalist Christian. As such, he had strong ideas about right and wrong, correct behavior and sin. Many activities considered mundane by today's standards, were viewed as instruments of the devil in the Case home. For example, "standard playing cards" were deemed sinful vehicles of vice by Charles.

Fortunately, his eldest son, Paul, had a strong personality and, like many young people, rebelled against many of his father's limiting opinions. Paul secretly bought a deck of cards, as well as a variety of books on sleight-of-hand and card tricks. These first independent steps, and rejection of outward arbitrary pronouncements, would lead Dr. Case to become one the world's greatest authorities on the Tarot.

Often his family would escape the severe New England winters by vacationing in Nassau in the British West Indies. These experiences not only broadened Paul's views of the world, but also supplemented his otherwise limited cultural exposure. The exotic climate would later hold a fond place in his memories. Often Paul would reminisce about how the meals cooked by their chef Dillett would be brought to them carried in great baskets, balanced on the head "of the blackest boy on earth," and kept hot by little pans of live coals.

These winter sojourns exposed Paul to the religion and culture of another country, a more romantic, evocative world. He stated frequently that he was not afraid of magic as he had studied and observed firsthand the power of some of the practices of Obeah, as the native religion was called.

Paul's mystical experiences started early in life. By the age of seven, young Paul found he could consciously manipulate his dream states by making objective selections. Looking for validation of these events, Paul wrote to the famous Freemason and author Rudyard Kipling *(left)*, the author of *Kim, The Man who would be King*, and *The Jungle Books*. Kipling assured Case of the reality of these inner states and verified the legitimacy of these "fourth dimensional" experiences. Thus was established an inspiring friendship and correspondence between these kindred souls.

Once, while shopping with his mother, Paul had a sudden feeling that his inner reality was shifting. First, it appeared to young Paul as though

9

everything in the world was "outside" of himself. Then his perception "flipped" and he discovered that the entire universe was actually inside of him. To Paul, it was a new and "total" reality. Later Ann Davies would share with a group of students that this personal experience led to Case's unshakable belief in the unity of all things.

Case would have many such spiritual occurrences in his early years. Frequently he felt that his consciousness would "turn inside out" as he described it. His center of Selfhood, instead of being inside his body, was an all-encompassing periphery surrounding the entire universe.

Paul's love of cards, sleight-of-hand, magic and illusion, led him, in his teens, to perform at several local exhibitions. He was quite skilled and his shows were well received. At age sixteen, while performing at a local charity event, he met author and occultist Claude Bragdon *(right).* Claude Fayette Bragdon was a resident of Rochester and one of the nation's leading architects. He was also the author of numerous popular books on mystical themes, such as *Old Lamps for New, The Eternal Poles, More Lives than One*, and others.

Backstage, between shows, Paul and Claude were entertaining each other by sharing card tricks. As Paul finished a trick, Bragdon turned to him and asked, "Case, where do you suppose the playing of cards came from?" The question struck Paul like a lightning bolt. Case would later relate, "It was as though an inner explosion had taken place." Truly, that simple query propelled Case into a lifelong quest into the mysteries of the Tarot. Bragdon and Case remained friends until the former's death in 1948.

Soon after that exchange, Case combed the local the libraries, patiently sifting through the written history of cards. He quickly discovered that at that time very little had been written on the subject. Paul also found that much of what was published contained blinds, myths, and gaps. If not for his inner determination, Case could have easily have become discouraged.

Eventually Paul found mention of the Tarot in a variety of texts including the famous 17th century Rosicrucian Manifesto, "Fama

Fraternitatis." Here, he discovered that the name, "Tarot" is actually a cipher for the Latin word "ROTA" or wheel. In other writings, Case learned that this ancient esoteric system was originally referred to as "The Game of Man," by early occultists. and that playing cards were fashioned from this intriguing set of designs.

Filled with questions, Paul collected every available book on Tarot. Where did the Tarot come from? What was the origin of the Tarot? How does the. deck work? Why? Case spent every spare moment looking for the answers.

During his research, Case would stare at the cards for hours, unconsciously entering into a meditative reverie. What he didn't know at the time was that the symbology of the Tarot is designed to stimulate the deep consciousness, expanding it into new levels of awareness. His attentive questing for the true meaning of the Arcana did what it was created to do, Paul was systematically transformed.

These expansions of consciousness were so profound that they literally altered the course of his life. This great awakening did something else significant. Paul Case began to hear an inner voice.

The Voice of Wisdom

Even in his teens Paul Case was no stranger to modern psychological theory. Through classes and extensive reading he was quite familiar with psycho-pathologies. Thus, he knew his "voice" was something to avoid sharing with others. In his day, people who heard voices were generally confined to mental institutions. Fortunately, being a rather reserved person, keeping quiet wasn't difficult for Paul. Regardless, he believed the voice to be a manifestation of his own subconscious mind.

Paul noted that his internal voice differed in several important ways from the typical delusional voices of psychosis. First, it didn't flatter his ego. It didn't say, "You have been chosen for a great mission." It didn't demand obedience or interfere with his personal life. The voice never gave him orders. Those who are mentally ill often describe voices that command or isolate. *His* inner teacher did neither. Moreover, personal experience with his inner voice provided a "question and answer" framework that he would use years later to guide thousands of students through the pitfalls of self-delusion.

11

The "voice" also assisted Paul with many esoteric endeavors. For instance, when Case conducted research at the Library the voice would often direct his studies. He would hear something like, "If you will reach for the third book from the left on the top shelf, and turn to page ___ you will find the reference you are looking for," or "if you look at a particular author's book on the top shelf and turn to page ____ in the third paragraph you will find the commentary, quotation, or attribution you need to clarify the ancient translation you are now studying." Invariably, when the instructions were followed, the prompting proved correct.

This Inner Voice guided Paul for years to come. As we all know, youthful exuberance and naivety can often lead to awkward or uncomfortable situations. When this would happen to Case the Voice would speak up and gently chide him, saying, for example, "Now wasn't that rather foolish?"

Case was, as previously mentioned, quite well-read in the theories of Freud and Jung, thus he assumed this inner voice phenomena to be a manifestation of his own subconscious mind. It even became a source of pride for him. How well he must be doing in his studies and meditations if his subconsciousness is cooperating and integrating with his self-conscious mind!

When we review his notebooks and diaries, we see that for years Case made a daily habit of researching, meditating on, and studying the Tarotic symbols. Indeed, Paul discovered that the designs of these pictorials actually channels and evokes specific archetypical energies, thereby transforming the consciousness of the seeker into that of an illuminated adept.

Throughout his life, Case was fond of quoting the 19th century mystic Eliphas Levi *(right)*, who wrote:

"As an erudite Kabalistic book, all combinations of which reveal the harmonies preexisting between signs, letters, and numbers, the

12

practical value of the Tarot is truly and above all marvelous. A prisoner, devoid of books, had he only a tarot of which he knew how to make use, could, in a few years, acquire a universal science and converse with unequaled doctrine and inexhaustible eloquence."

Case would devote most of his life to helping earnest students learn how "to make use" of this extraordinary system.

Chapter 2
Past Life as a Rabbi

Although Case was born of mostly Christian, New England stock, he was unaccountably drawn at an early age to the Kabalah, the mystical tradition of the Jews. As he progressed in his studies, he soon found that all he needed to do was review the Hebrew alphabet in order to know the meanings of most Hebrew words. It was as if, Case would later relate, "He was remembering the ancient language."

This faculty was of course a great resource when studying the Kabalah and the Kabalistic texts. As Ann Davies once suggested, "the very fact that he had this ability to almost immediately pick up something that should have required much study, would in itself, indicate that there was a past incarnation in which it had already been learned." Confirmation of this fact came dramatically.

Around the age of 23, Case entered a meditative state and suddenly experienced the following:

While engrossed in the many attributions between the symbols of the Tarot and the Kabalistic Tree of Life Case found that instead of being Paul Case, he had become the Jewish, Kabalistic Rabbi Wolff of 18th century Poland. He was sitting in his study pouring over the treatise, The Sepher Yetzirah. The right hand side of the text was in Hebrew, while a literal translation in Latin was on the left page. Amazingly, he was able to read both languages perfectly. Unfortunately, he felt distracted and unable to concentrate. His attention kept wandering back to his daughter, Rebecca. She was already sixteen years old and rapidly approaching spinsterhood; a serious problem! How would she provide for herself in her old-age if she didn't marry? He knew he needed to make a match for her, but he would also have to provide a suitable dowry. As a Rabbi in a very poor community that was going to be difficult. He turned the problem over and over in his mind. In the midst of his anxiety, he again became Paul Case. But now he had the full recollection of his earlier life as a Rabbi.

The meditation was so vivid, so real, that Paul knew without a doubt that he had been this other person. Not only did he retain the memories of this other existence, but he was aware of all the details, concerns, worries, emotional stresses, and attachments that are so much a part of daily life.

As Ann Davies expressed it to her Thursday night class, "He was aware of those little factors that human beings are always aware...their sense of 'I.'"

Harriet Case would later share with this author that Paul frequently visited one of the libraries at the University of Illinois in Campaign/Urbana. One day he related this personal mystical story to a librarian there (who was also a friend). While telling his tale, the friend looked up at Paul abruptly and asked him what the title of the book had been. Paul answered that it was a bilingual translation, Latin-Hebrew, "a book from my own library."

His friend then explained that the library had just received a bequest from an estate that contained many rare books and manuscripts. "There is one or two in Latin," he explained, "that look like they would be old enough to fit into that time period. Let's take a look."

He retrieved a key and dispatched one of his assistants to go down to the rare book vault and bring out the book under discussion. Once it was found, Paul's colleague asked, "Do you remember any additional details that would help authenticate the book?"

Case readily responded with the page number of the passage he had been reading. He also explained that the text related to a particular aspect of the Kabalah and that in his vision he had made a note in the margin.

His friend turned to the indicated page and began reading to Paul in Latin. "Is this the text?" he asked Case. Paul answered, "My God, yes." There were also notes in the margin, just as Case had mentioned. When they turned to the back of the book they saw Rabbi Wolff's name and a date from the 1700's.

During the winter of 1972, this author was on assignment with the United States Air Force at Chanute Air Force Base, near Champaign/Urbana. I decided to visit the University campus and to do some research at the library. I specifically remember seeing an entry in their rare book catalogue for a Latin/Hebrew translation of "The Sepher

Yetzirah," published in 1570. Although I did not see the actual book, I can verify it was in the collection, a significant fact given that this story was relayed to me several years later.

Chapter 3
Yoga in Chicago

During his early twenties, Paul, as his journals reveal, kept himself to a very rigid, self-disciplined regimen. He worked daily with the Tarot and the Tree of Life, and he maintained a strict vegetarian diet. His journals also reveal that at this time he started experimenting with various Yogic Pranayama techniques (breathing and meditation).

A copy of *The Gheranda Sanhitu* (purchased in New York in 1905) found in his library, reveals that Paul methodically tried over twenty exercises, each of which he checked off in the margin. *The Law of the Rhythmic Breath,* which he procured in Chicago in 1908 (also in his library), contains another fourteen exercises Case practiced. Unfortunately, Paul did not realize the significance of his Gypsy blood (and his corresponding sensitive, psychic vehicles) and didn't foresee the effects these experiments would have on his consciousness. He later realized that, for him, these exercises were foolhearty, as he would caution his hundreds of students in his later years. He, indeed, had opened wide the doors of perception.

Pranayama is an advanced component of both Hatha (physical) and Raja (meditative) Yoga. It appears that Case was largely self-taught, using as we have discussed, various published sources. His "success" in these practices activated his inner sensorium and psychic vehicles. Case also learned through his readings to attune his consciousness to subtle, lower astral levels and influences. Conversely, his studies neglected to instruct Paul how to control, limit, or protect himself from unwanted psychic intrusions. Later, he would relay this story of an incident of intolerable sensitivity.

One day, while riding on a bus, he received the "paranoid" impression that he was surrounded by rapists, murderers, arsonists, and thieves. Obviously, this was not the case, but Paul had unintentionally tuned into the basest level of the "mob-consciousness" of all who had previously ridden that bus.

Shaken, Case fled the vehicle. His Inner Voice instructed him to go to a restaurant and order a large piece of rare steak! Case promptly followed this direction and the meat effectively shut down his psychic senses until he could reestablish his equilibrium.

To follow-up and control his oversensitivity, he would take at least two drinks before dinner. And to desensitize rapidly, he started eating large amounts of garlic, which, incidentally, did nothing to promote his social life. Ultimately, Case realized vegetarianism was not for him and returned to adding meat-eating to his regimen.

Finally, what he discovered was that Pranayama, though an effective system for activating and increasing alternate states of perception, is not designed for use in Western culture, nor is it particularly suited for the Western type of mind and body. He also noted that his Tarot meditations did not have this limitation.

Chapter 4
Destiny's Crossroads

In the years 1909-1910 Paul was 25 years old. His life had settled into a strict routine.

He studied the Tarot diligently every day. He earned his living by playing the organ in several theatrical establishments in the Chicago area. He had a special route he took to the Swartz Theater where he regularly rehearsed and performed. He took the same streetcar at the same time so that he would always be punctual. Each day he would arrive at the stop 10 minutes before the streetcar was due to arrive.

One afternoon, as he waited for his ride, he was approached by a stranger. The man was well dressed and had refined manners. Without introducing himself, he spoke directly to Case:

From Ann Davies Thursday night class notes:

"I have been sent here by someone, my teacher, to meet you. Your name is Paul Foster Case. You were born in upper New York State. I also know you are here waiting on a streetcar to take you to your rehearsal, but you are actually ahead of schedule and do not have to be at the theater quite this early. You have about a half-hour before you need to go. Won't you wait and take the next streetcar? It will give you a little less rehearsal time, however, if you are interested, you could spend that time, sitting down with me in the park."

What would most people think of such a speech? Today in the twenty-first century we would assume the man had hacked our identity or was stalking us. But Paul was living in the early 1900's and life was quite different. Case didn't hesitate. He was nervous (he would admit later), but he acquiesced.

As they sat in the park, the man continued to present Paul with a list of personal facts, details of Case's own thoughts and experiences. Paul recognized the stranger as a person of exceptional powers of telepathy and knowledge of occult techniques. Below is a recorded excerpt from that unique conversation:

> "The reason I have told you these things is to let you know that I was requested by my teacher, who is a Master of Wisdom, to come here and deliver a message, a very special message. These things I have related to you because he told me what to say to gain your attention so you will know that he has knowledge of your comings and goings, thinking and doing since childhood. This is done so that you may give careful consideration to the message."

He had Paul's attention, as he continued:

> "The message is basically this: You have come to a crossroads in your life. At this point, you are now approaching a very important time where you could go in either one of two directions. If you go in one direction you will continue in your theatrical work, you will become relatively successful on the whole, though never famous in the musical field. You will never know any want. You will always be quite secure and have a pleasant, satisfactory and contented life, but you won't do any extraordinary amount of growing on the spiritual levels. However, if you choose the other path, you will be dedicating yourself to fully serve humanity and to play a vital part in its evolution for the coming Aquarian Age. Your life will be hard. You will eventually retire from the musical field. You will have many problems and disturbances. You will not have a very pleasant life because you will meet sorrow, disappointment and be subjected to forces difficult to withstand. Tests and trials will be with you throughout your incarnation. Sorrow will walk with you often. You will face many obstacles and have times when you feel utterly lost, completely alone. But you will be in a position to leave a treasure for humanity. You will be a channel or source through which untold thousands of human souls will be helped along the road to higher evolutionary levels and you will do a great deal more growing yourself spiritually. However, you will not receive any recognition or glory, anything that can be called

20

acknowledgement of your abilities while you are alive. The recognition of your contribution to the evolution of humanity will start to come only after you have left your physical body. All we can tell you is this: That we make no promises if you choose the hard road. We make no promises at all except to give help in every phrase of spiritual teaching. All we can say is that, hard though your life will be, in the final analysis, you will not starve to death, although it will surely look like it and more than once. Now I know you must go to your rehearsal."

He seemed to know the exact time.

The Unreserved Dedication

Essentially, Paul Case was being asked to take, what is known in the Mysteries as, the Unreserved Dedication; a commitment to utterly and inexorably make the spiritual path and service to humanity his first priority. To who is this dedication made? To the Higher Self. When a mystic decides to take this critical step there is no turning back. The dedication may not be revoked, ever.

Remember, Paul was only 25 at the time. He had his whole life ahead of him. How many of us would be ready to take such a pledge? His life would change dramatically no matter what decision he made. He stood at Destiny's Crossroads.

What choice did he make? The answer is obvious to any student of Dr. Case's teachings.

The stranger then introduced himself as Dr. Fludd, the chief surgeon of one of Chicago's major hospitals. Their friendship blossomed and they met one another afterwards on a regular basis.

Dr. Fludd instructed Case in various aspects of Occultism, just as he had received them from his own teacher. Paul found that following this meeting, he experienced a dramatic intensification of his inner, mystical life.

Chapter 5
The Three Initiates

In 1907, Case met William Walker Atkinson, author of the New Thought classic, *The Secret of Mental Magic.*

William Walker Atkinson

William Walker Atkinson (December 5, 1862 to November 22, 1932) was an attorney, merchant, publisher, and author. He was also a Yogi, occultist, Hermeticist, and a pioneer of the Unity School of New Thought Christianity founded by his colleague Charles Fillmore.

Due to his desire to keep his mundane careers separate from his mystical interests he made extensive use of pseudonyms. Thus much of his work is now largely forgotten. He did however author more than 100 books over a thirty year period and many of his works remain in print today.

Theron Q. Dumont, Swami Bhatkta Vishita, Swami Panchadisci, Theodore Sheldon, and Magus Incognito are just a few of the pen names Atkinson used. Writing under the name Yoga Ramacharaka, William authored no less than a dozen books on various aspects of Yogic philosophy and practice. These books may still be purchased through his Yoga Publication Society of Chicago, Illinois. They are considered by many to be the best and most easily readable introductions to these topics.

After reading, *The Secret of Mental Magic* (published in January, 1907), Paul contacted Mr. Atkinson. Case had been writing articles for the *New Thought* magazine to which Atkinson was a regular contributor. Most likely they met each other at one of the publisher hosted author receptions.

In the summer of that year, while performing in Chicago, Paul made numerous grammatical corrections to the text and showed them to Atkinson. William was impressed by Paul's clarity of thought and ease of expression and they soon became good friends. Together they conceived the idea for a book on general principles of Hermeticism and decided to call it, *The Kybalion*.

Philip Deslippe, in his book, *The Kybalion: The Definitive Edition*, states:

"The claim made on behalf of Case as a co-author of 'The Kybalion,' suffers greatly for the reliance on undocumented and unseen evidence, anonymous sources, and accounts of Atkinson that are riddled with factual errors..." [Page 24].

Well, I can assure Mr. Deslippe that Paul Case's longtime associate and successor Ann Davies related to this author that Dr. Case told her *personally* how he and Mr. Atkinson (and an unidentified third person) authored this book. Additionally, the same information was independently confirmed to this author by Paul Case's widow, Harriett.

Further support of their authorship is suggested in Case's journals which detail the decision to name the book, *The Kybalion*. According to these references the title is a synthesis of the words "Kabalah" and "On" as a reference to the Egyptian, Hermetic teachings of Alexandria. Additionally, according to Jacob Fuss, Ann Davies widower and successor, in the 1960's, the Yoga Publication Society proposed to republish *The Kybalion* with the authorship by line changed to just William Walker Atkinson. Builders of the Adytum, the organization founded by Paul Case, objected, and the publisher withdrew the project, instead continuing to attribute the work to "The Three Initiates."

While Atkinson and Case's involvement in the project is relatively well known, the identity of the "third initiate" remains a mysterious controversy. Some allege that the third initiate was simply Case's inner voice. Yet, at this time Paul still thought this phenomenon was a product of his own subconsciousness, making this explanation very unlikely. Other sources suggest that the unknown contributor was Dr. Fludd, whom we discussed in the previous chapter. Still others attribute the third authorship to one of Atkinson's students.

Harriett Case confided to this author that the third initiate was in fact, Michael Whitty, Paul's later-time mentor in the Alpha et Omega. However, some students will point out that, according to certain accounts in the Order, Paul did not meet Michael until after *The Kybalion* was published in 1912. Perhaps the dates cited in these accounts are inaccurate, perhaps not. I have not been able, as yet, to make that determination. I will, therefore, content myself with simply presenting the leading contenders.

The significance of the *The Kybalion* is that it sets forth, in easily understandable terms, an explanation of the seven great Hermetic principles, the so called, "Pillars of Hermes." 1) The Principle of Mentalism; 2) The Principle of Correspondence; 3) The Principle of Vibration; 4) The Principle of Polarity; 5) The Principle of Rhythm; 6) The Principle of Cause and Effect; and 7) The Principle of Gender.

It is interesting how these seven ancient principles are being adopted, with slight change, by today's theoretical physicists.

Chapter 6
The Tarot Revealed

As we have mentioned, Case studied the Tarot on a disciplined, daily basis. He assiduously followed any clue uncovered in study or meditation. Eventually Case began to record his discoveries in personal notebooks, one such being titled, *Day by Day*. These physical notations and commentaries were critical in developing his realizations in regards to the Tarot, many of which had direct impact on his own growth and development.

Paul would later record about this formative period:

"During those years when I was a musical director on tour with road shows, I had plenty of time for reading, reflection and study. Soon I discovered the writings of those two great occultists, Papus (Gerard Encausse) and Eliphas Levi (Alphonse Louie Constant), but their attributions did not satisfy me. So, I puzzled over the attributions, until I noticed that all Hebrew codices of the 'Sepher Yetzirah,' disagreed as to the planetary (the so-called double letters), but agreed as to the pairs of opposites assigned to the planetary letters."

He then continues:

"Then, it struck me that 0 logically precedes 1 in the numeral series and I tried out 'The Fool' [Tarot Key #0] to Aleph [the first letter of the Hebrew alphabet], 'The Magician' to Beth, and so on. This, of course, made the zodiacal attributions clear, for all copies of the 'Sepher etzirah' agreed as to these. For a while, the 'blind' of transposing 8

and 11 puzzled me, but the symbolism of 'Strength' so obviously corresponded to Leo, and that of 'Justice' to Libra, that I was sure that this was an intentional 'blind' for exoteric packs.

"Then I noticed that 'The Sun' fell to the pair of opposites 'Fruitfulness' and 'Sterility,' and I thought of the contrast between deserts and gardens, both produced by the Sun's rays. After this some consideration of Keys 1, 2, and 3 (The Magician, The High Priestess and The Empress) convinced me that they could be none other than Mercury, Moon, and Venus. And, The Tower was so obviously Martian that I had no difficulty. I reasoned that Jupiter is Lord of Wealth and that we are free or slave according to the use we make of Saturn's power of limitation.

"All this took several years, but when Waite published his pack and Key, I was delighted to find he had transposed 8 and 11, and in spite of his reticence, the change mattered greatly to me. So did his hints as to the placing of 'The Fool.'"

And, in another place:

"The symbolism of Mr. Waite's pack, which has just appeared, set me right about the cards for the signs Leo and Libra, and I had no difficulty in seeing that his Magician was Mercury, his High Priestess—the Moon, and his Empress evidently Venus. Symbols on the cards made this clear. But I was still undecided about Saturn, Jupiter and Mars, although it was evident enough that the Sun was represented by the 19th Tarot Key. As soon as the magazine article appeared, my doubts were set at rest, and though I have seen other attributions since, I am perfectly sure that in connection with the Hebrew Letters, the Tarot Keys represent the elements, planets and signs as they are

26

attributed in these lessons. I am the more certain, because I succeeded in locating all but three of the cards without any help or teachers, and then found my conclusions confirmed by the magazine article I have spoken of, (i.e. Waite's article in 'The Occult Review')."

Chapter 7
On the Road

According to Ron Ferrara's research and Paul Case's personal itinerary, starting in 1914 and for several years, Paul performed primarily in New York City as an orchestral director with the Keith-Slogel vaudeville circuit. At that time he was earning from $100 to $300 a week, which in those days, was considered quite a bit of money.

In 1917, America entered World War I. In that year Case played organ accompaniment to the ever popular silent motion picture. At the beginning of each performance, he would conduct an overture, which would then be followed by a vaudeville act. A newsreel would then show before the start of the feature film when Paul would again play the musical accompaniment on the organ.

Case wrote, "In the theatrical environment, as you may suppose, there was little encouragement to do occult work, and few persons to discuss the work with."

He relates, however, that this line of work enabled him to earn a nice living working only three hours a day. Most of his spare time was then spent at the public library. Here, he found an abundance of free resources for his researches.

He continued filling his notebook with copious notes detailing esoteric subjects. An analysis of these journals reveals a young man of 30 or so, passionately involved in a quest for mystical truth. Moreover, not only did his writings solidify his own revelations and understandings, but they also served to refine his technique and train his consciousness to properly transmit this knowledge to others.

With the guidance of his Inner Voice, he was entering a new phase of achievement.

We read from a 1914 journal:

Oct 26, 1914: "Make a collection of practical methods, jotted down in a notebook like this. Make a similar collection of illustrative material. See reference books on homiletics for this. In this collection paste all cuttings short enough to quote or rewrite. Also apt phrases and stories of people who have achieved. Another book as an 'aide memoire,' for letters and conversational uses."

Oct 29, 1914: "In formulating what you want; find out what you really do want—no greater mistake than making a picture of what you supposed to be the conditions that will give you what you want. The Creative Energy is <u>unconditioned</u> remember, and can express itself in any form."

Nov 7, 1914: "I must revert again to an idea that has been mentioned elsewhere in these pages. It is this: The One Spirit or Life is the Great Teacher. It works unremittingly to bring each of its personal expressions to self-realization, which, in its perfection, is Cosmic Consciousness, Nirvana, or the Kingdom of God. To each, in due season, it brings whatever lessons may be needed. Some of this teaching is from books. Some of it comes from conversation with enlightened men, and this is, perhaps, the most illuminating form of instruction, because God himself speaks through those who know him with a force and power greater than that which is expressed by any other means. Other lessons come through experience and through direct revelation."

On November 15th, Case comments in his journal on the process of channeling his Inner Voice:

"These jottings seem to be almost automatic. I am not conscious of any forethought. The words rise into my field of attention without any particular volition on my part. I am not stopping to think either about the matter or the form. Very likely the latter can be considerably improved in spots by revision. But I am constrained to think that whatever imperfections there may be are the result of my own personal interference with the dictation of the indwelling teacher.

"What utter foolishness this would be to the great majority: Sheer insanity-megalomania-paranoia. But it is what follows from combining the idea of God with the discoveries of psychology. If God

29

is omniscient, omnipotent and omnipresent—he must be the essential fact or reality of my life. He must be able to communicate any part of this perfect knowledge. Semi-automatic writing would be the ideal method. It can be accounted for by this.

1. Subjective mind is constantly amenable to suggestion.

2. The conception, hypothesis, or premise of an eminent, all-wise and all powerful being constitutes a powerful suggestion.

3. The subjective mind, accepting this suggestion can express Divine Wisdom through automatic writing."

Feb 5, 1915: "A set of hand drawn and hand colored Tarot cards with checkered backs. A design for such backs employing some symbolic geometrical arrangement."

Feb 12, 1915: "1. A Tarot Book I wish to write is one that will enable the general reader, who has heard nothing of the cards, to understand their theosophical meanings. This book is not intended to convert you to any system of religion or philosophy. My sole aim in writing it is to show what doctrine is concealed in the ingenious symbolism of the Tarot; to explain the manner in which that doctrine has been veiled from the profane; and to show some points of agreement between this doctrine and others that have preceded and followed it."

The next three selected entries are a glimpse of the profound insights Paul generated during this period:

Feb 26, 1915: "Is there anything unreasonable in supposing that if there is a God, He should be able to make his aims and nature known to men? For example, the Qabalistic calculations which I am so constantly engaged seem to be arbitrary. Yet they do bring knowledge to me. Is it too much to say that this knowledge is a revelation? Not a 'special' revelation, although there are doubtless many degrees of capacity for perceiving and expressing the truths imparted to man by

God, but a genuine revelation, all the same a communication of knowledge or wisdom to man by God Himself.

"Indeed I am inclined to think that all human discoveries are really direct revelation–that God thinks in man's minds–that Edison, for example, is a center of the divine knowledge about the possibilities of applied electricity and chemistry–that Wagner and Brahms are instruments for materializing the divine gift of music."

Mar 21, 1915: "The key to the correct interpretation of the Trumps Major is antithesis. Each of the Trumps is the antithesis of the one that precedes it."

Especially revealing is the entry of April 28, 1915 which was a communication in the form of "automatic writing" from his Inner Voice:

"Why are you trying so hard to master your circumstances? What reason have you for making all this strenuous effort to impose your will on men and things? What you need is to grasp the truth that you are, right now, the builder of your own conditions and place in the world.

"You are like a tapestry weaver, and what comes out of your loom is your own future. What you produce depends wholly on the pattern you are carrying in your head. When you have a beautiful pattern you can weave the threads of present action correctly. Nine out of ten people have no patterns. They don't know what they really want. So they fail.

"Cautious people seldom succeed as well as they might be expected to. In prudence is a twinge of fear that checks the highest manifestations of human power. That fine daring which throws caution to the winds without being fool hardy, is rare, but whoever exhibits it is always a success."

Case published his first articles on Tarot in January of 1916 and immediately attracted favorable attention. We read:

31

"Finally, in New York, Howard Percival of 'The Word' magazine lent a sympathetic ear, but manages to persuade me that swords are better symbols for fire than wands. So my maiden work on Tarot, published in 'The Word,' while it gave correctly the attributions of the major keys, was at fault in its attributions of the elements to the suits. 'The Word,' however, suspended publication before I had gone past my analysis of 'The Hanged Man.'"

In 1917, Paul had several communications with Harvey Spencer Lewis, the United States Imperator of the Ancient Mystical Order Rosae Crucis (AMORC). After attending a lecture at the then headquarters in New York City, Paul wrote a letter to Lewis on May 9th. In the letter he discussed the validity of certain facts relating to a numerical symbolism published by AMORC.

Spencer Lewis replied a few days later, assuring his critic of the authenticity of the attributions. He then continued with this interesting comment:

"I thank you for your compliment and assure you that so long as there is breath in my body, I will continue to concentrate my efforts on that very good part of the public which Lincoln said could be fooled all of the time. I hope thereby to someday enable them to rise upon that condition where they can no longer be fooled. Those, like yourself, who cannot be fooled, do not need our teachings or our help. With all good wishes for Peace Profound. Yours very truly, H.S. Lewis."

H. Spencer Lewis

In 1917, The United Stated entered the European War in support of the Allies. Case, believing it to be his patriotic duty worked for a little time in the office at a munitions factory. The armistice was signed in 1918.

During this year, Paul expanded his esoteric career. He met Michael Whitty, then founder and editor of *AZOTH*, a new occult magazine. He relates, "Michael opened to me the columns of AZOTH, and once more I published the attributions of the Major Trumps, and corrected the elementary attribution of the Minors."

Chapter 8
The Alpha et Omega

In 1918, Case was approached by a very tall, distinguished looking gentleman. The man explained to Paul that he was interested in Case's published Tarot attributions. After asking several questions the stranger affirmed to Case that his esoteric revelations were indeed correct. But, he also wondered at Case's possession of such knowledge, given that such information at the time was considered "secret" and transmitted only to those duly initiated. The man assumed that Case had either broken his own solemn vow or that someone else had. Case assured the gentleman that neither was true and that he had recovered these keys via his own meditation and research.

The mysterious individual was none other than Michael James Whitty, Cancellarius (Archivist) of Thoth-Hermes Temple #9 of the Order of the Alpha et Omega, and a later day version of the Hermetic Order of the Golden Dawn.

The Golden Dawn was founded in 1887 in London by three high grade Rosicrucian-Freemasons: William Woodman, William Wynn Westcott, and S.L. MacGregor-Mathers. Their ritual system was based on the legendary Cipher Manuscripts. [For more information see *The Secret Cipher of the Golden Dawn*, by Paul A. Clark and J.B. Morgan, Jr.]

Around the turn of the century, the original Order, due to personality conflicts, split into three splinter groups: The Stella Matutina, headed by Robert Felkin and W.B. Yeats; The Holy Order of the Golden Dawn under the direction of A.E. Waite; and, The Alpha et Omega which stayed loyal to MacGregor-Mathers.

It was this last section that had expanded into the United States nine years after the initial founding of the Golden Dawn. As Mathers said:

"It may do some good to extend to America this work for if we only gain ten adepts in one hundred years, we are doing much." [Address to Thoth-Hermes Temple #9, Boston, quoted in January 25, 1923].

Michael James Whitty

To his American Fraters and Sorors, Mathers was the Arch Magus, the unquestionable teacher and authority in Order matters. Elsa Barker, under the pen-name of "Chesed" gave the following account of Mathers in an obituary in the February, 1919 issue of AZOTH Magazine:

"S.L. MacGregor-Mathers had been a resident of Paris for many years, and he was one of the most interesting figures in that city of light and learning. His beautiful wife is a sister of the philosopher Henri Bergson. At their picturesque home in Auteuil on Sunday afternoons, they used to gather an interesting company: The Army, the Church, the ancient aristocracy of France, the world of art, the world of scholarship and letters were all represented, and there was generally a sprinkling of distinguished foreign visitors.

"Sometimes in summer, when the party gathered in the garden, the host would appear in his Scottish Kilt, looking twenty years younger than his age. On such occasions, he carried his learning lightly. A delightful storyteller, he was a great lover of laughter, and he was fond of saying that the occultist should always have some lighter interest, so as to not become one-sided. For prigs and pedants he had a special aversion, and never seemed happier than when surrounded by animals and children. For the little ones he had a collection of marvelous tales—simplified versions of the great myths whose deeper meanings he would patiently reveal to children of a larger growth. We used to smile at the length of his visiting list, for he found his 'lighter interest' in the social world. Many who knew him as a charming friend had only a vague idea of the deeds of his erudition, embracing subjects of whom the ordinary man and woman have never heard...he was never too busy or too weary to elucidate the mysteries of the Cabala."

Seven years elapsed between the time Thoth-Hermes received its warrant, and an actual working temple was formed. Ritualistic paraphernalia, such as the banners, scepters, pillars and officers' lamens first had to be acquired. It was therefore not until 1904, with Michael J. Whitty (Frater Gnoscente et Serviente) as Cancellarius, Mrs. Lockwood as Praemonstratrix, and Mr. Lockwood as Imperator, that the doors of

Thoth-Hermes Temple #9 were opened as an active First Order temple, conferring the grades 0=0 (Neophyte) through 4=7 (Philosophus).

By 1914, the transplant to America was complete with the establishment of the Second Order, "Ordo Rosae Rubeae et Aureae Crucis."

Israel Regardie

In his letter to Israel Regardie dated October 25, 1933, Case stated:

"Mrs. Lockwood, her husband and Michael Whitty (the three Chiefs) had the benefit of whatever magical knowledge was possessed by Elsa Barker, who is supposed to have earned the grade of 7=4. She knew S.M.R.D. (Mathers) and Vestigia (Moina Mathers) intimately, and made all her own magical weapons under their personal supervision. Thoth-Hermes Temple had some very fine members and there was great attention to detail in all the ceremonies. The Vault was beautifully executed, and Vestigia herself painted the lid of the pastos. Thus, the original Chiefs had direct instruction from Elsa and all the magical work was carried out in strict conformity to the methods used in Europe..."

Michael Whitty was, in many respects, the American counterpart of the English Magus, William Wynn Westcott. Whitty was described in AZOTH ["In Memoriam: Michael J. Whitty," by H. Kellet Chambers, Feb, 1921]:

"Born in 1862, he was the grandson and namesake of the Michael James Whitty who established the first penny newspaper in England, the Liverpool Daily Post. His grandfather stood 6' 3", his father 6' 2"; but Michael topped the family record, and ducked doubtful doorways, with 6'4" of frank winning manhood...He addressed legislatures and medical societies in support of movements to put an end to deliberate and harmful medical experimentation upon the poorer class of hospital patient."

He became a significant figure in the Theosophical Society and was elected President of the New York branch, a position he retained for many years, during which he did much lecturing. His book, *A Simple Study in Theosophy,* is justly regarded as the most readable and lucid shorter textbook extant on the subject.

It was not until some years after quitting the Theosophical Society and entering a more advanced field of study that Michael founded *AZOTH*. He had long dreamed of fathering a magazine which should be an impartial clearing house of spiritual, esoteric, and psychic research and at the same time should not let its own course deviate from the polestar of classical occultism, as handed down in the Western world since the time of Pythagoras.

When Case explained how he had discovered the true, secret keys of the Tarot, Whitty offered him initiation. As Case recollects:

"A little later Michael Whitty opened to me the columns of AZOTH, and once more I published the attributions of the Major Trumps and corrected the elementary attributions of the Minors. The first article appeared in October. By November, I was invited to be initiated into the Alpha et Omega."

In another place Case reminisces:

"My own motto was the somewhat ill-fated one, Perserverantia (Perseverance), and I was admitted to Thoth-Hermes Temple in November 1918. At that time Charles Lockwood (Heraclion) and his wife E. Daniel Lockwood (Pophra) were Imperator and Praemonstratrix, and my good friend (Gnoscente et Serviente) was Cancellarius. Charles Lockwood held an honorary 7=4. Lockwood himself took only the most perfunctory interest in the Order, and never became a master of its most rudimentary knowledge. His wife, who had been associated with W.Q. Judge in the Theosophical Society, interpreted all the work in terms of theosophy. Towards the end of the spring of 1920 they suddenly announced their resignations–at a meeting of Neophytes–alleging that certain work required in the higher grades was contrary to what they conceived to be their moral obligations. The truth is that friction had developed

between them and the Cancellarius, to which I must admit having contributed, inasmuch as I supported Whitty in his contention that the Kabalah, of which Pophra knew little, and her husband nothing, is not to be confused with Madame Blavatsky's doctrines. And I fear that I asked a good many embarrassing questions of Pophra, who until my arrival, had been a center for a little circle of admiring worshippers."

Case continues:

"Well, Thoth-Hermes weathered that storm, Whitty became Praemonstrator, Vota Vita Mea (Howard Underhill) was appointed Cancellarius, and Whitty's sister, and Mrs. Tom Wise (Non Mihi Solum) was made Imperatrix-Deputy. I had, in the meantime, become a Z.A.M. (Zelator Adeptus Minor or 5=6, on June 6th, 1920) and was made Sub-Praemonstrator; Then began a period of seeming prosperity, although I felt at the time that admissions were being made on somewhat too large a scale. But our numbers increased, and interest in the work was pronounced."

A student at Thoth-Hermes by the name of Lilli Geise who would become the future bride of Paul Case made the following observation:

"I know Mr. Whitty very well and know that he recognized fully the privilege which our Temple had when Mr. Case became a member of it. Michael Whitty was big hearted and modest, a real student, and he realized that Mr. Case would make a better teacher than himself. When he made him Sub-Praemonstrator he intended giving all the work over to him and he followed Mr. Case's advice in everything. He died, knowing that the Temple was in capable hands. And soon he found out he had judged right. Michael thought only of the teaching and how and through whom the members could get the most out of it, never of himself."

Lilli became a Second Order Initiate and later the Praemonstratrix of the Alpha et Omega Temple in Philadelphia.

After becoming a sub-chief in 1919, Paul began a correspondence with the Head of the Order in Scotland, Greatly Honored Frater Sub Spe or Brodie-Innes. Most of their communications centered on the Tarot and Paul's researches. On July 9, 1919 Brodie–Innes counseled Case:

"Care Frater, thanks for your letter regarding the Tarot. I have only seen one or two of your articles on the Tarot in AZOTH. It may well be that there is a workable correspondence of the Keys to both Sephiroth through their numbers. It would, however, take a great deal of careful working out for both with the Keys, and with the Sephiroth. Its symbology is so vast and intricate that errors may very easily be made.

"I agree, however, that different points of view, if only their accuracy is carefully established, are very valuable, as only in this way can we approach ultimate truth. You will have apprehended by this time that, like the Scriptures according to the Orthodox Church, the Tarot is not of any private interpretation...your analogy of the Shield [i.e. on Key #7] is quite a good one. You will remember, of course, that our attribution of the Keys with Hebrew Letters is strictly private and on no account to be given to outsiders."

The Book of Tokens

About this time work was started on *The Book of Tokens*, a true classic of Qabalistic symbolism. What is generally not known is that Paul Case did not author this great occult text. In fact, Paul always maintained that *The Book of Tokens* was a recovery of a much earlier work by an unknown Qabalist. Together Michael Whitty and Case collaborated on the work in the year 1919. Paul explains how this was accomplished: [from the original 1924 typewritten manuscript].

"The Book of Tokens: A Recovery of Certain Meditations on the Secret Wisdom–with a Brief Commentary by a Brother in L.V.X."

"As the title shows, The Book of Tokens is a recovery, not an original production. An outline of the meditations was first obtained in 1919, through the joint labors of two of the Brothers, but the completion of

40

the work has been delayed until now by a series of events beginning with the death of the older of these two."

Neither Case nor Whitty knew the source of this channeling, but credited it to Paul's 'auditory hallucinations,' a phrase Case used when referring to his Inner Voice. We have included, in one of the appendices of this present work, a copy of the complete "communications" received many years later by Paul, Ann Davies, and Harriett Case, so that the reader may have an idea of how these teachings were received. The opening phrase refers to the session received by Case many years before the later communications:

"We have waited long, Frater, for another to take up the work interrupted by the advancement to the Third Order [i.e. death or transition] of our Very Honored Frater G. et S. [Michael Whitty]...His passing into a higher field of action deprived us for a time, as you reckon time, of a balancing force for yours, Frater Perseverantia...Not a moment has passed since he sailed for California that we have not kept in mind the unfinished work, begun in the weekly communication of twenty-five years ago...You must remember that we are taking up a project which was broken off by the passing of Frater G. et S. Furthermore, we shall later give you much the same kind of outline as with the 'Book of Tokens,' which, you will remember, you received only in skeleton form, which served later as a sort of springboard for the writing of the complete text."

In the first printed published edition, Paul stated:

"We do not know the name of the author. Internal evidence in the text suggests that he may have been one of the later Qabalists. Perhaps he knew the Tarot, perhaps not..."

The Passing of Michael Whitty

In 1920, Michael Whitty's health declined. He sailed to Los Angeles in hopes that the climate of sunny Southern California would improve his situation, but to no avail. His last days were described in *AZOTH*:

41

"During the greater part of last year [1920] he struggled desperately against the pleadings of those who loved him, to keep himself in harness despite the encroachments of an irresistible debility. His work meant everything to him, his health nothing...As if by a miracle, the beloved patient rallied sufficiently to put his affairs in order for a voyage to Southern California...

"Most important of all in the mind of the stricken editor and teacher, was the uninterrupted continuance of the magazine [AZOTH] was assured by the loyalty of his valued friend and fellow student, Mr. Paul Case, author of 'An Introduction to the Study of the Tarot,' already well known to the readers of AZOTH...Mr. Case unhesitatingly abandoned the lucrative practice of his profession of music and hastened here from the South to relieve Michael Whitty... thus getting him free for, as it proved, 'the great adventure.'"

The exertions of the long sea voyage from New York to Los Angeles exhausted Whitty's strength and his decline rapidly continued after making port in Southern California. Renewed medical treatment failed to reverse this condition and he "fearlessly crossed the threshold" into the measureless regions, on December 27th, Saint John's Day. This was the arena wherein he had long studied to function as a conscious servant of humanity.

On his death, as was customary with an initiate of his Temple, all of his personal writings and Order manuscripts were sent to the Cancellarius, his fellow Chief, Howard Underhill, with some notable exceptions:

"The notes of these sittings [of Paul Case and Michael Whitty] were, except for those having to do with the 'Book of Tokens,' kept by Mrs. Whitty until after the passing of Frater G. et S., at which time she saw fit to destroy them, she never having been in real sympathy with his deeper occult interests..." [Communications]

Chapter 9
Trouble in the Temple

In February of 1921, Vestigia (Mrs. Mathers) confirmed Paul Case as Praemonstrator (teaching Chief) to fill the vacancy left by Whitty's passing. Case wrote, "Although I received no honorary grade [i.e. 7=4 or Adeptus Exemptus—see Appendix 3 for Alpha et Omega's grade structure] as it having been decided by herself and Sub Spe (Brodie-Innes) that such practice was unwise."

Moina Mathers

Case's status in the Order as a teacher is revealed in a letter from Elma Dame, Imperatrix of Ptah Temple in Philadelphia:

"Before Michael Whitty died, he had discovered in Paul Case erudition in the Kabalah and a teaching ability that eminently qualified him to take the office of Praemonstrator and to carry on the teaching of the Temple in Michael's absence. Michael died satisfied that he had left the work of the Temple in competent hands. During the following five months [Feb-Jun], the growth and inspiration of the Temple was phenomenal. Mr. Case taught practical occultism and Miss Geise offered her home as a place where prospective candidates could be interviewed, and where the real meaning of the step they were about to take could be explained to them.

"It was also a place where encouragement could be given to students already in the Order. They came here for their examinations and went back to their work and studies refreshed and enthusiastic. Frater Vota Vita Mea [Howard Underhill] and I aided with our counsels. Mrs. Wise was away, but wrote continuously of her happiness in the progress of the work and her looking forward to the time when she could be with us again. Dr. Kenny was a visitor several times a week and was regarded as an intimate and loyal personal friend. We had a united Second Order, who shared the sacred things of our lives and feared no misunderstandings."

Lille Geise, the Praemonstratix, writes in a letter:

"Last winter under Mr. Case's leadership the Temple blossomed as it had never done before. It was a surprise and joy to all to see it and the visitors from other towns remarked on the 'life' which was in this group. It began to spread to other places outside of this city. Our home became a center such as Michael's once had been. New members were interviewed and old ones were encouraged to stay, for the teaching in the First Order is mystifying, not to say clumsy and many were ready to give it up. Mr. Case and I even traveled to the suburbs and spent time and money to talk to members who needed help and all of them began to study with renewed efforts."

44

Another example of Paul's influence is found in a letter he wrote in answer to a question by Soror Fortiter et Recte on February 23, 1921:

"Here at last is the first of the series of letters required to answer your questions. In this letter I shall take up the points you have covered in the section of your inquiry under the Roman numeral I, referring to the 1=10 Ritual...Try to realize that in all magical operations you make no effort to <u>acquire</u> powers, or to <u>gain</u> control over any external force. Your problem is merely (but oh, how much is included in that 'merely'!) to learn what powers are <u>already</u> yours, and to <u>exercise</u> them...May the Lord of the Universe bring you speedily to the recognition of His presence in your heart of hearts. My next letter, which will be sent as soon as possible, will take up the second series of your questions.

Yours fraternally,
Perseverantia."

Unfortunately the harmony at Thoth-Hermes would be short-lived. The initiatory process is not an easy one. It requires dedication, diligence, and most importantly, self reflection. In order to become a clear channel for the Divine Will, one must transform the consciousness. In the early stages this process often involves dealing with personal and emotional issues. These issues are often painful and can be overwhelming, hence many choose to project these shortcomings unto others rather than face them within. Chiefs are often the target of these projections. As Paul wrote to Vestigia explaining:

"As you probably know, during our V.H. Imperatrix' absence in her professional work, practically the whole administration of the Temple fell to me."

And, later, in a letter to A.E. Waite *(left)*:

"...For the rest of the winter I had on my hands one of those tempests in a teapot which can be raised by two women [Vestigia and Mrs. Wise]

who hate each other, and prod their husbands on in the ensuing warfare. On my hands, because Mrs. Wise, the Imperatrix, was in Chicago, acting in one of David Belasco's productions, and Vota Vita Mea was spared most of the trouble, both parties centering the efforts on me. Eventually my attempts to bring about reconciliation had the effect that such attempts often invite. Both parties turned against me..."

That Look, Full of Meaning

"Various petty jealousies and rivalries disturbed our peace during the winter and no sooner had I succeeded, or as I thought, in bringing these to a peaceful conclusion than our First Order began to be permeated with innuendoes and accusations directed against me and our Heirophantrix [Lilli Geise]. Now, no member of the First Order had one iota of evidence to back up these accusations...I want to make this point especially clear. None of these scandal-mongers had any more foundation for their stories than the sort of thing I have cited, coupled with the fact that I had spent a great deal of time working at the apartments where Soror Nunc Et Semper [Lilli Geise], Frater Vota Vita Mea [Howard Underhill] and Soror Aude Sapere [Elma Dame] share their expenses together. Thus, no matter what the facts might have been, every one of these persons spoke of random matters concerning which they had no actual knowledge whatever.

"Unfortunately, Soror Nunc Et Semper and I had so much confidence in the honor and discretion of our Second Order, that we admitted to some of its members, including our Imperatrix and V.H. Frater Honore Et Virtute [Dr. T. B. Kenny], an affection which I am glad to admit to you also. We found ourselves in a most difficult situation, confronted by circumstances which we had considered long and prayerfully. We had considered our problem from every angle and the decision we reached was based upon a better understanding of all the points involved than any other person could possibly have.

"Most of these points we discussed with our V.H. Imperatrix and with G.H. Soror Unitas [Elsa Barker]. One evening we discussed ways and

means for averting an open scandal. Finally to satisfy V.H. Soror Non Mihi Solum's idea of the necessity for speaking literal truth, we both voluntarily pledged ourselves to refrain from relations more intimate than that of close friends. Because of this renunciation, which at the time, seemed to affect our Imperatrix most profoundly she felt able to make the explanatory speech in the Temple which you have in your possession."

In another letter referring to this speech, Soror Aude Sapere (Elma Dame) explained:

"Mrs. Wise read an address in Temple, in which she made the mistake of denying the conditions instead of silencing the evil tongues and reminding them of their obligation not to stir up strife or mischief making. Her defense was so half-hearted that a story spread that she was trying to 'white-wash' her Second Order members. She had pleased nobody, not the scandal-mongers nor those whom they were vilifying. The Imperatrix had assumed that it was her sphere to regulate the 'personal' conduct of her Fratres and Sorores and had openly shown her allegiance to external conventions, with disregard for the Cosmic Law which must be paramount for all true occult students. This, of course, invited all the troubles that followed."

To Paul it was clear that the situation was escalating:

"This whole situation in Thoth-Hermes has been complicated by matters which, in my opinion and in that of several who know all the facts, have no proper connection with the affairs of the Order. I have been accused of teaching things I have never taught, of holding opinions I have never held and of being actuated by motives that never entered my head."

Evidence for this scandal was based on flimsy rumors and ridiculous observations. For example, it was whispered that Paul and Lilli exchanged a "meaningful glance" over the altar during the mystic repast (part of the closing portion of the Order's ritual).

What a difference a hundred years makes. In 2013, two initiates dating would not only be accepted, but would most likely be celebrated, given that such unions are infrequent. But in the early 1920's such behavior was looked upon as outrageous.

It should be observed that this mutual affection led to Case's and Geise's eventual marriage–a not altogether dishonorable end.

Chapter 10
Expelled

Elma Dame continues in her letter:

"The fictitious 'scandal' instead of being hushed, was shrieked through the ranks of the First Order and became so noisy, that Mr. Case saw the futility of attempting to continue an association with an Imperatrix who did not have the courage to support him. His resignation from Thoth-Hermes [on June 22nd] was accepted by Mrs. Wise. The third Chief, V.H. Frater Vota Vita Mea was not consulted by her in this matter!"

Paul relates in his letter to A.E. Waite:

"Following Mrs. Wise's speech of June 15 or thereabouts...less than a week later I was subjected to the violent attack of a First Order member...and found no course open to me but resignation from office...In the house of our Imperatrix, and in the presence of G.H. Soror Unitas and the present Praemonstrator [Dr. T.B. Kinney] (whose appearance on that occasion I am still at a loss to understand), I have been subjected to what Americans call a 'third degree' cross examination at the hands of a First Order member, himself only of the 2=9 Grade, who admitted at the onset that his accusations rested on nothing but opinion and belief..."

Because of his quick advancement and young age, Paul had evidently aroused jealousy among some of his fellow members at the Alpha et Omega. Moreover, as later recounted by Harriet Case, Paul was subject to a certain native bluntness. It seems he had a reputation for, "not suffering fools gladly" and was often criticized for his candor by members of the First Order.

In another letter, he writes:

> "Recognizing that my usefulness to Thoth-Hermes was at an end, because our Imperatrix would not support me in the only course which could have saved the situation, viz. the expulsion of the scandal-mongers, I resigned my post and ceased to attend meetings: and Miss Geise, who was then Heirophantrix, also ceased attendance."

In Lilli Geise's journal we read about the subsequent events:

> "Mrs. Wise, although fully aware of Mr. C's unusual ability, called it in my presence and that of the Cancellarius [Howard Underhill] a personal insult if he [i.e. Case] were ever to be a Chief again. This opened our eyes. For personal reasons she closed the channel of his knowledge to the First Order, even claiming to one of the discouraged fellow students that there was no teacher. But, one by one, they followed their own way and came to our own home to ask questions of Mr. Case. And we went on encouraging them as before, never betraying any of our own doubts, which had arisen meanwhile."

Sex-Magic

Shortly before Paul resigned as a Chief of the Temple, he gave a short talk on the symbolism of the Tree of Life and the stations of the Temple. Case pointed out that the altar is situated in the position of the Sephirah Yesod, which is attributed to the genitals of the archetypal man. And that as such, he explained, the altar is a symbol for the creative energy of the Cosmic.

Almost immediately, his comments prompted gossiper's tongues (and pens) to wag. His critics chose to write, not to Brodie-Innes, the teaching head of the Order, but again to his junior, Moina. Case's words were reported to Vestigia by some First Order members as "teachings concerning sex magic." Her reaction was predictable. Anything even remotely connected to sexual expression was considered taboo in her eyes. Indeed, she frequently commented to friends that she and her husband found even the thought of physical sexuality repugnant, and that they practiced strict celibacy for the entire duration of their marriage.

She had even criticized Dion Fortune for giving out esoteric secrets on sexuality.

Moina responded to these accusations by writing to Case directly:

"...I have seen the results of this superficial sex teaching in several occult societies as well as in individual cases. I have never met with one happy result."

Vestigia advised Paul:

"This need not touch the private life of the individual. We are not supposed to interfere with the moral, civil or religious duties of the members of the Order. But a member's practices must not touch the Temple or the teaching.

"You evidently have reached a point in your mystical Way where there would appear to exist certain crossroads. You will certainly have to take some definite decision as to which path you will pursue. The artist in you, which I recognize and with whom I deeply sympathize, would probably choose to learn the Truth through the joy and beauty of physical life.

"I am convinced that great Truths may be learnt through the rhythm of Physical Beauty. But these are nothing compared to the depths of those to be gained through suffering and renunciation. You who have studied the Pantheons, do you know of that enchanting god, the Celtic Angus, the Ever young. He who is sometimes called–Lord of the Land of Heart's Desire.

"The artist in us may have lingered in that land for a moment. But you and I who would be teachers and pioneers in this Purgatorial World must be prepared before all the gods to be the servant of the Greatest of them All...That is to say of the Osiris, the Christ, the God of the Sacrifice of the Self."

But to Case, sexuality became an increasingly important subject. In his *Book of Tokens,* he comments on the sex function:

"You must alter your conception of sex in order to comprehend the Ageless Wisdom...It is the interior nervous organism, not the external organs, that is always meant in phallic symbolism and the force that works through these interior centers is the Great Magical Agent, the Divine Serpent Fire." [Commentary on the Meditation on Nun].

In his books, *The True and Invisible Rosicrucian Order,* and *The Masonic Letter G,* Case writes of certain practices involving the redirection of the sexual force to higher centers of the brain where experience of supersensory states of consciousness becomes possible.

Case responded to Vestigia, in the following letter:

"Your letter of July 18 requires a careful and detailed reply, because it shows plainly that when it was written you had not yet received all the correspondence which by now has been put into your hands by H. Frater Veritas Victoriam Portat.

"Let me make it very clear that while I held the post of Praemonstrator in Thoth-Hermes Temple, I never discussed any aspect of the sex theory in open temple. Nor have I expressed any personal views to any of our members further than what follows:

1. I have said that certain of our symbols show plainly that one of the great practical secrets of occultism has to do with the control and direction of that force which, on the physical plane, is chiefly employed in the reproduction of the species. Note, please, that I never ventured to give any sort of practical instruction. At most I have asserted (as do such writers as Eliphas Levi and many others) that <u>one</u> of the Arcana known to Adepti relates to the control and direction of the nerve-force (let me call it) which ordinarily energizes the reproductive centers.

2. In speaking of the four Kabalistic worlds, I have said that Assiah, as well as the three higher worlds, has its place and use in our Work. This, to combat the opinion that our Order demands of its members the false asceticism insisted upon by many self-appointed teachers. What I have intended to convey (and what every right-minded person who has ever heard me speak on this subject has understood me to mean), is that every function of man has its appointed use, and that the business of the occultist is to <u>control</u> himself on all planes."

Case, then turned his comments to his relationship with his future wife, Lilli Geise:

"I do not know what your judgment of our case will be. I <u>do</u> know that this is no sordid affair of the senses, that I have led nobody astray nor been led astray by anybody. What has been done has been done through principle, not for the mere satisfaction of an ephemeral desire. The situation in which we find ourselves is extremely difficult and involves renunciations and deprivations that I have no wish to parade before you. It undoubtedly includes, among these renunciations, my resignation from a post that brought me much happiness along with the responsibilities and enmities that it also involved.

At the same time, I must beg you to believe that I have no desire to be 'a teacher and pioneer in this Purgatorial World.' What prominence I have had has been thrust upon me. What exploration of undeveloped fields has fallen to my lot has been more the result of guidance than by choice; and now that guidance seems to have removed me from the high place to which I have never really aspired."

"The relief is great. I am now free to pursue my studies and my life without incurring some of the dangers that beset more prominent members of the Order. I no longer occupy a conspicuous place in a group of persons among whom there are some who, it seems, so little understand or recognize the meaning of their obligation and the seriousness of their work, that they can occupy their minds with

thoughts and their tongues with words more appropriate to the gutter than to a Temple dedicated to the service of the Gods.

"These are strong words, but I pray that you will distinguish between my condemnation of thoughts and actions and my feeling toward the thinkers and actors. Those who assailed me most bitterly have, I am sure, acted according to the best light they have. Who am I to judge them?

"My conscience acquits me. I feel that I am living up to my obligation to lead a pure and unselfish life, even though people seeing only what I do, without knowing why, may judge otherwise. No argument, occult or otherwise, has yet convinced me that I am a miserable sinner, or that what seems to me to be the correct solution of a difficult ethical problem makes of me a charlatan and an imposter.

"Forgive this long letter, which has been read by V.H. Soror Nunc et Semper before it was mailed to you. We submit to your decision in all affairs concerned with the Order and its Temples. Our relation to each other we submit to no other judge than that Lord of Love and Justice who we all adore.

> *Sincerely and fraternally yours,*
> *Perseverantia 5=6"*

Enochian

Mrs. Mathers soon ratified Case's decision to resign his position as Chief. Paul for his part, asked pointed questions about the Order's Enochian and Tattwa systems; systems that Moina stated her late husband S.L. MacGregor Mathers had written. Case, however, pointed out that the Enochian system (a system of spiritual astral magic developed in the 16th century by Dr. John Dee and his associate Edward Kelly through the practice of skrying or crystal vision) could be found in Meric Casaubon's book, *A True and Faithful Relation,* and the Tattwa discourses were lifted, word for word, from Rama Prasad's *Nature's Finer Forces,* all found in the New York Public Library.

S.L. MacGregor-Mathers

Further, Paul questioned the reliability of a system received through the mediumship of someone as disreputable as Edward Kelly (after reading Benjamin Wooly's excellent biography of Dr. Dee, *The Queen's Conjuror,* I'm inclined to agree with Case in his opinion of Kelly). Case stated that he knew of at least three other individuals who, in his opinion, had suffered severe illnesses because of the use of Enochian Magic. Additionally, Paul attributed Michael Whitty's relatively young death to his extensive involvement in the Order's uses of the Enochian system.

As upset as Vestigia was about the reference to sexual teachings, it was nothing compared to her response to these criticisms. Case and Geise were peremptorily expelled from the Order.

"January 11ᵗʰ, 1922

Dear Mr. Case,
I have just heard from the V.H. Imperatrix of Thoth-Hermes Temple, Non Mihi Solum that you and V.H. Soror Nunc et Semper have sent in your resignations to Thoth Hermes Temple.

"I regret that at the same time that you both did not send in your resignations to the Order in general. On several occasions since the recent unfortunate dissentions in Thoth-Hermes, I have received reports and accusations against yourself. These I hitherto ignored.

"But now on the definite authority of one whose word I cannot doubt, the V.H. Imperatrix Non Mihi Solum, you yourself have deliberately made certain statements which leave me no choice but to erase your name from the Roll of the Rosicrucian Order A∴ O∴ for no Member

believing and circulating such statements <u>could</u> remain with us. He would be of no use to us—we should be so to him. I have been told among other things that you state that:

'the Order is a spurious arrangement made by the Count MacGregor, who was either deceived himself or willfully did it;'

'that the late S.R.M.D. has not left behind him the true and real Rosicrucian Order.'

'That you state as a fact, that except for the Minitum Mundum and for the Ceremonies of the Portal and the Vault, every other single teaching can be found in the Public Library.'

'That you declare the Enochian Tablets are absolutely false and that you can prove it. And that you speak in great 'grief' of the responsibility to those whom by bringing into the Order you have helped to deceive.'

"I will retain no Student in my Order who makes an attempt to dishonor the memory of our late Chief. Therefore I repeat again, that with deep regret I must erase your name from the roll of our Order and I ask you to return your M.S.S. etc., etc. as soon as possible to the V.H. Soror Non Mihi Solum.

Yours Sincerely,
Vestigia Nulla Restorum
(M. MacGregor Mathers).
External Head of the Order"

To quote my Frater, the late Ron Ferrara:

"With these developments, the stage had been set for the final act of the old drama and the beginning of the new; as things were to turn out, they were inextricably blended, in a process that was equally gradual and decisive in its result."

Chapter 11
The "Voice" on the Telephone

After having his name "erased from the rolls of the Order" early in 1922, Case with a number of other high-grade initiates, almost immediately began to form, *The Builders of the Adytum*.

One evening, the telephone rang at Case's home:

"I presume you recognize my voice?"

Imagine Case's astonishment when he realized that the voice on the phone was the same he had heard in his head for years. Apparently his Inner Voice had not been that of his own subconsciousness.

"Yes! Yes I do," he stammered out.

"Would you like to meet me?"

"Yes. Yes, indeed."

The "voice" instructed Paul to go to the Waldorf Astoria Hotel located at the corner of 5th Avenue and 33rd Street (now the site of the Empire State Building). At the time, the Waldorf was considered one of the most luxurious hotels in Manhattan. Its old world charm was famous, as was its fine cuisine prepared by the head chef, Caesar. The Astoria even had a railway station beneath it where preferred customers could park their private Pullman railcars. We read a description of it in the magazine *Peacock Alley, p.26*:

"It was a joint operation of two hotels, The Waldorf and the Astoria...it opened on March 13, 1893 and was demolished on October 1, 1929.

"The hotel had been provided with costly and artistic accoutrements worthy of an Old World palace. All the refinements of the Old World civilization had been drawn upon. There were magnificent tapestries, paintings, frescos, wood carvings, marble and onyx mosaics, quaint and rich pieces of furniture, rare and costly tableware. There were beautiful chandeliers, palms and ferns, roses and violets heaped loosely on the tables or banked on the mantles..."

The Old Waldorf Astoria (circa 1920)

No doubt Paul was both nervous and unsure when he arrived at the appointed suite. Who would be on the other side of the door? What would be expected of him? Would he be able to live up to those expectations? While he knocked on the door he held his breath and mentally prepared for the encounter.

The door was opened by an olive complexioned, dark haired man with a slight build and a neatly trimmed beard. Paul guessed his age to be somewhere in his forties. Ann Davies would later describe him:

"Master Racoczy is not some towering vast giant, but actually a man with quite small bones, his height approximately between five foot seven and five foot eight...and with a delicately-boned structure...He always looks like he's in his prime, anywhere around forty to forty-five...

"The Master R. has been called the Prince Racoczy, a Polish nobleman, who is said to have been born close to 400 years ago. At that time the Polish areas were part of the region of Hungary, in which he came from. He was born of aristocratic parents."

During Racoczy's incarnation in Hungary he both discovered and perfected the Alchemical Elixir of Life, becoming one of the "deathless adepts," well known in mystical literature. Racoczy subsequently used various pseudonyms to preserve his anonymity. For example, he is said to have been the Count de Saint Germain during the reign of Louie 16th, and the "Professor" active in the events of American Independence.

Case relates that when the door was opened, he found himself in the presence of a, "small, well dressed man (who nevertheless gave the impression of great height) with such brilliant eyes that I thought he was some kind of holy being." Paul stammered, "Good evening. I am Paul Case." Rococzy answered, "I am the Count de Saint Germain."

Awed beyond words, Paul immediately began to bow before the Master. Racoczy stopped him cold. "Do not kneel before me. I am a man, just as you."

Paul described the event years later, in his book, *The True and Invisible Rosicrucian Order:*

"Some years ago I met a man who I believe to be one of the Greater Adepts. He made no such claim. Indeed, he made no claims at all. Yet, I have good reasons for my belief. Like another Teacher, this man told

me all the things that ever I did. Yet he was in no sense a striking personality. You would not turn to look at him on Fifth Avenue. He could sit unnoticed in any hotel lobby. His dress conformed to the ancient Rosicrucian rule, 'Adopt the customs of the country where you dwell...' this man's dress was beautiful and his outlook on life was a perpetual recognition of the beauty in everything and the lesson he taught me—a lesson I shall never forget— was a lesson of beauty too...This is the reason Magi are always teachers and healers. They heal by their presence. They teach without speech. In their circle of influence, ignorance is dispelled, as darkness flees before the sun...he who is most truly self-possessed, i.e. 'possessed by the Self' is the ruler of the rest. For in his thought there is a strength, a positiveness, a clarity, which imposes themselves by induction upon the minds of all others in the company.

"I have enjoyed unusual opportunities for direct, objective instruction from a person who has demonstrated to me his possession of the practical and theoretical keys to the Rosicrucian mystery. Thus, what I am offering in this explanation of the Rosicrucian allegories is by no means the result of my own personal interpretations only. It is largely a development of instruction received from one who merits, if ever a man did, the august title 'Rosicrucian.' The identity of this man is beside the point...I am simply confessing my personal inadequacy to the unaided production of such an interpretation and humbly acknowledging my everlasting indebtedness to the source of my enlightenment. From that same source I have received assurance that we are now in a period of human history when much that hitherto has been forgotten by the world shall once more be brought to light."

Paul spent most of the next three weeks in the presence of the Master. Racoczy's vibratory state (developed through lifetimes of work and discipline) so heightened the awareness and receptivity of Case, that the development and instruction that would have generally taken a lifetime, was accomplished in less than 21 days. An analogy would, perhaps, be like a swift computer download of a complex program.

This phenomenon of "impartation" whereby an Adept heightens the perception of the students around him, and in some cases even triggers illumination, is well known in parts of Asia. Paul would write years later:

"A whole system of initiation and mystical teaching and the keys to accessing their use was implanted in my mind."

Case further stated that although he could not claim to have completely understood the knowledge at the time, he could, even after several years, repeat the instruction, word for word.

Ann Davies relayed to her students:

"He was also told about the outline material which he and Michael Whitty had received for 'The Book of Tokens' in 1919-20 because of their special training. He received verification of the source of the material, along with much else in the way of instruction and commentary. Every possible verification, certainly was had, from the Master R.

"The Master told him that he had been the one who directed its interpretation in the language of our own culture. Here was a very amazing and interesting verification of the actual contact.

"Dr. Case learned that the reason he had been given help to unravel some of the intricacies of the Tarot and Qabalah and had put them into print was because the time had come for much more to be given out...which had been kept esoteric. Had he come into the Golden Dawn before he had discovered and made public these attributions, he too would have had an obligation not to give it out and this was the way it was done..."

During their time together Master R. informed Case that he had been watching him for a long time. When Paul asked why he had been chosen for this great responsibility Master R answered (as summarized by Case):

"That while he was not particularly impressed by Paul's personality, he was absolutely the best they (i.e. the Masters) could find for the job they had in mind. They had to work with what they had at hand!"

Case later wrote that Master R. shared with him a set of personal Tarot designs. They were esoteric in nature and much more elaborate than any published at that time (even more so than the deck Case would create through B.O.T.A.). Ann would later relay to this author that Paul noted that the cards somewhat resembled Tibetan "Tankas" or Buddhist's "Mandalas." The Master asked Case to base his own Tarot on this esoteric version, and that in doing so he would correct the exoteric designs such as those published by the Golden Dawn and Waite-Rider. In 1929 Case did this when he published his B.O.T.A. version, drawn under his instruction, by Jesse Burnes Parke (photo page 89).

The Master relayed to Paul that Mystery Schools, like people, go through incarnations and, after a while, go into periods of withdrawal from form, only to be reincarnated into a new vehicle, suitable for the needs of a growing humanity. He explained that one of the main reasons he made personal contact with Paul was to prepare him to formulate the next incarnation of the Western Mystery Tradition training system, eliminating the impure, outworn elements that dogged the present schools.

The Master clarified to Paul that Case's own unique combination of talents and skills, developed in past incarnations using the Qabalah, had already been integrated into his psyche. He also told Case that he had been gifted with the special genetic makeup needed to serve as a useable channel to transmit the spiritual teachings they [i.e. the Masters] had in mind.

Enochian—Again

Master R. related to Paul that the material channeled by Edward Kelly was dangerous. The Enochian Tablets had, due to an error on Mather's part, been incorrectly brought into the Order system. I examined copies of the original Cipher manuscripts, which are the source Mathers used for the construction of the First Order Rituals and found the following; The Cipher manuscripts refer to a set of tablets from the "Old Manuscript" but do not specify Dee or Kelly's work by name. Mather's had been doing much research in the British Museum where the Dee manuscripts were housed. It was natural for him, perhaps mistakenly, to assume these were the ones referenced in the Cipher manuscripts. Unfortuantely, this was not necessarily the case. Dee was very excited about some tables found in the *Soyga Manuscript,* a manuscript that predates the Enochian work by centuries—a work based on the Qabalah. Paul once wrote to Dion Fortune that the Enochian tablets were a *caricature* of an earlier system.

Case further writes about his views on the Enochian system:

> "…Among this knowledge was the fact that protective methods were nowhere included in the instruction sent from Europe to Thoth-Hermes Temple…Thus the Hierophants of Thoth-Hermes, as well as those of other Temples…were obliged in the Grade Rituals to perform elemental operations (using the Enochian invocations) which were by no means safe. These Hierophants and all members present at these operations were therefore permitted, nay obliged to run great risk of obsession…I have personal knowledge of more than twenty-five instances where the performance of magical operations based upon the Order formulae led to serious disintegrations of mind and body. From this last I have been preserved by the fact that my elevation to the office of Praemonstrator came just before my advancement to the office of Hierophant so I never performed the Hierophant's part of the rituals. Perhaps the most conspicuous example of the use of these formulas is A.C. [Aleister Crowley] himself, but there are plenty of others that I have personally witnessed, whose personal shipwrecks have been just as complete even though their smaller tonnage, so to say, makes the loss seem less deplorable…Whitty's health failed as a direct result of magical practices based on Order formulae, but sadly deficient in adequate protection."

Chapter 12
The New Dispensation

In accordance with the new "Aquarian" dispensation, Paul was instructed to take special care that those who followed the work would do so for the sake of spiritual service and not service or devotion to a particular leader, as had been the case in much of the older, Piscean dispensation. Because of the evolution of humanity as a whole, much knowledge that had been released only under severe vows of secrecy would now be much more easily accessible. It was critical, he was instructed, to make this knowledge much more widely disseminated, so that those spiritual aspirants who were ready could be exposed to it.

Paul was told that his mission would involve restating the ancient wisdom in terms more easily understood by the modern person. The use of blinds, commonly used in ages past to hide the true teaching from the uninitiated, would no longer be used. If a certain teaching was too advanced for common distribution, it would simply be withheld until the seeker would reach a suitable level of spiritual maturity. The Ageless Wisdom would be restated and taught in such a manner that it could be accessed by the modern person. To accomplish this, Paul was to state it in terms of modern psychology.

The Tarot was chosen to be the primary vehicle of this teaching, as it is a uniquely suited instrument for training the consciousness. The Adepts of the Inner School (the Third Order) had long realized that there would be many centuries of "narrow dogmatic and unhappy control of the minds and spiritual thinking of the masses…" Thus, the Tarot would provide a safe method to train the consciousness of modern people to progress toward spiritual unfoldment.

Case was told:

> "Because from cycle to cycle, as language changes, as the cultures change, there needs to be certain changes made—not in the training— but in the presentation and the interpretation from one language to another."

During the time that Master R. spent with Paul, the contact with the Inner School was stabilized. Extensive oral training was given regarding methods of purifying the teachings, as well as to the extent that these doctrines could be released to the public. Much information on Spiritual Alchemy, or techniques to purify the body and activate its hidden potential as an instrument for spiritual evolution was imparted.

Ann Davies once explained:

"While he was under this special contact and training with the Master, a great deal of information was instilled in his consciousness. It was also rather peculiar. He said that being with 'the Boss' so enhanced his consciousness that he was like a blotter. He absorbed an enormous amount of ideas, information, and interpretation...Indeed, there was so much he couldn't even understand at the time, but it was there. His awareness was 'so heightened that there wasn't a single thing he was taught, which did not remain as bright, as new, as vivid as the moment it was given to him'... A Master of Wisdom has such an expanded consciousness, such an intense and forceful magnetic field that he can naturally stimulate to an extraordinary degree the spiritual element in whatever disciple or pupil he is working with and this, of course, is what happened to Paul Case. As the years went on, every time it was needed—suddenly another group of reinterpretations would be remembered—a sort of enhancement which kept the wisdom alive and available. Although he was not able to contact everything he'd been taught all in one remembering, it was there at all times as he wrote the various lessons and courses."

The Master divulged to Paul a great deal of information in relationship to the Hierarchy, and its functioning. For example, he explained how a Master of Wisdom would not serve as a teacher for a group of students, but would rather work though one or more disciples. Thus, the Master would use the teacher as a channel for spiritual teaching. Additionally the Master emphasized how important it is for the group charged with the disseminating and grounding of the teachings, to be harmonious. He lamented that the internal strife present in the Alpha

65

et Omega had largely rendered that particular school unusable by the Hierarchy for this purpose. He emphasized the need to maintain fraternal harmony above all else, for the continued success of the spiritual work.

Ann Davies further related that:

> "It had been made known to Dr. Case during the face to face instruction by our elder Brother that the Mystery School to which he was called to head was a direct lineal and hierarchical descendant of similar Spiritual Schools reaching back to antiquity. Furthermore, that the leadership of Dr. Case was fully authorized and in the accredited line of descent, as would be that of the leaders chosen to succeed him, provided that the teachings were kept intact and pure and the school and its leadership free from all taints of commercialism and power drives.

> "Master R. also told Paul that the Inner School does not concern itself with the financial requirements of its outer Temples. It feels, and rightly so, that it is up to the members who are being helped along the spiritual Grades of the Path of Return to take care of the material needs of the Great Work, in accordance with their means.

> "Master R. relayed to Case that the Work was to be kept more or less quiet, until at least four decades had passed, in order to give the destructive forces a chance to die down and for the nucleus of the new incarnation of the Western Mysteries to grow strong—to become a powerful center in and of itself.

> "Dr. Case was instructed to organize the more esoteric elements of ritual and ceremonial—the basic Mystery training which still remains oral, because this is where the emanation of spiritual force comes from...At first, even the existence of the new organization was to be secret and then it would become more visible."

Chapter 13
The Hermetic Order of Aquarius

Following this meeting, Paul began earnest work on his correspondence courses and publications. His mission now well defined, he began translating the ancient teachings into a form more accessible to modern humanity. From his personal editorials in his magazine *Tarota*, it is easy to see that a very important part of Case's vision was to establish working groups to practice the ancient system of initiation.

To comply with the Master's instructions the new group was named "The Order of Aquarius." However, even at this time, the inner group referred to itself as, *The Builders of the Adytum*. The "Adytum" was used in reference to the inner shrine of a temple, a place where the priest is able to commune with God. This outward physical adytum corresponds to the in-dwelling physio-psychic body of the aspirant, which is completed and activated by the disciplines of the Great Work.

The designation, "The School of Ageless Wisdom" was conceived to serve as the name of the outer correspondence school. It was dropped when the work moved to California.

Many years later in another communication, Master R. states:

"As Frater P. knows, all of our former communications had to do with the forming of an outer vehicle for what he knows under the initials ____ and one of the most important things is to do everything possible to correct the errors which have disrupted so many spiritual movements. One of these errors—one of the worst, and one of the subtlest—is against which the subject matter of this instruction is directed. This error springs from the supposition on the part of the aspirant that <u>he</u> is doing something to raise himself—to life, or sublimate, some of what he mistakenly to be his personal powers— physical, emotional or mental. The truth is that nothing originates in, or is directed from the personal level. Right understanding of what really goes on requires this basic realization...Because any pride or even spiritual vanity, vitiate the work of the student who has not

grasped the basic principle. This misunderstanding leads to the substitution of purely personal prejudices for judgment and is colored by unresolved complexes. It may comfort you to know that even <u>we</u> must ever be on guard against this same delusion. For though you may think of us as being Masters, we are really only your fellow students and as we are still human beings, incarnate like yourselves, the necessary illusions which are inseparable from physical embodiment affect us as much as they do you..."

Paul and his associates were very secretive about the early days of their new order, referring to it, as we have pointed out, as the "Hermetic Order of Aquarius," or H.O.A. Case outlines this policy as follows:

"With the exception of the three people whose names appear in the publications of the Hermetic Order of Atlantis, no person is authorized to declare in public the fact of his or her affiliation with the organization. If you hear anybody making such declarations you may know beforehand that you are listening to falsehoods. Every person now in good standing with the Order has agreed not to claim connection with it, nor reveal such connection to any person whatsoever who does not demonstrate by the secret means at our disposal, the right to be accepted as a fellow member.

"Not everyone will approve this course. But the founders of the Order do not care to have everyone for members. There are certain people with whom we expect to get in touch. These people will understand why even the fact of membership is to be kept a secret. But it is only right that we should explain our reasons for such a course. They are:

1. The peculiar character of our teachings.

2. The desire to obviate the danger of having unworthy members cast reflections upon the Order.

3. The desire to concentrate the activities of each member upon demonstration."

During this period of transition many letters were passed back and forth. The following are a selection:

From Lilli Geise to Moina Mathers:

> "We, who hoped for a second Temple (in New York), which was the only way out at the time, are now grateful that it never came into existence...You allowed the real leader to resign (in June, 1921) while there was nobody who could hope to fill his place in the near future. He was driven to this step through the pettiness of a few jealous First Order members and especially through the inability of two fellow Second Order members (Mrs. Wise and Dr. Kenny) to cope with the situation. On that day the death warrant of Thoth-Hermes was signed. Since then, the First Order has reigned supreme. You and Mrs. Wise absolutely ignored the fact that we might have a strong personal following. Naturally those who began to love the work through our encouragement and who for the first time understood it under the guidance of their leader were attracted to us. That is only human. While I do not claim any special knowledge, I had many friends in Thoth-Hermes; Paul Case was generally known for his great gifts (naturally despised in some quarters by envy) and Miss Dame was his close second in the understanding of the teaching, and simply worshipped by the Philadelphia group, which she founded."

Elma Dame to Mrs. Mathers:

> "...I wrote you in August in reference to the need for a new Temple, which would avail itself of Mr. Case's ability and would hold together those members who were above personalities and looked for Principle...you ignored the principles at stake in the matter of a new Temple in New York. That new Temple would have saved the situation and nothing else could. You had been misinformed about the extent of personal following that Mr. Case had and entirely underrated the degree to which his constructive teaching had promoted the growth of the Order in New York. Mrs. Wise's assertion that the formation of such as temple in which she would not be a Chief, would be a direct insult to her, and her consequent recommendations against such a

69

course, are immediately responsible for the wreckage that followed. Two Temples could have shared the rent that the one Temple finds itself unable to meet. There was a double exodus from the Temple, including those who were positive loyal believers in Mr. Case and those who were too indifferent to come to anything that was not proving itself a live organization with a positive message...you never answered Mr. Case's letter of self defense. [July 29, 1921]"

Mr. Wiggs' Rosicrucian Side Show

As Mrs. Dame's letter revealed, the A.O. was in a steady decline. Case related such to Dion Fortune, a famous British occultist, in his letter of August 31, 1936:

"Then began a period of disillusionment. If V.N.R. [Vestigia] had a full account of what had happened she would speedily set things straight.

Our confidence had been shaken somewhat, it is true, by the discovery that Mr. George Wiggs (Amor Lux et Labor), whom S. M. R. D. had appointed Group Chief with headquarters in Chicago, was sending out knowledge lectures to almost anybody who would pay $10.00, but we thought even that might be remedied in time...Wiggs has never been through any ceremony of the Order. He sends all the initiation fees to V.N.R. and horrified

Dion Fortune

Mrs. Wise by telling her how he thought it was a 'poor month' when he did not admit 15 or 20 persons to his mail-order Rosicrucianism...it was this that set some of us checking up on our supposedly secret manuscripts. The New York Public Library has Isaac Myer's collection of occult books, and it didn't take long to track down most of the supposedly Rosicrucian material, sometimes to very un-Rosicrucian sources. And 'The True Relation' (of Dr. John Dee) exposed the whole genesis of the Enochian Tablets and language.

"Then, for the first time, I began to examine the evidences we had as to the claims G.D. Brodie-Innes [Oct. 26] had made solemn assertions

70

that he had verified them but offered nothing in the way of evidence. And just at this time I began to examine the rituals and knowledge lectures, etc. that were supposed to be in the direct line of historical descent from the original foundation. I found nothing that was not in print prior to the establishment of the G.D., except certain negligible contributions to the Flying Rolls, and the material on the Tattvas. But the Tattva instruction was so evidently pirated without the slightest acknowledgement from Rama Prasad's Nature's Finer Forces, that Brodie-Innes himself recognized the necessity of a revision of the text."

The story continues in the following letter of Dec. 1921, from Lilli Geise to Brodie-Innes:

"Now as to the question you ask me about the Temple in New York and how we are getting along; the situation of the A.O. in America is a long and sad story! Of course, we feel that you, as Praemonstrator of the Grand Temple, ought to be fully acquainted with what happens to the M.S.S. here and be able to judge, if the various channels are worthy to receive them. But I do not feel quite at liberty at present to tell anyone the plain facts, as I would naturally have to name names, including those of some of my Chiefs. If I do so it may be considered as breaking my Obligation, as 'tale bearing' or disloyalty and until I have your personal advice about the matter and what you feel to be my duties in this, I would not like to make a detailed account of things, as I can judge them. Neither would I like to have my statements used officially as complaints, for reasons which you probably can understand perfectly!

"As the present policies of Thoth-Hermes Temple here in N.Y. apparently endorsed by our G.H. Chief Soror Vestigia, were entirely against our principles, most of us 2nd Order members, who have stood by Thoth-Hermes in many storms of the past, have now retired from active work in it. Some of us now belong to Ptah Temple in Philadelphia, a very harmonious group of good students, and others will probably remain just members at large. Mr. Howard Underhill is

only staying until someone else can take his place on the lease of our Hall.

"The other two present Chiefs are: Imperatrix–Soror Non Mihi Solum (Mrs. Wise, Mr. Whitty's sister). Praemonstrator Frater Honore et Virtute–Dr. Kinney.

"Our G.H. Soror Vestigia has been in constant correspondence with Mrs. Wise and the Group Chief in Chicago, Mr. Wiggs, and is acquainted with all that is going on, but from a very different angle than ours. We have tried to warn her and explain matters as we saw them, but without result. So all we could do is to 'look on', without being able to help and it has been a heart-breaking spectacle to us, as 'Rosicrucian Teaching' means a great deal to us.

"But this has gone entirely in the background here, only the 'outer organization' is kept up, with very little real occult knowledge left in it. The heads in this country have hardly seen the 'outside' of any Second Order book."

And, in a letter from Paul Case to Mrs. Mathers, dated January 31, 1922, we shall end this chapter in his life:

"Dear Madam,

"Your letter of January 11th was expected. I was sure Mrs. Wise would give you some account of my conversation with her. As I anticipated, your reaction to it was that of a person with something to conceal, rather than that of a sincere teacher willing to dispel the honest doubts of a student. If you had satisfactory replies to the facts which are available to any person capable of research work in the occult collections of a great library, you have been more short-sighted in failing to give them.

"Let me; however, enter a denial to your statement that I have circulated reports derogatory to the Order and its teachings. I have spoken of my doubts to Mrs. Wise, because she was my superior. I

72

must repeat that I hardly expected you to provide any other answer to these doubts than that of excommunication. This was the final test of a series which have conclusively demonstrated that whatever the validity of your late husband's claims, you are not to be seriously regarded as the representative of true Rosicrucianism in this day and generation.

"Mrs. Wise is not more than usually inaccurate in reporting a conversation, when she says that I declared that no <u>single</u> teaching of the Order apart from the Minitum Mundum and the ceremonies of the Vault and Portal is peculiar to the A.O. which cannot be found in a public library, unless one is willing to consult the works of that thorough-paced rascal, Crowley.

"What I maintain is that the essential teachings of the A.O., if not by actual explicit statement, given to the members as traditional instruction handed down from the days of Christian Rosencreutz, are neither secret nor peculiarly Rosicrucian.

"I challenge you to refute any of the statements following. You must, unless you are of a particularly confiding and uncritical temperament, know as well as I do that they are statements of plain fact.

"The requirements for advancement given in Book A (which neither yourself or the former head of the A.O. ever sent to America) show that as a 7=4 member, you should have demonstrated to competent examiners your possession of powers, which would enable you to gain first-hand knowledge of events in this country. If you have such powers, you have not exercised them. Of this more than sufficient demonstration is given by your regrettable maladministration of the affairs of the A.O. in America. This course you have adopted is rapidly disintegrating the society in this country and there is grave danger that as the immediate results of your own mistaken delegation of authority to unfit persons, your name and that of your husband will become a byword and a hissing here. That you can permit what purports to be the true channel of the ancient wisdom, a supposedly sacred Order, to degenerate into a mere mail-order business, which

every Tom, Dick and Harry, [can enter] without anything like a personal interview (provided he has $10) is proof enough that even if the claims of the Count MacGregor were true, the Secret Fratres no longer regard the A.O. as their instrument, nor you as their link with the Order.

"I do not know the exact grounds which your husband claimed his authority. I do know that several sincere occultists in England and on the Continent have questioned those claims. The evidence I have cited convinces me that the A.O. is not a channel of Rosicrucian teaching, and the only logical conclusion to be drawn from this evidence is precisely what I said to Mrs. Wise. From this dilemma there is no escape. I fail to see wherein I dishonor your husband's memory in recognizing the logical outcome of the facts. I repeat he was either deceived, or else he was a deliberate impostor. My belief is that he was deceived. But by refusing to make any attempts to dispel my doubts, by acting as you have acted for the last eight months, you weaken even that belief. It is you, not I who blacken the memory of the Count MacGregor. It is you who are even now pursuing a course, which bids fair to drag his name in the mire.

"I am glad to be freed from allegiance to a Head incapable of exercising the proper functions of a Head. Your action has condemned itself in the eyes of those who have worked hardest to build up the A.O. in America. You have freed me and I thank you that I am now in a position to conduct a thorough investigation of every claim of the A.O. Be sure that I shall do so, and that the results will be made known to every person who has entered the Order through my representations, or has been encouraged to remain in it by anything I may have said or written.

"I fear no punitive current that you may attempt to invoke against me. You have no magic to combat me. You are impotent because you know that all I have said is true; that I might have said much more; that all I have here set down has the irresistible inference which shows how ill-founded is your right to call the True Rosicrucian Order 'My

Order,' and diverts you forever of everything but the tawdry, tinsel glory of an assumed authority which you do not possess in fact.

Yours truly,
Paul Case."

With these letters, Paul Case, Lilli Geise, and Elma Dame severed the last links with the Alpha et Omega.

Chapter 14
The Builders of the Adytum

On August 31, 1936 Paul Case wrote again to Dion Fortune:

"...Once one makes direct contract with the Inner Order, no action or Chiefs in the Outer makes a bit of difference, if the outer Chiefs act in error. This has been abundantly demonstrated since those same Inner Chiefs authorized me to make an adaptation of the Order's work with special reference to the practical situation in America. The result of this was the establishment of 'The Builders of the Adytum,' a society whose name is self explanatory. It makes no historical claims to connection with any earlier Order. Its five Founders were all members of the G.D and all but one were Chiefs of Temples in America for years before leaving the G.D."

It is important to note that Case did not found B.O.T.A. alone. He was assisted by several close associates who acted as co-founders and his support in the early days.

In a letter to A.E. Waite, he mentions some of them:

"1. Mr. Howard Underhill (Vota Vita Mea), whose name you may recall as Astrological Editor of 'AZOTH,' and who was Cancellarius of Thoth-Hermes Temple until very recently, when he resigned on account of what we had been able to discover, even at this great distance from Headquarters, concerning the pretensions of the A.O.

2. Miss Lilli Geise (Nunc et Semper) who was expelled by V.N.R. at the same time as myself, and on the same grounds and who was, at that time, Praemonstratrix of Ptah Temple in Philadelphia.

3. Miss Elma Dame (Aude Sapere), who resigned immediately upon the expulsion of N.E.S. and myself, although she was Imperatrix of Ptah Temple."

The identity of the fifth founder, Ann Davies informs us, is uncertain, although it may have been a Mr. Brown. He wrote to Vestigia, using rather forceful words in an attempt to resolve the situation, 'so that the teaching might be saved.' Vestigia removed him from the Order for his efforts.

In a small booklet titled, *The Builders of the Adytum: A Little History* published in January 1929, the goals of B.O.T.A. were enumerated:

"History: THE BUILDERS OF THE ADYTUM began their work in New York City in 1921. The original founders had given years to the study of the Ageless Wisdom and had been working for some time under the leadership of Paul Foster Case, who had brought them in touch, through Tarot, with a teaching which they had found to be of inestimable benefit to themselves. This teaching they were eager to make known to others and they established the B.O.T.A. with these objectives:

1. To disseminate dependable knowledge concerning the forces and laws expressed through human personality, correlating what is best in the wisdom of the past with the most recent developments of modern science;

2. To give specific instruction in methods of personal development based upon this knowledge, to the end that every affiliate may become a more efficient and more serviceable unit of the social order;

3. To afford all earnest aspirants opportunities to cooperate, in the spirit of true brotherhood, in making the personal and social adjustments demanded by the New Age."

In his notebook, *Notes on Tarotic Systems,* Paul wrote his introduction to the first lesson of the B.O.T.A. curriculum:

"The Tarot is a book that can never be exhausted. It will teach you new truths, new aspects of Truth, every little while as you develop the capacity to understand. For this same reason there will never be a

book that explains all the Tarot means. The present work makes no such claim. Its purpose is to point out some of the arrangements of the cards designed to bring out the deeper meanings of the cards that are not explained herein...None of these things will be written. But if you have a penetrating mind and are worthy, you will find out how to be instructed in the Unwritten Law. For every person worthy to become a pupil there is a Teacher whose services are given without money and without price to those who come up to the standards required for initiation. With this introduction we invite your attention to the following pages, representing years of investigation by the present writer, partly independent and partly under the guidance of a Teacher to whom this work is gratefully dedicated."

The way was now cleared for the official founding of a new vehicle for the Inner School. Thus, on the Vernal Equinox of 1922, the outer and public founding of the Builders of the Adytum took place. Like many start up organizations, its members' enthusiasm had to make up for the scarcity of physical resources. The fellow founders encouraged Case to give up his career in music and devote his full efforts towards teaching, lecturing, and writing.

From its inception, students of the B.O.T.A. curriculum were divided into different divisions. There was a probationary, composed of dedicated students who received correspondence lessons and attended Paul's lectures on Tarot and the Tree of Life. This group studied their lessons and performed their meditations in their own homes. Advanced students prepared themselves for eventual initiation into the Chapters.

Paul writes:

"Many references to the Inner School abound in the literature of the secret sciences. Mistaken conceptions of it also abound, but none is more mistaken than the notion that any organization which publishes its existence, however limited may be the circle to whom the announcement is made, is the official representative of that School. We make no such claim, although it is within our personal knowledge that the Inner School is a reality and that in certain parts of the world

are colleges where very ancient records of teachings received from that school may be seen by those who are 'duly and truly prepared.'

"The main object of this fraternity is to help you do this very thing. To bring this hidden gold of wisdom to the surface of consciousness is one of the great works of the students who have united their efforts in this fraternity...every member of the B.O.T.A. is required to provide himself with a set of the Tarot.

"For members of the B.O.T.A....the chief interest of the Tarot is the fact that it is really a book, written in the universal language of symbolism. Thus it conceals from the profane, while preserving for true Sons and Daughters of the Doctrine, the essentials of that ancient wisdom, or knowledge of cosmic law, which it is our aim to learn and apply to constructive action.

"Now and then, we hear vague hints of a 'real tradition' concerning the Tarot, supposed to be in the possession of certain sanctuaries of the 'very occult,' and having their headquarters in Europe. The founders of B.O.T.A., have firsthand knowledge of this tradition, but are not convinced that it has any particular historical value. The opportunity to examine this claim was given to us under an obligation of secrecy which we shall respect; but the reader of these pages may rest assured that he suffers no great loss through our decision that we are in honor bound not to publish this 'real tradition.' Turning then from speculation and the grandiloquent pretense of the 'very occult,' let us examine the Tarot itself to see what evidence it offers concerning its origin...many of the pictures show the distinct influence of Christian thought. Closer examination reveals the presence of many symbols of 'Rosicrucianism.' Here, too, are traces of Gnosticism and the number philosophy of Pythagoras..."

Paul Case was very highly thought of by his early students. For example Lilli Geise, writing to Brodie-Innes, remarks:

"...A few of us have been his daily fellow workers for the last years and feel that he is by far the most promising Occult leader in this whole country...

"He has an unusual amount of knowledge and is so over-modest, that we, as his friends, often feel quite helpless to overcome this feeling and try to make him think a little more of himself. A modern psychoanalyst would tell him at once that he is suffering from a 'humility-complex.' He has kept his knowledge under a bushel all his life, until we have convinced him that it is his duty to give it to the world now, and to take his place as a teacher and leader at last...I think it is quite possible that you and we would become splendid friends, if we were to meet personally and had a good heart to heart talk, even if we study along different lines from now on. If we are searching for the truth, we are certain to reach the same goal."

In the 1930's, this comment reveals a picture of Paul Case:

"...He is invariably called 'Paul' by his students and they look upon him as a true friend as well as a teacher...He not only writes the materials for his courses, but stencils, mimeographs, and assembles the lessons. He spends the minimum of the return of his works on everyday needs—the balance goes for books, materials, etc...Schooling stopped before the completion of High School but he is one of the best informed men on general subjects one could meet and in his specialty he is an outstanding authority. His education is certainly used for the good of others...

"During the years when he did lecturing or was in the theater, he did not own a home. When he started devoting his entire time to correspondence work, a student-friend bought the house in which he now lives, as a contribution to 'the work.' The place is used almost exclusively as a workshop and the living room is also the 'lecture hall.' The only wholly personal rooms in the house are the bath and the kitchen. From the point of view of character, we can say that the spiritual job he has been entrusted with has been the greatest contributing factor to a foundation for his being. His whole life is

focused...on studying and teaching those things which have to do with the higher mind."

It is worthy to note that Paul would later supplement his early formal education by receiving a doctorate from a Bible School in the South.

It was about this time that Lilli and Paul decided to get married. That "meaningful glance" was finally formalized and Case joined the love of his life.

Chapter 15
The Fruits of Adeptship

Paul Case wrote about the Alpha et Omega:

"No clearer statement of the Chiefs of the R.O. of the A.O. could well be made. It says the work of the Order leads straight to Adeptship. With this in mind, those who wish to form a notion of just what kind of Adeptship it leads to, should consider the following..."

Thus begins one of the opening paragraphs of a paper written by Paul in response to assertions made by the Order he left. It was during the spring of 1923 and it was in the form of on "open letter," written to the remaining members of the A.O. in New York: I'll quote it, at length:

THE FRUITS OF ADEPTSHIP

At a meeting of Thoth-Hermes Temple, No. 9, the V.H. Imperatrix, Non Mihi Solum, speaking of the curriculum of the Rosicrucian Order A.O., said:

"HERE IS ALL. Here is all knowledge collected for you—knowledge that might take you years and years of research to try to find and not succeed. Ages ago, others did that for us. Here, ready for your hand and heart, arranged for you step by step, is all—leading up to what? Adeptship, if you will!...Remember that, if you will, you may even in one lifetime become an Adept. And with all my heart I tell you that the straightest, clearest, best ordered road thereto is here in the Rosicrucian Order."

This was reluctantly written, in response to a number of plagiarisms, Mrs. Mathers had made from Case's own writings and others that had appeared in a set of lessons to the Los Angeles Temple.

To continue the quote:

"During the winter of 1922-1923, the Chiefs of A-TOUM Temple, No. 20, Los Angeles, California, announced that they had received from London some new lessons on the Qabalah. From these, they said, they were permitted to select certain more or less exoteric matter, which they would give in a series of public talks. Members of A-TOUM Temple were urged to bring perspective candidates to these public meetings so that the taste of Qabalistic doctrine there given might arouse an appetite for further knowledge and thus lead to an increase in the membership of the Temple. The lessons were not supposed to be part of the A.O. curriculum; but it was intimated that they were written by the G.H. Head of the Order, Soror Vestigia Nulla Restorum. Thus, they were invested with the prestige of high Rosicrucian authorship. Such was the claim. The facts are as follows:

"Six copies of these lessons are in my possession. All but one contains extensive plagiarisms–not from any ancient source, but from books by modern writers. The books are listed below and the numbers in parenthesis indicate the number of thefts from each:

- *'Tarot of the Bohemians by Papus' (3);*
- *'Numbers: Their Meaning and Magic,' by Isidore Kozminsky (4);*
- *'Pictorial Key to the Tarot, A.E. Waite' (1);*
- *'Introduction to the Study of the Tarot,' Paul F. Case (11);*
- *'Hidden Way Across the Threshold,' J.C. Street (2).*

These plagiarisms are not small speculations. In some instances whole paragraphs have been stolen without the alteration of a single word. The thefts from Doctor Kozminsky are thinly disguised, perhaps because he is (or was, at last accounts, a V.H. Frater of the A.O.). Practically all matter having a direct bearing on the Qabalah is from the books by Papus and Case. A whole lesson, dated Dec. 28, 1922, is from Street's, 'Hidden Way.' It is copied without change from pages 46 to 49...

"...Your Imperatrix warns you to study nothing but A.O. curriculum. Why? Because if you do, sooner or later you will find out that you are caught in the meshes of a lying imposter."

You may Google this for the complete text. However, it is apparent that this defense was the last tolling of the funeral bell for the Alpha et Omega in America.

Chapter 16
The Pattern on the Trestleboard

Paul began mailing out his lessons to his affiliates in the fall of 1923, under the title, *The School of Ageless Wisdom*. The first set of lessons detailed the Great Magical Agent and dealt with occult psychology. This set was followed by courses dealing with the symbolism of the Major and Minor Arcana of the Tarot.

In 1920, Case, while in communication asked 'the boss' for his summary of the meaning of the ten Sephiroth of the Qabalistic Tree of Life. The answer would be known later as, *The Pattern on the Trestleboard*. In this author's opinion this is one of the most important documents in the Western Tradition:

This is Truth about the Self:
0. All the Power that ever was or will be is here now.
1. I am a center of expression for the Primal Will-to-Good which eternally creates and sustains the Universe.
2. Through me its unfailing Wisdom takes form in thought and word.
3. Filled with Understanding of its perfect law, I am guided, moment by moment, along the path of liberation.
4. From the exhaustless riches of its Limitless Substance, I draw all things needful, both spiritual and material.
5. I recognize the manifestation of the Undeviating Justice in all the circumstances of my life.
6. In all things, great and small, I see the Beauty of the Divine Expression.
7. Living from that Will, supported by its unfailing Wisdom and Understanding, mine is the Victorious Life.
8. I look forward with confidence to the perfect realization of the Eternal Splendor of the Limitless Light.
9. In thought and word and deed, I rest my life, from day to day, upon the sure Foundation of Eternal Being.
10. The Kingdom of Spirit is embodied in my flesh.

By 1923, these ten affirmations of the Life Power were integrated into the daily practices of all students of the school.

Paul made the following comments in regard to the Pattern:

> "...each of the ten affirmations used by the Builders of the Adytum leads by suggestion to a specific change in personal consciousness. True affirmations must be patterns. To say 'all is beauty' is true enough in the absolute sense, but it will not make your world a whit more beautiful. But to say, 'In all things, great and small, I see the Beauty of the Divine Expression,' and to follow up this initial statement with specific images of beauty, is to bring about a change in your consciousness that shall eventually modify for the better all things in your world."

In 1924, Lilli Geise contracted a kidney disease known as "chronic diffuse nephritis." After being admitted to St. Luke's Hospital on May 2nd her conditioned worsened and she died a week later. Her cremated remains were interred at Fresh Pond cemetery three days later.

Although Lilli had expressed, to many of their close associates, that she intended to leave the bulk of her estate to B.O.T.A, they could not locate a Last Will and Testament. Paul began searching through her desk, drawer by drawer. Finally, weary and full of grief, he held his head in his hands. Suddenly, she was there beside him. Lilli told him of a secret drawer in that desk, one that he didn't know about. She instructed him to touch a specific spring and that he would find the Will in a secret compartment together with the papers naming him as executor. Lilli then smiled at him and faded away.

The following year, Case completed and published the first edition of *The Book of Tokens,* together with his commentary, which as he wrote:

> "... To afford clues which will enable students of the Qabalah to trace certain details of the text to their sources."

Paul made great use of Gematria in these commentaries. Although an artificial system, it has been used for centuries to train the conscious mind to think in a relational manner. The effect is a synchronizing of the conscious with the subconscious mind, enhancing communication and efficiency. As Case explained it:

"It will presently appear that in many instances the Author of these meditations has made use of that branch of the Literal Qabalah termed Gematria…As a rule, Gematria is dry as dust and it has been used by so many text-twisters that not a few Qabalists are disposed in modern times, to neglect it. These meditations, however, contain many examples and they are such excellent ones that the present author believes their presence in the text are a sufficient reason for publishing it, were there no others. During the five years which have intervened since the outline of the meditations were received, many of these hidden instances of Gematria have been discovered in the text and they will be explained in due course…It may also be said that many who have had access to the manuscript of 'The Book of Tokens' have found that some of the meditations are particularly uplifting when read aloud…"

Secrets of Meditation and Magic

During the course of his life Paul made friends with many authors of occult works. He knew Charles Stansfeld Jones, who as "Frater Achad" wrote, *Q.B.L.* or *The Bride's Reception* in 1922, *The Chalice of Ecstasy* in 1924 and, in 1926, *The Anatomy of the Body of God.* He knew Walter Russell, who gave him a personal copy of *The Universal One.* Paul was also a good friend of Alice Bailey and, according to Ann Davies, was the source for much of her book, *Initiation: Human and Solar.*

In 1925, Paul wrote his next installments of the correspondence courses. *Concentration* was first, quickly followed by *Meditation*, *and then* finally by *The Way of Return* (these three were later consolidated into Section C). Section D soon followed with its lessons on the theory and symbolism of Ritual Magic.

In 1925, Case also met the woman who would become his second wife, Astra Fleming. She has been described as, "an intellectually brilliant, energetic, emotional and quick tempered woman of about 36." Records suggest that she also had a personality disorder (using today's

terminology). Theirs was to be a rocky relationship. Astra *(below)*
emigrated from her native
Norway to pursue a writing and
theatrical career in America.
She met Paul in New York City.
Soon after, they married and
settled in Fairport, New York,
Paul's home town. The School
of Ageless Wisdom
headquarters remained in New
York City.

That same year, Paul
embarked on an intense
missionary program, carrying
his message to all the principle cities of the Eastern United States. As a
result the School expanded and its membership rose to several hundred
affiliates.

In each city, Case would speak at one to three public lectures. Then,
depending on the response, the lectures would be followed by an
extended class for several weeks. Those attending would be offered a
chance to sign up for the correspondence courses. Via these reach out
"campaigns," study groups were formed in Boston, Rochester, and
Worcester in Massachusetts, among other locations.

In 1926, Paul entered the Masonic Fraternity by taking the three craft
degrees in his local Fairport Lodge #476 (He was initiated an Entered
Apprentice on March 26; passed to Fellowcraft on April 12; and raised to
the sublime degree of Master Mason on June the 28th).

Paul's status as a Mason provided him access to various great
Masonic research libraries, such as those of the Grand Lodge of New York,
of Massachusetts and of the Scottish Rite at the House of the Temple in
Washington, District of Columbia. He also now had a receptive audience
for his unique approach to esoteric symbolism.

Chapter 17
The School of Ageless Wisdom

While in Fairport, Paul prepared for the reactivation of the esoteric initiated ritual group work. This was, as we have previously pointed out, an important part of the vision imparted by Master Racoczy. These groups, besides providing a vehicle for the ancient tradition of initiation and the training for future adepts, also acted as powerful centers of light. From these centers healing energies could be sent forth to all those in need, whether known or unknown, friendly or hostile.

Although Paul had returned all of his manuscripts and rituals to the A.O., as per the terms of his obligation, he had access to the versions found in Aleister Crowley's, *The Equinox*. Additionally, using the instruction from Master R., and his excellent memory, he was able to reconstruct and purify the rituals used in the esoteric system of group work. In fact, Case's version, with his extensive commentaries (it could be argued), were superior in many ways to the versions he returned to his former Chiefs.

The Enochian system of the A.O. was removed and replaced by a set of elemental tablets based on Qabalistic formulas given to Case by Master Racoczy. Color and sound attunement and healing techniques were fused into the group work. The rituals were purged of the verbose, Victorian verbiage, characteristic of the older Order. Masonic elements were incorporated where deemed appropriate. Finally, the emphasis on authority was changed from rulership to that of instruction. For this reason the senior chief was no longer the Imperator, but the Praemonstrator. To emphasize this change, this office was renamed Prolocutor, or "he who speaks for." It carries the connotation of Chief spokesman and teacher of ritual, as opposed that of "guide."

In 1927, Paul published his first version of what would much later become his "magus opus," *The True and Invisible Rosicrucian Order.* This book analyzes the system of inward initiation as presented in the Rosicrucian system of grades. It also studies the inner alchemical disciplines illustrated in the manifestos of this Order. This Work, in its fourth and much expanded edition was published in the 1970's. It is a must for any serious student of these subjects and is considered to be the best presentation of these studies.

In 1927 Paul published a second book, titled, *An Analysis of the Tarot.* This volume contains a short interpretation of the greater trumps, the symbolism of numbers, and a short instruction on Tarot divination. The book uses the Waite-Ryder version of the Tarot (The B.O.T.A. deck had not been yet developed). These two publications drew much favorable attention to the fledgling organization.

In 1928, Paul began communicating, via a series of letters, instructions to the new working groups (called Chapters). His opening comments lend insight into the mind of a humble, yet true teacher of spirituality:

> *"You are under no compulsion to accept your Prolocutor General's knowledge as final. You need not even assume that it is absolutely accurate. He simply transmits to you, through your Chapter Prolocutor what he knows, as he knows it now..."*

Before long, five Chapters were working in the New England area. B.O.T.A. was achieving its purpose.

Later this year, Case made contact with a well known artist (perhaps also a member) in the Boston area, Jessie Burns Parke *(right).* Here, finally were the hands to make manifest Paul Case's images of his Tarot pack. These cards, initially printed on a single sheet called a Tableau, accompanied the first course on the Tarot in 1929.

During this same year a new course was introduced, *Seven Steps in Practical Occultism,* a study of occult psychology and its practical application. Ann Davies would later describe these lessons as, "one of the most advanced courses in the eventual curriculum." Before it was released Paul and his senior initiates debated as to where the new courses should appear in the series. After much discussion, Paul finally decided that it should be the first course, hidden in plain sight!

"After the student has had these preliminary lessons, he will be ready to understand and apply the new Basic Tarot Course which is being prepared to supersede the First Year Course now in use..."

Chapter 18
Tests and Trials

The period of 1930 to 1933 was a period of growth, development of curriculum for the Order, and disappointment. The economic situation of the Great Depression drastically limited the income students had to spend on non-essentials, like spiritual development.

Additionally, Paul's health began to suffer from the high levels of stress, intense schedule of lectures and writing, and the constant "drama" of being married to Astra. Many of his associates tried to explain the reasons for her instability by using terms like, "lower vibrations," "over-development of the mental and emotional bodies," etc. But, as mentioned previously, she was most likely suffering from a personality disorder.

R. J. Meekren, one of the members of the school's Board of Directors wrote to another, Craik Patten on Feb. 24, 1933:

"I like Astra immensely. She has extraordinary powers and capabilities. But her mental approach to things is so unusual, so different, that she is hard to deal with, hard to keep at work in a team. Perhaps it is impossible. But, I frankly do think this much. She has driven the thing, she has held it up, she has pushed Paul (and perhaps half killed him in doing it) and I do not see quite who is to take her place if she be forced out..."

The situation was not conducive to Paul's work. Although the School was prospering, the administration was in disarray. Astra was making demands for money and making demands on Paul's energy, ones disproportionate to the needs. At the end of the year, because of the economy and for his own survival, Paul reevaluated his plans for the Order and his life. It was decided that he and Astra should separate and he left New York by train for California. The School was left in the hands of Astra and the Board. Paul followed Horace Greeley's advice to "Go west young man!"

Chapter 19
The Sage, The Card Shark and The Lady of The Night

Ann Davies, in one of her Thursday night classes (*Qabalah and Reincarnation*), relates the following story:

"When Dr. Case was on his way, moving from the East to California, he stopped in Reno where he had to stay for a short period. Through some unhappy circumstances funds he expected did not arrive. On top of this he became suddenly ill. He had to spend what money he had waiting to recover and, after a month, he had no money left. Instead of recovering, he got worse. He became so ill that he lost consciousness in his hotel room.

"Fortunately, it so happened that about a week previously he had gone to one of the gambling establishments for several nights and had become acquainted with a card shark, with who he liked to talk— like Jesus, he too hung around sinners!

"They had some very pleasant conversations. Case was quite a prestidigitator and loved to entertain people. During one of his appearances, he mentioned to his friend that he didn't feel well.

"For three days he lay unconscious in his room. The card shark and a lady friend (who was a prostitute) noticed they hadn't seen Dr. Case for several days. Both the card shark and the prostitute had taking a liking to Paul and she felt intuitively that there was something wrong. 'Surely, he would have said goodbye or told us he was leaving,' she thought to herself. 'He seems like that kind of a person.' She was so worried that she spoke to the card shark about her concerns.

"He didn't know where Case was staying but he made inquiries all over town. Eventually he found out where Paul was registered. When they went to Case's room they found him unconscious. He thought:

'My God, I have to go back to my job and this man needs care and attention.'

"They decided they would have to help him. So the card dealer sat with Dr. Case at night and the prostitute (who, naturally, had to be free nights to earn a living) took care of him in the day time.

"When Dr. Case came out of his delirium (he had been in that state for about ten days) he found the prostitute, sitting next to him taking his pulse, wiping his brow. He didn't know what had happened. She explained to him that he had really been sick. They had called a doctor and had indeed paid for the doctor themselves. For a long time Case was on the verge of death, and it was their care, that saved his life. He started to recover; she fed him by the teaspoonful, every two hours. They generously gave him funds so that he could continue to Los Angeles."

Henry Donaph, an old member, recalls that, after he was back to normal, he put a quarter in one of the "one-armed bandits" and hit the jackpot. He then divided up the winnings between the three of them.

Ann continued:

"During one of those periods when he became conscious, he had a glimpse of this prostitute's past incarnations. He saw her as an oracle in one of the temples, well-versed in the stars. She was guiding the various noblemen of that period. With this heightened vision, he saw into her soul and saw that hers was a highly evolved one. As he became stronger they talked a lot about astrology and other esoteric subjects. He never preached to her about being or not being a prostitute—he loved her. She knew, in the words of Jesus, 'I was hungry and you fed me, I was thirsty and you gave me to drink, I was homeless and you took me in.'

"When he got to Los Angeles, in view of the vision he had of her past life, he realized what he could do for her. He went to Llewellyn George and bought her a complete set of astrology books. He sent it to her as *a gift of love and thanks because she was so interested. She had a fine educational background and was previously interested in sociology.*

"When she received these books, she had pretty much the same experience that Dr. Case had with his memory of being a Qabalistic Rabbi. The memory came to her quickly and startlingly. Something in her vehicle at that time was able to tune into that development. She studied the books and with her old technical training, which had been considerable, picked it up so rapidly, that in two years, she retired from being a prostitute to become a very fine and successful astrological counselor. She became a profound follower on the Path of Return and her spiritual growth was staggering. Everything she needed was already there and she needed the experience of being a prostitute in this life, as special preparation.

"Later, Dr. Case used to tell his classes, 'Remember, if this work has value for you, if it is helping you on the Path of Return, if it is bringing you spiritual riches, don't forget to send love and gratitude to a prostitute and a very dishonest card dealer, who had so much love in their hearts, that they went to a man they did not know at all. They spent their own money to feed him. They gave up their sleep and their time to nurse him. And they gave him money to get to Los Angeles where he had followers waiting for him. Please remember this when you start evaluating what is and is not highly evolved. It can be misleading.'"

Chapter 20
Meeting with Soror Resurgam

Reverend Ann Davies

Soon after moving to Los Angeles, Paul and Astra divorced. His finances significantly depleted, he would have to rebuild his financial fortune. That same year he met Dorothy Spring and, after a whirlwind romance, married her.

But perhaps his most important relationship would not be romantic at all. Paul would also meet Ann Davies in California. I'll let her describe the events, as related to her students of her Thursday night class:

"There is a destiny which shapes our lives. It happened to me when I reluctantly agreed to accompany my sister Rosalie to a lecture given by Dr. Paul Foster Case, whom I later learned was the world authority on Tarot and the Holy Qabalah.

"I was practically dragged by force to hear Dr. Case and I didn't go to really listen to him. I didn't know what he was all about. I didn't know

what Tarot was all about. I had been nagged into it by my sister who was an extraordinary clairvoyant, clairaudient and psychic.

"So, I went under duress. I did not want to go and did not like to be bored with a lot of various claims. I was almost allergic to it! The one thing I did assiduously was to avoid all occult teachers and lecturers.

"I was a lone eagle. For many years, I spent either as a complete or semi-invalid. What I did during this entire period was to get ten books at a time from the library (that was all they would let me have), take them home and study them. I started off with Buddhism, and then went on to Vedanta and Yoga. I was already familiar with Christian Science and Unity, and had looked into New Thought. I did this very thoroughly, because I did nothing else. My only interest was to find out who I was and why I just didn't like the idea of being alive. I was very much an atheist—dogmatic and prejudiced. It was difficult for me to give up some of my ideas. I saw nothing but pain and sorrow, and it tore at my heart.

"My whole approach to occultism was different from what we usually find. When I first started to study the Buddhist philosophy, I did it in order to cure a friend of mine from his superstitious belief in it and I thought I would attack him from the inside! I didn't start off with occult reading to try to prove something; I much preferred to disprove it. When some of the ideas were presented to me in these books, I was disturbed for I didn't like the idea that I might be wrong. I preferred thinking that life was an accident and that when I was dead; I was 100% dead—no more consciousness.

"After spending years of doing nothing but studying books, investigating and testing the various claims, I was very shaken up to discover that they worked. I started to have many strange awakenings and experiences and was never very happy about it at that time. Nevertheless, what I wanted was Truth.

"Then in 1944, when I was about 32 years old, I walked into Dr. Case's class. People came in and all sat down. There were about 15 to 20 people in the living room. I was confused and complained to my sister, who I was sitting next to, telling her about all that was wrong. Why did I have to get on a street car to be here? Why should I be sitting on this hard wooden chair and in this uncomfortable place waiting for a lecturer? Why are we surrounded by a bunch of Tarot cards and fortune telling nonsense?

"The door opened and lightning and thunder struck! Imagine my amazement when Dr. Case walked into a roomful of people, emanating an extraordinary spiritual power. As his eyes met mine, we both experienced an intense shock of recognition that was soul shaking. Along with this recognition, I was aware of many other elements. Infinitude looked out from behind his eyes and smiled into my soul. I knew him so well and yet I couldn't understand why. I couldn't immediately say, 'We've done this, that or the other.' It was a very shaking experience. I was telling my sister in a very hysterical tone that I knew this man so well.

"He rushed over to me in front of everyone, threw his arms around me, and said, 'Oh my god, I'm so happy to see you again! Oh, isn't this wonderful!' And, of course I knew him. I have known him throughout eternity. That moment there was thunder and lightning, but, in between, there was confusion.

"I said, 'Yes, I'm so happy to see you too.' But, I was a little embarrassed. When you know someone even better than you know your own sister, you certainly should know their name and I didn't know his name when he walked in! I knew who he was, but I didn't know who he was! That was the problem, and it was a big problem. He threw his arms around me like that and there was all this happiness. I threw my arms around him and we hugged each other.

"I turned to my sister and said, 'you see, I told you I knew him.' I turned to Dr. Case, 'I've been trying to tell my sister that we know each other, but isn't it odd–I hope you will forgive me–I'm trying to figure out from where.'

98

"He said, 'where have you been? Why have you been away for so long?' I looked at him in astonishment. I said, 'What do you mean?' He said, 'Why have you been away from the class for so long?' I said, 'No, I've never been to class.' Then he got confused and we both just stood there, bewildered.

"The thing that next shocked me was that he pulled out a large Tarot key, Key #5 [The Hierophant] and put it on display. I thought, 'Ye gods, this man is an extraordinary being. He couldn't be anything less than a very high initiate and adept, but he pulls out this nonsense!' He pulled out this 'nonsense' and started to speak about Tarot Key #5, The Hierophant, as being the teacher, in the most erudite manner...What he had to say was so interesting ...

"Instead of fortune telling, he really shared pearls of wisdom. I heard brilliance, beauty, it was the most astonishing, glorious and joyous experience that ever a human being could have. To everything he said, my intuition responded, 'Yes, yes!' I've never met anyone I could go along with like that before. It was a most beautiful, wondrous thing.

"During his lecture, time became non-existent. Knowledge and wisdom poured from him as from a fountain. Gone was my physical discomfort of the hard chair and my complaints to my sister at having dragged me out to this endurance contest. In their place a speechless astonishment swept over me. I was very impressed with the way he taught and what he was teaching, in the way he expressed himself and the ideas he held."

Years later, when Ann would tell me about this first meeting with her teacher, you could still see the ecstatic wonderment and enthusiasm light up her face and shine from her eyes. When she met Paul, it was instant recognition of a familiar soul, a family reunion. The joyous meeting recounting was contagious. I felt as if I had been right there.
Ann continues:

"At our meeting after the lecture, he invited me to visit him and thus started the 'Great Adventure.' So, I made an appointment for us to meet. When I came for the interview, I never left. I learned that he was the founder and spiritual head of Builders of the Adytum, a true link in an age-old chain of Mystery School training systems based on the Qabalistic Tree of Life. We both knew intuitively that we had not been brought together by chance. That indeed, a profound and meaningful destiny lay behind our meeting.

"We had a long talk coming to the inescapable conclusion that though this was the first time we had met in this incarnation, we were old friends. We knew each other well and that it would be my great privilege to work with him closely from that day forward. Dr. Case was my spiritual father, brother, teacher and friend."

Chapter 21
The Craftsman and His Apprentice

The relationship between Paul and Ann developed, not as a new association, but as a reconnection of old friends, friends that had known each other many times, in many lives before. Ann reveals the first few days of their working together in the following comments:

"There was something again very interesting and peculiar about the whole situation. It was Dr. Case's eyes. This was an entirely subjective experience for me. Looking out of Dr. Case's eyes I saw another being. Furthermore, I was quite sure that I was in communication with this being through Dr. Case. My entire impression was that Dr. Case was being used like a telephone, or, shall we say, almost like a television. It was also an eye for somebody else to look at me and love me. The love was tremendous. I'd never experienced such love in my life before or since...

"That first three days, I kept looking and looking at him, because I saw this vast soul whom I knew. My consciousness was absolutely able to differentiate, here was Dr. Paul Foster Case, whom I knew his personality, and, then, there was also from behind his eyes this fantastic being, this soul who had evolved the ability for divine compassion and love...

It was revealed later that Ann was psychically picking up on the channeled link between Dr. Case and his long time Third Order contact, the Master Racoczy. Paul waited to share this information with Ann. He first wanted to see if she could divine the connection on her own. On the third evening, while sitting in front of her mirror, brushing her hair, suddenly, there in her reflection, looking out from her own eyes, she saw this same consciousness, this same vast being. She said she almost collapsed.

She then received a message from the Master; that she was exactly where she was supposed to be, and would be entering training to establish the next linkage in the chain of contacts.

"Sure enough, it came in and out. Every time Dr. Case lectured, anytime he felt giving or compassionate…there it was…Those who have gone before us always symbolize the wise ones, those that are guiding us in order to be able to share the rapture, the love and the beauty…

"It was only after a good five or six days later that he [Dr. Case] told me about the Master of Wisdom he called 'the Boss'…

"…After that he told me that connections had been made this way for contact to be made… so he had been warned not to upset my vanity until I had better understanding of the work…

"…Dr. Case was not a very practical man. He was trying to take care of the entire work of Builders of the Adytum, printing the lessons, stenciling them, mimeographing them, taking care of the accounts while giving two classes, directing the inner esoteric work and so on. I think it was a little too much… I spoke to Dr. Case right away. Indeed, we were like old friends. There was no getting acquainted, just catching up with all the things between us. I never left. I knew I longed to be there and apparently so did Dr. Case. We worked shoulder to shoulder.

"He trained me in more than words could tell and usually the training didn't have to do with the sort of things we think training is. It had more to do with his fantastic capacity to help me see my personality. I could see the difference between his personality and that higher Self and it made me love his personality infinitely more because of the fact that his personality was a channel for that extraordinary divinity…"

In those days Paul and Ann did everything from writing the lessons, to typing and reproducing them, to mailing them, etc., not to mention the public promotions, classes and esoteric work. The work was great and the funds were small. To supplement their income, Paul drew on his days as an entertainer and developed a "mentalist" or mind reading act. He taught Ann the old "verbal code" technique, still used today in night clubs. Paul would have a member of the audience select an object from his or her purse or pocket and then he would hold it up and project its image (with a great deal of dramatic flair) to a blindfolded Ann, seated on the stage. He would then, with very carefully selected words, clue her, without the audience knowing, as to what he was holding. Their act wasn't a mega-hit, but it helped put dinner on the table. Ann once told me an entertaining story in connection with their theater days.

Funds were so scarce that sometimes they didn't have money for bus tickets. She told me to picture her in an evening gown and Paul, in a tuxedo, trying to get a free lift. Ann would often "thumb a ride." She didn't have much trouble, being young and attractive. Then Paul, who had been hiding out of sight nearby, would jump out, and Ann would ask, "Oh, won't you give my poor old daddy a ride too?" What could the guy say? He had already stopped. Times may have been desperate, but chivalry was not dead, at least in those days.

*　*　*　*　*　*

Ann found that Paul could see through her subtle methods of persuasion. Often she tried to make it seem as though her thoughts were actually his ideas. One time when she did this Ann noticed a strange look on Paul's face. He then broke out in a fit of uncontrollable laughter. *"Ann,"* he said to me, chuckling with indulgent affection, *"I knew what you were up to from the very beginning. But I was so impressed with the cleverness of your technique and the sweet tact and patience you were displaying, that I would not have stopped your magnificent performance for anything in the world! You are a rascal, but you shall have your reward for entertaining me! Come, let's get that job done!"*

"I became more than comfortable around Dr. Case, despite the fact that he saw through me. He taught me that laughter is an important ingredient in love and acceptance of oneself and others."

Chapter 22
Green Apples on the Tree of Life

Ann Davies recalled:

"Dr. Case used to love to call the undeveloped, less evolved, immature, tantrum throwing, egomaniacal levels of humanity the 'Green Apples on the Tree of Life' because, when you bite into a green apple it's sour and will give you a stomach ache...

"Dr. Case also used to say that going off on what is called 'The Search,' is often just an excuse for some aspirants to become 'Metaphysical Tramps.' I thought that was a rather interesting term— Metaphysical Tramp...

"He said that unhappily, there were quite a few seekers who are more metaphysical tramps than aspirants. They give the illusion of being aspirants because they could...spout metaphysics with such vast ability, any phase of metaphysics you could bring up; whether it is Persian Occult Thought, or Japanese Zen Buddhism, or other forms of Buddhism. Whether it be the Hindu forms of metaphysics, The Vedanta Abstract or the various Yoga disciplines or some of the Western Elementary Metaphysics, there were many who could give a description of each of these schools of thought."

Ann recalls:

"Dr. Case used to get into all kinds of trouble with people who didn't know what was happening to them. He was a fabulous channel and true spiritual aspirants, for example, would pick up his energies and interpret it in their own ways and levels. You would be amazed at how many women decided he was their 'soul mate'. He wasn't a handsome man, but his eyes did channel infinity...I was amazed to discover how unaware he was of why he kept having so many

problems...at the time Master R. brought me to Dr. Case, he had about five 'soul mates' chasing him. He loved—and loves—humanity and certainly there wasn't anything handsome about him from the usual point of view, but there was this emanation."

Paul would be married many times. According for various sources, he would stand before the altar either on four or five occasions in his lifetime. As mentioned previously, he was first married to Lilli Geise, then Astra Fleming, then Dorothy Spring. His last wife was none other than Harriet Bullock (Case), who he married in 1943. Some accounts state that he was married twice to Dorothy Spring. Others suggest that there may have been a short marriage after Dorothy to another woman. Whatever the truth may be, Harriet was definitely the final spouse.

After marrying Harriet the stress of these "soulmate" pursuers relaxed a little. Also, with the addition of Paul's new wife, the Master Racoczy now had the perfect combination to renew the work of transmitting a lost, esoteric, Qabalistic text. The instrument chosen for these communications was an Ouija Board, an unusual one. Significantly (and I personally saw it) it had a slide planchette, unlike traditional boards. Additionally, it had a Sacred Pentagram painted on the back in certain initiated colors. This communication device proved to be a very serviceable tool. Paul acted as the operator, Ann as the sensitive or receptor, and Harriet served as the scribe. Master R. explained that this was a much more stable and dependable combination for the transmission of such information; meaning literal word for word. I have made the complete transcripts of this operation available in Appendix 2 of the present work.

Chapter 23
An Adept Passed this Way

One of the vows a Rosicrucian makes is to look for a worthy successor to replace him, after he is gone. It will be seen from the account of the forgoing chapters that a replacement for Paul Foster Case would be hard to find. Ann Davies, his successor, would have agreed. She may have succeeded him, but she never replaced him. He was an Adept of unique qualities and capacities; a shining link in the Golden Chain of Initiates. But Paul was conscientious. He trained his successor to carry on the Great Work of the regeneration and enlightenment of humanity, even if in doing so he would have to forgo duties and tasks that he dearly loved.

Ann tells us:

> "Then, in the last year or so before he passed on, he announced to me: 'I'm not going to lecture anymore. I have no intentions of having any more classes. You are going to have to start teaching, Ann.' This sounded ridiculous to me. I couldn't really accept that.
>
> "I said: 'I can't lecture.'"
>
> "What do you mean, you can't lecture?"
>
> "I said, 'Well, I can't remember words. I can't–I have no ability, I've just never been trained.' He said, 'Well, you don't have to; No one is going to force you. But, if the work is going to have a group anymore, it's going to have to come from you. It's not going to come from me...'"

Ann and Harriet would attempt, time and again, to tempt Paul into fulfilling his old role of teacher and lecturer. Ann even faked a bout of laryngitis to persuade him to fill in. Paul outsmarted them both by going to a "Gentleman's Only Card Club" on the evenings when the classes were given. The ladies knew where he was, but they couldn't gain admission to try to convince him to come out of retirement for the evening.

Thus, Ann was forced or "encouraged" to fill his place as the spiritual guide and leader of The Builders of the Adytum.

Then, on March 9, 1954 the friends and students of the B.O.T.A. received this letter:

"To the Friends and Pupils of Dr. Paul Foster Case:

"The Founder and Leader of Builders of the Adytum, Ltd., has left his physical body and entered into the Higher Life. Though our hearts are heavy with the thought of our own personal loss, we do rejoice with him in his glorious release

"Dr. Case was born in New York State October 3, 1884, and passed on Tuesday, March 2, 1954, in Mexico City, where he was vacationing with Mrs. Case. His physical body was cremated within 24 hours, in accordance with the laws of Mexico. Mrs. Case is returning from Mexico City and will bring the ashes with her, to be interred in Forest Lawn Memorial Park.

"In his young manhood, Dr. Case was a professional organist and orchestra leader. Later, as his mission in life became more apparent to him, and his Inner Powers developed he entered into his life's work. His mission—to translate the Techniques of Tarot and Qabalah, teachings of the Ageless Wisdom, into terms understandable to the modern mind, to assure that this and coming generations will have available a Way towards Spiritual, Psychological and Philosophical integration. The Western Occult techniques will remain alive, due to a lifetime of dedication to this end. Forty-five years have been given to study, research, writing, lecturing and teaching.

"He was a member of the International Brotherhood of Magicians, and of the International Guild of Prestidigitators, having served as Recording Secretary and as Chaplain of the latter group. A Doctor of Sacred Theology; a Master Mason, holding membership in Eagle Rock

107

Lodge #422, F.&A.M.; a Priest of the Liberal Catholic church, whose presiding Bishop is the Rt. Rev. Frank W. Pigott of London, England; a deep scholar with knowledge of Hebrew, Hindu, Chinese and Christian religions and philosophical teachings, his influence was widespread and his friends and pupils were many. As a man who taught the oneness of God, the brotherhood of man, and the unity of all Life, he has never been known to sit in judgment on a fellow creature. With deepest humility, he always insisted that he was only a channel for something higher than himself, to assure that the modern world will have available a practical method for Spiritual unfoldment.

"He was the recognized world authority on TAROT, such credit being given to him in the writings of many prominent Occult authorities, including Manly P. Hall. The headquarters of B.O.T.A. was moved from Boston to Los Angeles in 1933, and the work will go on now, still guided by him. For we know that he is more alive than he was when we knew him in the flesh, and he will continue working with us from the Larger Life upon which he has entered.

"We rejoice—our hearts are filled with gladness for him, that his sojourn in the flesh has been so rich in accomplishment and that his release came so easily and painlessly.

"In accordance with his expressed wishes, a Memorial Service will be conducted on TUESDAY, March 16th, 1954 at 11:30 A.M. in the Church of the Recessional at Forest Lawn Memorial Park. We know that you, his friends and pupils, will want to be present to wish him Godspeed and to add your thoughts and blessings to those of others who love him and to whom he gave so much.

THE BUILDERS OF THE ADYTUM. LTD."

Well, the journey ends—or does it? Paul certainly has achieved immortality. His writings and teachings, his system of initiation, attract more and more students each year (I have included some of these teachings in the appendices of this book). He is probably better known

108

and more influential now than he was at any time during his life. It is certain that he was an Adept of the Western Mystery Tradition.

Years after his transition, in my presence, when questioned by some students about the persistent rumor that Paul had merely had a "Hermetic Death", his widow Harriet answered, cryptically, with a twinkle in her eye:

"Well, all I can say is, I brought someone back in that box."

She then turned, smiled and winked at me conspiratorially!

Appendix I:

Thirty-Two Paths of Wisdom

This is the Communication received, in skeleton form, By Paul Case and Michael Whitty from Master R., in 1919:

In the name of Adonai, shall the nations be blessed!

1. The paths of the Tree of Life indicate the order of manifestation after the primary expression of the powers of the ten Sephiroth, indicated by the Lightning-Flash. Not until the Paths of the letters are manifested do the Sephiroth come into full expression. Prior to this, they are like unrealized ideas. The Paths of the letters make them active.

2. Now consider the order of the Paths. The eleventh, *Aleph*, brings Wisdom into activity; the twelfth, *Beth*, Understanding; the thirteenth, *Gimel*, brings Beauty into activity and thus Beauty begins to be active before Mercy and Severity. As in creation, the beauty of visible nature was manifest before creatures to which Mercy or Severity could be shown, were brought forth.

3. Beauty being established, the fourteenth Path, *Daleth*, unites Wisdom and Understanding, and the central point of this Path where it crosses the thirteenth is Da'ath, in Hebrew, Knowledge. For all knowledge has its roots in the Divine contemplation of the perfect primal Beauty.

4. Wisdom or *Chokmah*, which includes the idea of skill in construction, then projects the *Path of Constituting Intelligence*, fifteenth path, *Heh*, and through this path Beauty, which has received only the influx of power from *Kether*, the Crown of Primal Will, now receives the influence of the *Illuminating Intelligence* of the Father, *Chokmah*, The *Constituting Intelligence* of the letter *Heh,* with which creation took place.

5. Hence the next Path, that of *Vav*, joins Wisdom to Mercy. For when creatures begin to exist, Mercy becomes active. This is the passage of Wisdom, *Chokmah*, into the Self-impartation of the Divine Spirit through the Self-contemplation of his or Its limitless possibilities as an eternal Spirit of Life.

6. Mercy, *Chesed*, is prior to Severity, *Geburah* for reasons that will appear shortly. Do not confuse this sequential manifestation of the Sephiroth with the instantaneous one indicated by the Lightning-Flash which brings them all into at once into actual manifestation.

7. The Path of *Zain, Disposing Intelligence*, suggests by its name the operation of the Supernal Understanding, *Binah*, in separating the creatures produced by the Constituting Intelligence into species, classes, etc. The fundamental separation is that of sex and hence this path is indicated by *Zain,* the sword and by the Lovers in the Tarot.

8. Not until this *Separating Intelligence* has projected the power of Understanding into Beauty can the activity of Severity be manifest through the path of *Cheth*, which, setting off definite fields of operation of the Divine Understanding brings into effect the *Radical Intelligence* of *Geburah*.

9. At this point in Spirit's full realization of Its powers as a limitless, self-imparting principle manifested in limited forms of expression unites the potencies of Mercy to those of Severity through the Path of the letter *Teth*, called *Intelligence of All Spiritual Activities*. This Path is also called *Intelligence of the Secret*, because the Great Arcanum is based upon the fact that Limitless Light expresses itself in limited form. Therein you may discover the Great Secret of all magical operations, the Arcanum of the equilibrium between Severity and Mercy.

10. Notice also that this Path crosses that of *Gimel*. The central point of the magical equilibrium is the realization that the Primal Will eternally projects itself in Beauty and this Path of *Gimel*, being that of the *Uniting Intelligence*, the implication is that true equilibrium can only be attained

by means of the conscious, self-identification of the personal will with the Universal Self-direction toward the realization of Beauty.

11. Now comes the Path of the letter *Yod*, which carries the influence of Mercy into Beauty, concentrated in a complete realization of the cosmic purpose indicated by the name of the Path, *Intelligence of Will*. In the Tarot the Hermit, far from being a conventional type of priest, illustrates the masculine expression of beneficence, *Chesed*, through *Yod*, the letter of the Father. This will be clear upon examination of the ninth Key of the Tarot.

12. The Path of the letter *Lamed*, by contrast, shows a feminine influence, that of the ruler of the sign Libra, the feminine planet Venus, in the activity of *Faithful Intelligence*, which perfects or completes the static manifestation of Beauty through equilibrated action or work, karma. But this static manifestation of Beauty is not effected until after the Path of *Kaph*, or *Conciliating Intelligence* has brought *Netzach* into activity as the projection of the influence of *Chesed*. Because Karma does not begin to operate until the turning Wheel of Manifestation has brought into the field of the unfolding Universal Self-consciousness a definite conception of the victorious end towards which it's Self-impartation is directed. Karma cannot be supposed to work without an objective, and the Maker of Spirit assures us that Its objective must be the successful outcome of the creating process. Hence, *Lamed* and the twenty-second Path follows *Kaph* and the twenty-first.

13. The static expression of Beauty being realized, Severity projects Splendor to balance Victory. You will observe that Understanding, Severity and Splendor are, as it were, reflections of Wisdom, Mercy and Victory respectively.

14. The Path connecting Severity and Splendor is that of the letter *Mem*, called *Stable Intelligence*. The fixed, unwavering self-contemplation, proceeding primarily from the Supernal Understanding is associated with *Mem* because it is the reflection in the creature of the Creator's Self-understanding. This Path refers to a condition of human consciousness. In the Tarot it is the Hanged Man, that is, the suspended mind or Man as in

112

the state of freedom from activity, which the Hindus compare to a perfectly calm body of water. When this state of the Universal consciousness finds expression through a personal form complete realization of the Divine Splendor is made actual.

15. The Path of *Nun* is the first manifestation of the dynamic or projective aspect of *Tiphareth* as contrasted with the static or receptive aspect. It is called *Imaginative Intelligence* because the primary activity of Beauty works through imagination by bringing about new modes of expression. This involves the passing away of the forms which are supplanted by those which imagination calls into existence. The passing away of supplanted forms is indicated in symbolism of the Tarot Key entitled Death, and the fact that the new forms are developments of the old is suggested by the nature of the harvest gathered by the reaper in the picture. The result is the perfection of *Netzach*, for through the transformations wrought by the power of Beauty the final Victory is attained.

16. The Path of the *Intelligence of Probation and Trial*, attributed to the letter *Samekh* follows the Path of Imaginative Intelligence because it signifies the testing of the ideas and innovations suggested by the imagination. It joins Beauty to Foundation because only by experiments, trials and tests can the harmony of *Tiphareth* become actualized in the established certainty implied by the term Foundation. Note that Foundation is the propagative Sephirah and you will have a clue to many problems.

17. The Path if *Ayin* is perhaps the most obscure of all. *The Renewing Intelligence* completes the dynamic expression of Beauty by uniting it to Splendor on the side of the Pillar of Severity. The Key to the mystery of this Path is the word limitation and it is the Renewing Intelligence because it is the source of human consciousness of limitation, incompleteness, lack personal achievements the essential perfection and bondage. Our sense of bondage, after all, is the reception of our intuitive knowledge of the freedom of That which is the essential Self of every man. When we consider the small extent of our personal achievements the essential perfection of the One Self seems to be an unattainable ideal.

113

Millions of people personify this ideal as an externalized deity. Its opposite, to which they attribute limitation of all kinds, they personify as a hostile and malignant agency, the Devil. The sense of bondage, however, is what drives man to seek freedom and thus it leads at last to the Splendor which is the consequence of the strict justice of *Geburah,* and the outcome of the dynamic impulse towards Beauty which pervades creation, while at the same time this splendor is the reflection of Victory.

18. The Path of *Peh*, which joins Victory to Splendor, is analogous to the Paths of *Daleth* and *Teth*. It is the *Exciting Intelligence*, and it follows the Renewing Intelligence because the sense of limitation sooner or later gives way to the conviction that this limitation is not permanent. This conviction is man's chief incentive to the kinds of action which will lead to freedom. It originates in an inanimate perception that the spirit of man is one with the Universal Spirit which, as we have seen must necessarily succeed in carrying out the great purpose for which it projects itself in a universe. This intuitive perception comes suddenly like a Lightning-flash and usually overthrows the whole conception of the meaning of life held previously by him to whom it comes. This is an experience, not only of a single person but also of whole races at certain stages of their development. It is the great influence which effects sweeping changes in the thought and work of the world.

19. This sudden inspiration is followed by the calmer influence of the next path attributed to the letter *Tzaddi* and called the *Natural Intelligence.* This Path represents the gradual unfoldment of man's instinctive knowledge of truth. This knowledge begins to find expression in his thoughts as soon as he comes to know that he is not the bond-slave of external conditions. It is the projection of Victory, which the divine Spirit in the heart of Man recognizes as inevitable and this is the root of all man's hopes.

20. The next Path is that of the letter *Qoph*. In Hebrew the meaning of this letter *Qoph* is somewhat obscure. Usually it is given as "the back of the head," and there is no doubt that this agrees with occult tradition and also with certain facts. But the word Qoph is also translated "ape", and is apparently of obscure foreign derivation. If it means ape in the alphabet

it suggests knowledge of evolution on the part of Qabalists antedating Darwin by some thousands of years. For the Path of *Qoph* is that of the *Corporeal Intelligence* which "informs everybody in the influence of the solar orb and is the root of all growth." The word "informs" as here employed has the sense, now obsolete of "to form, vitalize, make or inspirit." The Corporeal Intelligence is that mode of consciousness which builds the physical vehicle of the soul and it is the consciousness which has its bodily location in the back of the head in the cerebellum and the medulla oblongata. In the latter, particularly, consciousness is active at all times, even when higher brain centers are asleep, for it controls all the physical vital functions.

21. Now the letter *Qoph* is associated with sleep in the *Book of Formation* as a hint that the Corporeal Intelligence remains active even in sleep. Furthermore, as the Intelligence which informs everybody it is that which effects all structural transformations and thus it is the immediate agency in evolution. Hence the Corporeal Intelligence unites the Occult Intelligence of *Netzach*, the Supreme spirit's hidden knowledge of Its limitless potentialities which must find expression sooner or later in the perfect manifestation of itself implied by the noun, Victory, to the *Resplendent Intelligence* of *Malkuth.*

22. Note also that this Path corresponds to the zodiacal sign Pisces, which rules the feet and that it ends in *Malkuth* wherein are placed the feet of the Grand or Macrocosmic Man. The Corporeal Intelligence acts in response to desire even in the lowest forms of living organisms. All structural changes in the evolution of higher types of life from lower ones, as Lamarck long ago pointed out are brought about by efforts to gratify some desire by the entity in whose organism repeated action directed toward some definite end brings about such changes. In man these changes take place only, or at least principally within the range of the nervous organism. It is by the transformations so wrought during natural sleep, be it observed, that the latent powers of man find expression. In other words, the higher faculties which are hidden or occult in the masses of humanity are brought forth into the supernormal power of Adepts who have become partakers in the Heavenly Kingdom,

Malkuth, through the influence of this Path. And these powers constitute Resplendent Intelligence of *Malkuth*.

23. The next Path that of *Resh* is the complement, or reflection of the *Natural Intelligence*. It is called the *Collecting Intelligence*, because this Path corresponds to the Sun, which is a great storage battery of the Cosmic and Spiritual Fire. This Fire is collected in the Sun and there, lowered in vibratory speed, so that it becomes perceptible to our gross senses in the phenomena of Light and Heat. The Cosmic Energy itself is actually manifest in the *Absolute and Perfect Intelligence* of *Hod*. The sages unite to declare that the fundamental principle of our Universe is consciousness. Whence it follows that the energy manifested by all modes of activity, whether fine or gross is inherently mental in quality. This fact is the scientific basis of Magic. The Cosmic energy is collected or focused as Solar force in the Path of *Resh*, which communicates this Force to the ninth Sephirah *Yesod*.

24. The next path is that of *Shin*, joining the *Perfect Intelligence* of *Hod* to the *Resplendent Intelligence* of *Malkuth*. It is called the *Perpetual Intelligence* because it is subject to no change. Thus it is in direct contrast to the ever changing Corporeal Intelligence attributed to the letter *Qoph*. Since this Path is attributed to *Shin*, the third Mother Letter it also refers to the Primal Fire. This Path communicates the influence of the Pillar of severity to *Malkuth*. The *Perpetual Intelligence* is that which persists through the series of incarnations as the spark or core of individuality, around which the successive personalities are built.

25. The last Path is that of the letter *Tav*, the *Administrative Intelligence* which communicates to the *Resplendent Intelligence* of *Malkuth* the propagative power of *Yesod,* without which the *Resplendent Intelligence* would be barren and nonproductive. Compare this Path with *Ayin* and also with those of *Lamed* and *Tzaddi*. The pointed comment is the influence of Saturn, which rules Capricorn, *Ayin* and Aquarius, *Tzaddi,* and is exalted in Libra, *Lamed*; the power of Saturn is doubled.

26. Thus the Alchemists say that their Saturn, Lead, is corrosive externally and lunar internally. That is, it combines the form destroying power of

corrosion with the perfect reflecting power of that which the alchemists call the Moon. The corrosive power predominates in Capricorn or the Renewing Intelligence. This Natural Intelligence, through the letter *Tzaddi* is associated with meditation. The Path of *Lamed* represents the equilibration of the corrosive and reflective powers.

27. These correspondences are shown in the Tarot where Justice is a female figure like her who kneels in the picture called the Star, holds the sword of corrosion and the scales which symbolize the equilibrium attained through meditation. *Lamed*, moreover, corresponds to work and this is allied to the Assisting Intelligence, which as pictured by The World in the Tarot represents the perfection of the Saturnine nature. The Assisting Intelligence completes the sequential manifestation of the Sephiroth. In human consciousness, it is expressed as Self-identification with the Supreme Spirit and as the dedication of the whole personal life to the furtherance of the Great Work.

Appendix II: Communications

Sunday, February 16, 1947 11:50 P.M.

In the Name of ADONAI shall all the nations be blessed!

We have waited long, Frater, for another to take up the work interrupted by the advancement to the Third Order of our Very Honored Frater G. et S. (Gnoscente et Serviente). You should have recognized [the initials].

(P.F.C. answered that he did.)

His passing into a higher field of action deprived us for a time, as you reckon time, of a balancing force for yours, Frater Perseverantia.

(Question: Is Ann the balancing force? Answer: Yes.)

It was for this that we began this communication with a phrase that should echo in your recollection. Not a moment has passed since he sailed for California that we have not kept in mind the unfinished work, begun in the weekly communications of twenty-five years ago. The interval has seemed long to you, and has been packed With incident, but all this, from our point-of-view, has been just a brief interlude. Even then, this new instrument was in incarnation, and had been brought within range of your auric emanation.

The Second Order work had a more important consequence than you then realized, or have even yet understood. It is tremendously potent in opening a channel for the outpouring of the astral light, and, from then on, you served as the communicating link between us and Ann. This accounts for the sense of familiarity you both felt at your first meeting. In effect, you have been in communication all this time, although neither of you had any conscious knowledge of the other's identity.

118

By bodily inheritance Ann is in a direct line of Knowers of the Mysteries of the Reception. You have the same basic knowledge, but you do not enjoy the advantage of the unbroken physical chain. G. et S., like yourself, had brought over former knowledge, but this instrument, though without conscious [memory? knowledge?] - apart from what she has learned from you-has really been under our instruction, and this has been projected into her finer vehicles through you.

(The hour was very late, and P. and A. were tired, so we stopped at this point.)

SECOND COMMUNICATION

Monday, February 17, 1947 10:45 P.M.

When you become advanced adepts you will understand many details of the mechanics of communication which may seem obscure at present. It is not so important to know these now as to bring through what has been so long in abeyance. It might be well to say that those at the planchette are really pushing it to the necessary letters, for the words are actually rising from the stock in your Nephesh. What is important is the content of the message, and you will find that you often correctly anticipate the word before its actual completion.

It is inadvisable to let the group who meet on Tuesdays know about these sittings. First, because some of them are simply curious about the possibility of survival. Second, because the things we have to tell you are, in many details, distinctly not for indiscriminate dissemination. You must remember that we are taking up a project which was broken off by the passing of Frater G. et S. Much of what was projected then has dropped out of the conscious recollection of Frater P., and since the notes of those sittings were, except for those having to do with the Book of Tokens, kept by Mrs. Whitty until after the passing of Frater G. et S. (at which time she saw fit to destroy them, she never having been in real sympathy with his deeper occult interests), there may be need for a measure of repetition. Frater P. will, no doubt, recall some of these points as they arise.

(P.F.C. asked what explanation shall we give to the Pasadena group about not using the other board. H.B.C. suggested, or interpolated, that we just say we had been too busy to use it. THEY answered as follows:)

That would be somewhat less than exact. Why not say that Frater P. found it too much of a strain to use it? The fact is, of course, that he is so accustomed to this type of board that it offers almost no obstacle to free communication. After all, it is simply a device. Incidentally, it may interest you to know that this kind of board was a development from the earlier planchette which had a pencil at the point. The script so written was often

120

difficult to decipher, so this arrangement was projected into the mind of a sensitive who happened to have unusual business acumen; and he and his family made a small fortune from Ouija until the patent expired.

If we may offer a suggestion it may be well to keep the records of these sittings in typed form, and to do so regularly, day by day, because you will find that their volume will tend to increase rapidly as the two at the board get into the rhythm of the work. More and more you will find that a sort of shorthand will develop, and if any of you anticipate the coming words, you will save much time and effort by speaking it (them?]. Just that is what will develop. For a while, however, we shall continue the full spelling until the operation becomes easy. Furthermore, we shall later give you much the same kind of outline as with the B. of T., which, you will remember, you received only in skeleton form, which served later as a sort of springboard for the writing of the completed text.

However, you must not expect another Book of Tokens right away, although we have access to a vast store of equally valuable and beautiful material.

(Ann asked if she is a less valuable complement than Michael Whitty. The answer was:)

No. He had a greater technical training in literary form, and in Theosophical terminology, but no greater natural aptitude.

(Ann: "I wondered if as much could be brought through with me as with him.")

Certainly we can, for the balance of force between you is better, if only because you are of opposite sex. Frater G. et S. had a very strong feminine element in his personality, as you will recall. His attitude toward you and many others was always distinctly protective, to the point of being "mother-hennish."

(P.F.C.: "Is there anything further of importance tonight, or shall we go to bed?" Ann: "It is not polite to stop like this.")

You do not have to be polite-much. But nothing is quite so important as clear channels, so Good Night!

(Here Ann asked a mental question, but did not tell us at the time what it was, which was "to give us a good night blessing.")

HE is One and One alone. Rest in the shadow of his wings. Sub umbra alarum tuarum, I H V H.

THIRD COMMUNICATION

Thursday, February 20, 1947 9:35 P.M.

Ave Frater et Sorores!

(Then followed a wait of half-an-hour or more.)

Remember well that Great Arcanum, the true equilibrium between Severity and Mercy, for their unbalance is not good. The force of SAMAEL standeth not alone, for it is a force of terror and darkness, not to be withstood except it be in balance with its opposite. Yet is that opposite also unable to stand unbalanced, for TzDQAL (English Zadkiel), unchecked, expandeth even to the destruction of all form or outline. There must be a balance in all true creation—Mars against Jupiter, SAMAEL against ZADKIEL, Severity against Mercy. But the one Reconciler between them standeth at the apex of the triangle of which they are the basic angles, and behold, that apex dependeth downward on the Tree, and from it floweth into the worlds of formation and action the power of the great Reconciler, SANDALPHON.

(H.B.C.: "Is someone different writing tonight?")

No, we are simply keeping our promise. Two of you should recognize the opening phrase, for you have heard the words often enough. What follows them is from the same ancient source, and, if you will now permit, we shall continue:

And the first path of the descent of the Reconciler taketh the power of RVCh (Ruach) into ISVD (Yesod), from whence it floweth into the world of forms, and filleth the secret places in Malkuth. But when that descent of power hath its straight and narrow course deflected by the overpowering of either the waters of Hod or the fires of Netzach, then is the Life-Breath from above distorted, and it becometh either too cold and moist with the Mercurial reflections, or else too hot and dry with the emotional heat of

123

the Sphere of Venus. Deluded by the illusion of personal independence, the uninstructed mistake the descent of power from Ruach for an ascent of power from Malkuth. Know ye, that never does power have its beginning in that which is below. It doth ascend from Earth to Heaven, even as Hermes saith; and from Heaven it descendeth again to Earth, as also he hath it. Yet remember that whatsoever the Sages write is always veiled, lest the profane burn themselves with fires they know not how to direct. Thus one seeth often that they who read the words of the Sages with the outer eye alone mistake the inner import. Many there be who aspire to the height of the Sphere of the Sun, and worthy is their aspiration; but many are called, and few chosen, for only the few who understand the written word with their hearts perceive that even their aspiration cometh not from the levels of Guph and Nephesh, but is truly a reflection of the descending from power Ruach. Always, then, is the aspiration like a reflected image of the sun in a glass, which, if it striketh straight into the eyes, seemeth to be the sun itself. No man riseth to Ruach by his own power. Yet many delude themselves concerning this, and from that delusion spring up many weeds of error. Know ye that the least of thine impulses toward what seemeth to be above hath its source in that same Above. Avoid error by keeping fast to this: nothing in the levels of Yesod or Malkuth ever can, or doth, set power into operation. These are but as glasses, and the feelings and interpretations of the spheres of desire and intellect, directed downward toward Yesod and Malkuth, are as spectators, watching a mirrored reflection, wherein all is the reverse of the true images.

Now read the whole to this point.

What has been given thus far is only the beginning of a fairly long quotation from an ancient instruction. Until you all become more accustomed to this work, we shall not give very long excerpts. One comment may be useful, and it will also indicate why we have chosen this particular theme.

As Frater P. knows, all our former communications had to do with the formation of an outer vehicle for what he knows under the initials, ____. And one of the most important things is to do everything possible to correct the errors which have disrupted so many spiritual movements.

One of these errors—one of the worst and one of the subtlest—is that against which the subject matter of this instruction is directed. This error springs from the supposition on the part of the aspirant that he is doing something to raise himself—to lift, or sublimate, some of what he mistakenly believes to be his personal powers—physical, emotional, or mental.

The truth is that nothing originates in, or is directed from, the personal level. Right understanding of what really goes on requires this basic realization. Everything in one's spiritual unfoldment is, so far as personality goes, a tropism, an automatic response to impacts from the level of Ruach in Tiphareth.

Because many do not understand this, all sorts of variations of spiritual pride, or even spiritual vanity, vitiate the work of the student who has not grasped the basic principle. This misunderstanding leads to the substitution of purely personal prejudices for judgment, and is colored by unresolved complexes.

It may comfort you to know that even we must ever be on guard against this same delusion. For though you may think of us as being Masters, we are really only your fellow students, and as we are still human beings, incarnate like yourselves, the necessary illusions which are inseparable from physical embodiment affect us as much as they do you.

(We stopped. P.F.C. asked if there was any more.)

There is infinitely more, but while it may not have occurred to you, we have to expend far more energy in sending than you in receiving. May we suggest that you plan for an earlier hour, both for your benefit and ours? Thank you for giving us this channel.

125

(Question: How often a week should we sit?)

Twice a week.

(Question: If we have an extra day, would you like it?)

Yes.

(Question: Would Saturday afternoon be all right?)

Yes.

(Question: And tomorrow afternoon, too, if we can?)

Yes.

Sub umbra alarum tuarum, I H V H. Vale,

Frater et Sorores. May you rest, and be revived by the Light of the Eternal. Good Night.

FOURTH COMMUNICATION

Saturday, March 1, 1947 8:30 P.M.

Ave, Frater et Sorores.

There was interference last time, but you need not have been disturbed by that. You had enough intelligence to recognize it for what it was. The general conditions were not favorable, and the reaction of Frater P. to the Tuesday night seance did nothing to help. In the main, he is well advised to have nothing to do with objective phenomena.

(Ann asked: Do the objective phenomena come from him?)

To a certain extent, but there are others present at those sittings who can provide force enough, without his running the risk of disturbing a nervous mechanism which has been attuned to receive a quite different sort of impression.

It may be a little while before we can send you the full outline of the text which follows the Book of Tokens, but send it we shall, as soon as this battery has been adjusted. But let us continue from the point where we stopped.

You will remember that the burden of our comment on the ancient text was to the effect that it clearly indicates the danger of confusing personal opinion with truth. Even persons with high aspirations are more or less subject to this error. Only repeated meditation on the demonstrable fact that no personal thought, word or act is personally originated will overcome this delusion. One must remember also the fact that we are all affected by the race-mind and its long history of ignorant interpretation of the world of appearances. Basically, all phenomena of personality result from the interplay of completely impersonal forces; and a primary truth about impersonal cosmic forces is the truth that none of them belong to, or can be owned by, anybody. There are no property rights in spiritual powers.

127

Thus you may read in the Acts of the Apostles that the early Christians shared all things in common, and how far this went is seldom a subject touched in the modern pulpit. Theirs was not merely a community ownership of property. They went much farther. They had rid themselves of the whole notion of ownership and all the devilish pseudo-morality which is the inevitable consequence of this initial error.

(A. and H. commented that they probably shared their wives, too.)

In answer to your altogether twentieth-century comment, let us say that you are not to be blamed for its lamentable flippancy. We are trying to help you understand something which has been almost completely obscured by two thousand years of muddled thinking, from the time that the Roman State took over the outer organization of the Church until now. The materialism which is well nigh synonymous with Rome has woven a tissue of lies, spun from the thread of the greatest lie of all—the lie that any person has property rights in any other person. Consider the history of the Roman Church after it fell away from the original simplicity of the plain teaching of Jesus, and ask yourselves what the so-called morality of the doctrines of the Roman Church is likely to be worth. Then consider the fact that all modern legalism springs from this same impure source, and was almost wholly unaffected by the so-called Reformation.

Your agreement or disagreement with a principle of cosmic law affects the principle not a whit, but it does affect you. When you honestly consider this whole matter, you will not pain us, nor make yourselves ridiculous by such flippancies. Heaven knows that, in these days, it is terribly hard for us to find even passably suitable instruments for the propagation of Ageless Wisdom, and at least one of you has heard often enough that he has not been helped by us because of any superlative excellence of his personality.

(Ann objected to accepting this teaching or principle, basing her argument on analogies relating to chemical affinity.)

A little knowledge is a dangerous thing, and never so dangerous as when it mates with prejudice, and begets a brood of ego-satisfying fancies. Your chemical analogy might be plausible, Soror, but for the fact that every one of the elements has a great number of affinities, from which

128

spring all sorts of compounds. Furthermore, sodium, for example, which has been combined with chlorine to make common salt, may be separated from that very same chlorine, and re-mixed with some other element to form a totally different compound, or with a different lot of chlorine to make ordinary salt again.

(N.B. As received, the text said "with some other element to form a totally different batch of salt;" but as this is obviously untrue, the present transcriber [P.F.C.] has altered the conclusion of the sentence as above.) (Ann here interposed a question to the effect that some compounds are so stable that their elements are inseparable.)

Ask any competent chemist and he will correct that idea. There are absolutely no indissoluble compounds. Water is unusually stable, but electricity will split water into hydrogen and oxygen, and there is no cosmic law that makes more holy the union of oxygen. With hydrogen than the union of oxygen with iron. From the latter results iron oxide, familiar to you as rust; but rust is just as divinely ordained as water, and when iron oxide is the thing needed for some specific purpose, water will not serve that purpose.

(Ann said: "Yes, but while it is water it is water, and while it is iron oxide it is iron oxide, and not both at the same time." Further discussion followed.)

Furthermore, the Lord's Prayer includes a petition for the establishment on earth of the perfection already present in Heaven, and the author of that prayer stated unequivocally that there are no marriages in Heaven. For his "Heaven," as the translators render it, really in the sky, or free space [and in free space] the elements combine and dissolve their transitory relationships ["without reference to the suppositious holiness of any particular relationship?" This interpolation, or something to the same effect seems needed. P.F.C.] all of which is an invention of priestcraft.

129

Possibly, if you will permit us to send what we hope to get through, you may learn something positive, to put in the place of your echoes of the lies planted in the race-mind by the Blacks. But we are beginning to wonder a little when you are going to wake up to the fact that this kind of communication takes energy from us, as well as from you. <u>Verbum sapientibus.</u>

*The word "Blacks" here is not in reference to those beings who are part of the black race, but instead Black Adepts or those using the darker forces either ignorantly or with intent.

FIFTH COMMUNICATION

Friday, March 7, 1947 7:15 P.M.

Blessed be this place, and they that dwell therein. Ave, Frater et Sorores.

Blessed be this place, and they that dwell therein. Ave, Frater et Sorores, concerned with the building are not its owners. Not thine, but Mine, is the work. Not thine, but Mine, is the Temple. For Me, and for Me only, is it planned and built, and Mine are the ordinances established for thy guidance in the service of the Light. For truly is Kether in Malkuth, and in Kether I dwell solitary, without a second. What think Ye then? Hath any man or woman a right of ownership higher than Mine? Mine is your body, thou who seekest to find Me, Mine and Mine alone. Mine is the power in all that cometh into manifestation through the thought, or word, or action of any of Mine instruments. Never shall they who remain deluded by the illusion of separateness become clear channels for the outpouring of My power, until all follies of "thine" and "mine" are cleared out by the irresistible down pouring of My power.

So far the text for tonight. Read, and consider its import, before going on. Do you comprehend? You aspire to the highest. Take heed, lest you surrender to the world's illusion through seeing the Light through the colored lenses of your personal prejudices, and personal emotional trends.

(Ann: "As I see it, they mean that, at a certain stage of one's growth, mating is necessary to one's growth, but that one outgrows this necessity.")

Yes. Action is better than talk or thinking. By doing one learns more, and more quickly, than by any mental approach.

(Ann: "Is not doing also a form of doing?")

Yes, but no growth follows mere negation. Refusal to act is like keeping shut the gate which releases a stream of water into a pipe leading to a turbine. To be sure, no water is wasted so long as the gate stays shut, but

131

neither is power generated. Of what use are fine ideals about serving mankind, if one refuses to become a channel for broadcasting the power?

The whole world suffers in inexpressible agony, yet some who might do much to heal these festering wounds remain aloof, wrapped in the garments of their own self-righteousness. Yet, but for One whom all the world condemned, you would not be sitting here. "Except your righteousness be greater than the righteousness of the scribes and Pharisees," said the Master, "ye shall in nowise enter into the Kingdom."

Think well on these things.

Vale, Frater et Sorores.

SIXTH COMMUNICATION

Saturday, March 8, 1947 7:30 P.M.

Ave, Frater et Sorores.

Now, what is this Guph which hath its seat in Malkuth? Consider its three tokens. First, cometh the letter Gimel, which links Kether to Tiphareth. This, therefore, is the sign of the Uniting Intelligence, and from this you may learn that the body conjoins a man to the Highest.

Second cometh the letter Vav, and this is the token of the Eternal Intelligence which unites Ab with Ben.* From this token, know that thy body is the link between the true Self in Tiphareth and the universal life and wisdom of Chokmah.

Now the third token is the letter which signifieth the mouth of man, and this is also the token of the Active Intelligence which uniteth Netzach with Hod. So this, thy body, is the instrument whereon may be played the Song of Life. Nay, it is more than this, for on this harp of ten thousand strings, the wind of the Spirit moveth ever, and soundeth, night and day, the melodies and harmonies of that Eternal Song.

Yet few there be with ears to hear. For that hearing is too often dulled by the noisy clamor of the world's illusion. Yet he who hath eyes to see, and mind to remember, may see in the very word Guph (GVP) that the heart of its meaning hath to do with Hearing. For what else is Vav (V) but the heart of the word? And is not Vav at once the special letter of Ben and the sign of Hearing?

So far the text.

133

Now for a word (P.F.C.: "Are you giving us comment now?")

Yes. The body is the vehicle of the One Life. Its end or purpose is to express the power and wisdom that ever flows downward from the inner heights. The sages, therefore, begin the word (Guph, GVP) with the letter which is placed on the Tree in the channel through which the Holy Mezla descends from Yekhidah to Ruach the Ego, named Ben (BN). Think well on this. It tells you plainly that your body, physical though it be, and transitory may be its continuance, is actually your means of direct contact with the Height which is said to be above all other heights.

Do many think thus of the body? Well do you know that only the very few entertain this idea. The Brothers of the Shadow work incessantly to spread the lie that the body is something low; and since the influence of the perverted church has waned, so that intelligent men and women no longer believe themselves to be worms in the dust, the attack of the "Blacks" has become more subtle. Now materialism perverts the truth of physical evolution, to make it appear that man's body is nothing but an animal organism. It is, indeed, an animal organism. The perversion consists in the notion that a human body is nothing more than this. The poetic image of the text gives a better idea.

Note the stress on the second letter of the word. You could meditate for days on this one short passage. To hear, as often we have said through Frater P., in his lectures, one must listen. The Song of Life never ceases, but it does not blare like a jazz band.

One great error is that most persons let what is symbolized by the third letter run on, as it were, of itself, without due preparation from what is indicated by the first and second letters. How few persons are accustomed to think of their bodies as channels for the descent of power from the Most High! And how few there are who listen for the still, small music of the Eternal Song!

Now consider another aspect of the third letter. On the Tree, it is the channel of communication between the seat of desire in the seventh Sephirah and the seat of intelligence (intellect(P.F.C.)] in Hod. Here is a

134

plain indication of what human speech should be, the _balance_ between feeling and intellect. But how often do men really use the power of speech for this?

With his mouth man builds his towers of folly, and immures himself in these word-built prisons. Thus does he restrict his actions, and barter his birthright of freedom for a veritable mess of pottage. And what a mess it often is!

The mouthings of self-constituted authority, the articulate ignorance of centuries of superstition, the codified and almost deified verbiage of man-made laws and rules having no basis in actual fact—these are among the worst of the race's self-made prisons; and the shackles that chain men therein are chains of words without any real meaning.

Again we say, _verbum sapientibus_ for we have not the time for extended pointing of the application. Enough to say that all this is by no means a mere piece of generalized philosophy.

Vale, Frater et Sorores. We have no more to communicate. Digest it well. Our blessing is always with you. Good night.

*TRANSCRIBER'S NOTE: In what appears to be H.B.C.'s copy of the communications, the word "Ben" is crossed-out and these notes are added:
...the Mercy of God, that thy body is the living evidence showing forth the love of the Father in the Universal life and Wisdom of Chokmah."

Sunday, March 9, 1947 8:15 P.M.

(Before the sitting began, there had been some discussion of the poetical quality of the Book of Tokens, and the hope was expressed that something similar might soon result from the sittings. For some little time the planchette simply moved erratically, and even this followed a long period of tiresome waiting. Then, very quickly, came the following:)

There was a young man from IRAK, Whose face was exceedingly black. From his feet to his head He wore nothing but red. Strange creatures, these men of IRAK. (We thought this evidence of some mischievous interference, and there was some talk of abandoning the sitting. But, after a few more erratic movements, came what follows.) Well, you wanted poetry, didn't you? And how much wisdom can you extract from that? Well, then, what qualifications do you have for grasping the inner meaning of what seems to be more weighty matter, when you get no more than a laugh from this? Yet here is subtlety not **less** than that of the Fool in Tarot. Whence cometh the young man, have you ever considered?

No, this looks like what you are pleased to call "silly," so you think it a waste of time. Yet you miss all the points that are there in plain sight.

First of all, is this not rather different from the usual limerick in at least one respect? Nonsense you may think it, but you could repeat it anywhere without giving offense. And you may have heard that just such seeming nonsense, in Alice, veils weighty secrets.

Yod is 10. Resh is 200. Aleph is 1. Kaph is 20. Add these. (We did so. The total is 231.)

Now, add the numbers from 1 to 21.

(This is also 231.)

And what is 21? Frater P. certainly can answer that.

(P.F.C.: AHIH?)

Yes, and that is the divine name of Kether. And is not a young man the type of the Son who comes forth from Kether through the path of Gimel? Furthermore, is not one of the personifications of that Son the Egyptian Osiris, of whom it was said: "He is a black god?"

We are trying to give you a hint not to be so concerned with external form. Lewis Carroll was in touch with us in his day, yet he wrote no ponderous tomes on occultism. Tarot is just a pack of cards in the eyes of the world, yet the world has transmitted Tarot for seven hundred years, and the Alice books will be read for many generations to come, and thus will be preserved their deep wisdom.

The face of the Son is black because the Son (BN) is one with the Mother (AIMA), as you may see from the numbers.

He wears nothing but red, because all the manifestations of Binah are clothed, and thus veiled, in the operations of Geburah:

Consider now IRAK. The correspondences to the Hebrew we have already given. I is earth, because Yod is Virgo. R is fire, the solar fire. A is air; and Jupiter, the god of rain, stands for water in relation to K.

So there you may see who and what the young man really is—none other than Ben (BN), one with his black Mother (AIMA), working through the Perfect Law, and embodied in a vehicle formed of the four elements. Note also the phrase, "from his feet to his head," that is, from Pisces to Aries.

So, you see, we have been telling you about Guph all this time, and we do not think you will ever forget this occasion, or miss the point of the object-lesson. Now take some more of the ancient text:

The essence of Guph is the serpent-fire of which the token is Teth, and this fire cometh forth through the working of the Active Intelligence, of which the token is Peh. Thus the number of Guph (GVP) is 89, and this

137

9 is Teth, and its channel of outpouring is Peh, or 80. Add 8 and 9, and you shall see the power of Zain (7) coming forth through 1 to bring forth 8, or Cheth.

The Abode of Influence thus is Guph, but the outer working of that aspect of Mezla which descendeth from Binah through the path of Cheth.

(This sentence appears to be somewhat confused. I take it to mean that Guph, the body, is the outward vesture of the force of the path of Cheth, the House or Abode of Influence. The symbolism of Key 7 would seem to indicate this. P.F.C.)

Through the path of Cheth the power of Saturn conjoineth itself with the force of Mars. This power of Saturn descendeth also through the path of Tav into Malkuth, and thus giveth form to Guph in the World of Assiah.

Now, Guph is the body of the Lord, for is not the name of the Kingdom ADNI MLK, Adonai Melek? Behold, then, the Kingdom suspended from the cross of Tav. And what said the King, speaking through that Guph men know by the name of Yeshua? Said He not, "I am the living water?" And behold, MIM is 90, and so is MLK; and thus Yeshua stilled the waters (seas), for he knew that Adonai Melek is Lord of the Waters. ADNI MLK numbereth 155, and here is AL in fivefold expression, for AL$^{P."}$ is 31.

So far the text. We shall add only one comment.

AL in five-fold expression relates to man, and his body with its five senses thus also to the pentagram, which in magic is directly connected with Malkuth. Work this out for yourselves.

Our blessings upon you. Vale, Frater et Sorores.

EIGHTH COMMUNICATION

Thursday, May 8, 1947 9:30 P.M.

Ave, Frater et Sorores.

Just two cycles of the moon, yet in those two cycles a whole eternity. For whether in small cycles or in great, the whole eternity subsists. A millennium is as a day, and a day as a millennium in the sight of the ONE.

This afternoon, Frater, you spoke of the Fool's girdle as being a symbol of the duplex illusion of time and space; but your fluent speech should not make you too complacent. True was what you said, but do you realize its deeper implications? Far-reaching is that symbol.

First of all, any girdle stands for Venus, and thus for all represented by the Empress. Time and space are states of imagination. They are inseparable, because time is the measure of distance from one point in space to another. Yet there is really no distance, no separateness, and thus is the Fool's black garment of illusion fastened by this girdle of imagination.

Lay the girdle by itself on a table, and what have you but the sign of nothingness? This is the basic illusion, but the Lord of Life is not deceived thereby.

Even man's weak intellect can reason correctly that no manifestation could be without this time-space illusion. But manifestation **is.** Call it illusion, if you will. Saying that does not get rid of it.

Thus, at least, you know that some manifesting principle must exist. Indeed, that principle is all that has any real existence. There can be no satisfactory answer to the question, "Why does that ONE manifest Itself?" except the answer implied in the statement, "God is Love," and this answer is for the heart, not for the head.

The can opener of intellect is too dull to probe the secrets of the Heart of Life. Knowledge goes deeper than statement. Love, and you shall know. Hod, on the Tree, is lower, and more external, than Binah. Enter through the Door of the Empress, which is the Gate of Love, into the heart of the Mother, and you will not be plagued by that god of thieves who has his abode in Hod.

But this is enough of this. Let us go on with Guph. 89 is its number, and as the numbers are Sephiroth, this revealeth Hod as the instrument of Yesod. But, again, 9 is Yesod, and 80 is the numeration of ISVD. So, also, is 8 the seed of 9, because 1, 2, 3, 4, 5, 6, 7, 8 total 36, and 9 is the sum of 3 and 6. Yet see here the Mother, 3, and the Son, 6. Now look at Key 8, and see there before you the Mother, and her Son, the Lion of the Tribe of Judah. For ONE is All, and thus is Hod but another aspect of ISVD. There is but one Foundation.

So also is 89 Teth (9), operating through 80, or the spiraling light-power working through the Mouth of the Eternal (Teth through Peh). When lightning flasheth, thunder roareth, and thunder hath been, from time immemorial, a symbol for the Voice of God. So is thy body, 0 aspirant, more, far more, than an earthen clod. It is the intelligence that uniteth thee with the Crown. It is the Nail that joineth thee to the Paternal Wisdom. And it is truly the Mouth of the Lord. For in Guph are the letters G, V, and P and these unite thee forever with the Kingdom.

Yet is all this naught but words without the key supplied by the understanding heart. Love is that key. Love, not reason. For reason followeth after love, and when reason would enslave love, then is reason but a tyrant, punishing itself with the loss of what it tries in vain to enslave.

So is the rider in the Chariot really the Mother, as you may **see** from her yellow hair and its wreath of leaves. Besides, is not Cancer the sign of motherhood, and does not the path of Cheth descend from Binah, so that the influence of this path flows down directly from Alma?

This is the same influence that flows across from Chokmah to Binah, through the path of Daleth. And the rider in the Chariot is therefore the Empress. She unveils herself in Key 17, but our text has linked 17 with Guph. This is another approach to the same idea, for Guph is the vehicle or car, and the letter of the Chariot is Cheth, which is 8, which is derived from 89 through 17.

But if you take 17 for the Star, what is this Star but Venus-Urania, and does not Uranus share with Saturn the rulership of Aquarius? Now look further, and see Saturn as 21, the World, a yellow-haired woman, whose sphere on the Tree is Binah, and the same woman tames the lion, and sits on the seat of Justice, where, again, she is the Empress.

The emphasis on 3 takes you right into the heart of the secret. For imagination is the fashioner of form, and form necessitates both space and time. Space is 3, length, breadth and height being its dimensions of extension. The so-called fourth dimension is not extension, it being the internal center, or Tav-Saturn again. Likewise is time a 3. Past, present and future are its extensions; but eternity is to these three as a fourth dimension, and eternity has no extension, and is central also.

Now that should keep you busy for a while!

(N.B. The comment evidently begins at the paragraph which opens with the words, "Love comes first." P.F.C.)

Try not to discuss in the midst of transmission. It is better to rest than to speculate. You will find that what we send comes more easily if you wait for us to "sign off" before you discuss it.

Our blessings are with you all. Vale, Frater et Sorores.

NINTH COMMUNICATION

Thursday May 15, 1947 8:50PM

Ave. Frater et Sorors:

The text continues: See now, Guph is KLH, Kallah, the Bride, and in her name is shown the perfection of the Kingdom. For the Kingdom is 10, and KLH is 55, or the sum of the numbers from 1 to 10. See again, the Bride, KLH, is also HKL, the ALL. For in Guph is the whole creation made manifest. Therefore is Guph, the body, the whole [holy? P.F.C.] Temple of the Most High. And where standeth this Temple? Verily, it standeth in the midst, or center, and in it abideth forever Adonai Melek (ADNI MLK), our Lord and King, Holy is His Name, Blessed be He! Yet is our Lord one with His eternal dwelling, for, see now, ADNI and HIKL are the same in number (65), and HIKL is but HKL, with the paternal Yod (I) added thereto. The ALL is the Bride also, so that the addition of Yod to HKL (understand KLH), betokeneth the union of the Father with the Bride.

Note the statement that Guph is really the Kingdom, or the Bride who is the ALL. This is fact. Can anyone separate even the smallest body from the whole? Through a single atom course all the forces of the universe, and whatever body you may take for an example, whether it be small as an electron or great as a galaxy, this remains true. Moreover, whatever body you may elect to consider, that body is the mathematical center of an infinite expanse.

The paternal Yod spoken of in the text is Ab or Chokmah, the Sphere of the Stars, and the seat of Chaiah, the life-force. The Bride is Malkuth, and MLKVTh is 496, a perfect number. Furthermore, 496 adds to 19, the number of ChVH, Eve, the Mother who is also the Bride. In ChVH are beginning and end, for 1 is beginning and 9 is end, and their sum is 10,

142

the Kingdom. So is 10 the letter Yod also, and the Yod in IHVH stands for Chokmah, the Father.

The Kingdom dependeth from Yesod, and is linked to Yesod by the path of Tav, and this letter standeth for the Temple in the midst, as is written the Sepher Yetzirah. Thus is the letter Tav the special token of the Lord, and of His Holy Temple. But above Tav on the Tree standeth the Foundation, the seat of NPSh, Nephesh, and Nephesh signifieth the eternal utterance of the creative speech. For see, it first letter is Nun, which denoteth perpetuity, and its second letter is P, the sign of the mouth, while the third letter is Sheen, the sign of the Holy Spirit. Yet see that in all three letters is one power expressed; for in Nun is the seed-power of Madim (Mars), and Peh is the special letter of Madim, and in Sheen, the final letter of its name (ShIN) is N with which NPSh beginneth.

Above Yesod is the path of Samekh, descending from MLK, the seat of Ruach; and above the King, who is also BN, Ben, the Son, extendeth upward the Path of Union which descendeth from the Crown. Thus from Kether to Malkuth descendeth one unbroken path, though it hath three parts, Gimel, Samekh and Tav. For this is ARCh TzDIQIM (Erech Tzadikim, the path of the just), and the path of the just is the Middle Pillar of the Tree. Reckon and see.

(We did so, and found that the numeration of ARCh TzDIQIM, the path of the just, is 463, the sum of the values of the letters Gimel, Samekh and Tav, which are the paths of the Middle Pillar. In transcribing this, P.F.C. notes also that the paths of Gimel and Samekh are both blue, and that Tav, the lowest path of the Middle Pillar, is blue-violet, as if the blue of Samekh, after passing through Yesod, had become tinged with the violet of that Sephirah.)

Behold, in the descent from Kether through this path standeth before thee the way of recompense, and this is GML, Gimel. For GML, Gimel, the Camel, is also the bearer of reward and punishment. Yet is Gimel also 73, and this is the number of ChKMH, Chokmah. For truly the

143

Eternal Wisdom is the carrier of both reward and punishment. See also that GML showeth GM, conjoined with L—continuance with instruction and correction. For GM signifieth continuance, and LMD (L) is the goad of correction and instruction. All this is the paternal Wisdom, and its manifestation is the Son. See, too, that because 73 is 10, Gimel is a hidden Yod, and Yod is the letter of Chokmah. Below the Son descendeth the path of SMK, Samekh, which carrieth the power of the Son to Yesod. For the path of the just is the path of union and support, and it endeth in that center which is the abode of the Most High. Verily, in Guph doth the power of the Crown stand centered!

Is comment necessary? Meditate on this, and you will find the central doctrine.

Vale, Frater et Sorores.

TENTH COMMUNICATION

Monday, May 19, 1947 8:05 P.M.

Ave, Frater et Sorores.

The heart of NPSh, Nephesh, is the letter Peh, and this path carrieth the power of Netzach into Hod. From Geburah, the Sphere of Madim, the Holy Mezla descendeth into Tiphareth through the path of action, the sharp goad of Lamed. Yet is this path of Lamed of the quality of Nogah.

Then from Tiphareth the Holy Mezla descendeth into the Sphere of Nogah through the path of change, the path of Nun. Thus from the Sphere of Madim the channel beginneth with Nogah, then taketh on the form of Madim to enter the Sphere of Nogah; and likewise is the first path from Nogah a path of Madim.

Consider this well, and see how, on the Tree, the paths of Daleth and Peh are of like nature, though opposite in appearance. Now see further. Peh is the heart of NPSh, Nephesh, and Peh is also one with ISVD, for the number of P is 80, and this is the number of ISVD. Truly, P and L are one, for P is K with a Yod, as you may see by looking at the character, and K with I giveth the number 30. Thus is Lamed a goad, and if this be considered, what is the goad but the power of Madim? And in ISVD is concealed SVDI, Sod Yod, the secret of Yod. Now Yod itself is Kaph, and the Sod Yod is a mystery of the hidden paternal power of Chokmah.

Verily, IVD is the seed of all the letters, and if thou hast eyes to see, in IVD is the secret of the Covenant, and this secret is the Peh-Heh (PH), for PH is 85, or HISVD, Ha-Yesod, the Foundation, and 85 is also MILH, the Covenant which removeth concealment from the paternal Yod.

So far the text. First look up MILE.

The text outwardly reflects the influence of Jewish exclusiveness, but this is only in letter, not in spirit. The physical rite does, indeed, unveil the paternal Yod, hence the phrase, "if thou hast eyes to see," but the Covenant is not its symbol. What is hidden here goes deeper.

In MILE the first letter is MIM. Then comes IVD, then LMD, and, lastly, HH. MIM IVD spells MI, which is the Living Water, transmitting life. Of that life, the letter I at the end of MI is the sign, for I is the first letter of I H V H, the Name of the Most High. Thus I stands for Chaiah, the life-force in Chokmah, and the letters L and H which conclude MILE are referred to Venus (Nogah) and Mars (Madim) respectively.

The Covenant, then, reveals the paternal Yod in Chokmah. Yet is the symbol a clue to a fact, for the cosmic life-force is projected, generation after generation, into manifestation through human bodies, and the power of Mars is combined with that of Venus in the Vital Soul in Yesod. This **is,** even now, a closely guarded practical secret, and not even here may you expect to find it unveiled. If you can see and hear, you may come to know it. But how far do you see, and what do you really hear?

(This was discussed by R and A, and they asked if they had come to the right answer.)

Answer our question first within yourselves. Having done so, you will find what you seek. Not by words, but by inner sight and hearing does this knowledge come. Upward on the Tree runs the Way of Return. It begins in Guph, and rises to Nephesh through the path of Tav. And this path is named NOBD, Administrative. The number of NOBD is 126, and it has close connection with the symbols of the R.C. For 126 is the total length (in feet) of the boundaries of the Vault described. In Fama. This path of Tali is also closely related to all temple symbolism, as you have learned from previous communications. The word NOBD also calls attention to Mars in Scorpio, and Mars combined with Saturn, and these are combined with the letters of Mercury and Venus. Mars in Scorpio, Mars exalted in Capricorn, Saturn ruling Capricorn, these are N and 0. Mercury is B, and Venus is D. Meditate on this, and find out what you have to administer in the Temple of the Body.

Above these is Yesod, and this path is the Pure Intelligence. The first letter of ISVD refers, as we have explained, to Chokmah and the life-force. But on the Tree, the path of Yod is that of the Intelligence of Will, and the work is a work of Will, of universal Will, not the self-will which is its counterfeit.

Thus the second letter of ISVD is Samekh, and this is the path leading upward from Nephesh to Ruach in Tiphareth. Notice that these two letters are related to Mercury and Jupiter, respectively.

Then comes Vav, with its correspondence to both the Moon and Venus; and, finally, D, Venus also.

Thus in ISVD, Yesod, is the combination of Mercury, Jupiter, Moon and Venus; and these are, of course, the metals of the alchemists, or the interior stars. Mars impels the upward flow of power on the Way of Return, and this power is combined with Moon and Venus in the work, as it begins in Malkuth and sends the forces up through the path of Tav. But in ISVD, Yesod, Mars and Saturn give place to Jupiter, and the path of Samekh above Yesod is doubly related to Jupiter, as you may see from the letters S and K. But the "matter of the work" is designated by M between S and K, and this water will not wet the hand; it will not, that **is,** wet the Yod. For the "hand" is none else but Yod.

Here is the "fixed water," which is the First Matter, duly prepared, and in the Tarot this is the Hanged Man, suspended over a dry water course. Note that he hangs from a Tav. He is centered. The flow is stopped, or suspended, and all personal considerations are eliminated, like the lopped branches of the trees. But the glory is there, and the perfection, for MIM, though it is 90, is also 650, if one takes the final M as 600. Then the water is the "dry water," and the 650 is ADNI multiplied by Yod, or HIKL multiplied by that same Yod. And the Lord and His Temple are One, and this is centered in GVP, Guph, as you have learned. All this points Straight, if one finds the door; but few there be that find it.

Vale, Frater et Sorores.

ELEVENTH COMMUNICATION

Thursday, May 23, 1947 8:45 P.M.

Ave, Frater et Sorores.

One of the great arcana is the crossing of the three horizontal paths on the Tree. Consider first the numbers of the letters. They are 4, 9, and 80, so that their total value, 93, is a triple 31, that is, a threefold expression of AL. This is the special name of the fourth Sephirah, and because 4 is a concealed 10, Chesed is actually the whole Tree in germ; and there are many passages in Qabalistic writings, and in fragments of Ageless Wisdom which have survived the destruction of Hellenic Wisdom by ignorant bigotry, which indicate the importance of the number 4.

Now observe that 4 is the number of D, as well as of Chesed, and the path of D is the first one to cross the Tree. Now see, this letter is also DLTh, or 434, which reduced through 11 to 2. Likewise, ChSD is 74, which also reduces through 11 to 2. Likewise, Chokmah, which in Hebrew is 73, as is the letter-name Gimel, GML. Yet 2, as a letter, is B, so that the Value of B relates to Chokmah. In the Rota this is evident, for the Magician a personification of Wisdom, and is he not also a potential father, that is, Ab? Again, 4 is 2 multiplied by itself, and thus Daleth is the multiplication of Beth by Beth, and also the multiplication of Chokmah by itself is Chesed.

Now see. In Daleth are the letters of Venus, Libra and Saturn; that is, nothing but the powers of Venus and Saturn. Daleth itself is Venus, but her path ends in the Sphere of Saturn, from which the path of Lamed receives an influx through the paths of Cheth and Geburah. In the Rota, Empress, Strength, Justice and the World are but various aspects and manifestations of Daleth, as you can see, and so is the Star, where the ruling power is Saturn. Again, BINH is 67, and the seed of 67 is also 4, or Daleth.

149

When we come to TITh, the number of its name is 419, and this .adds to 5. Yet 5 is also Daleth with the paternal Yod, as you may see in the character for Heh. Doors first, then windows, was the actual architectural development; and the sequence of the letters was originally determined by this fact. Moreover, 419 may be read as 400 and 19, and in this reading, 400 is Tav, and 19 is ChVh, the Mother, or Aima. And Teth is the link between Chesed and Geburah, just as Daleth is the link between Chokmah and Binah.

These two paths cross Gimel above Tiphareth, but the third reciprocal path of Peh crosses the path of Samekh below Tiphareth. Now see a subtlety, PH, Peh, is 85, and this goes back to 4 through 13, so that the path of PH, Peh, veils Daleth again. Thus all the horizontal paths are feminine, even though the path of Peh is related to Mars, and the ruling power in the path of Teth is the Sun. Now, in the Rota, Samekh is sometimes   represented as Diana, so that there is in this path a lunar influence. SMK is 120, and this reduces to 3, that is, Gimel. But the paths of Samekh and Githel are vertical, or masculine, so that in the three crossings male and female powers are conjoined at the point of crossing. This is the clue to the secret. Venus and Moon at the upper point, Sun and Moon at the point.

9:00 P.M.

Ave, Frater et Sorores.

(We asked: "May we communicate with you on Wednesday evening, instead of Thursday of this week?)

Certainly. To give to our Brother and Sister what this dedicated place has to give is of utmost importance. You are stewards of this place, which we knew was here, long before you came to California; and our Eastern Brother, S.L.W., assured you again and again that it waited for you. Forget not that though his devotion takes forms that are not for you, the actual builder of this House of Beauty is as truly a son of the Sun as is any other. He planned it in love, and in love it was erected. See to it, then, that it shall always be a shrine of love, for love faileth never, and where love is enshrined, nothing but beauty can abide. Not yours is this place, but Life's.

(H. asked: Did you inspire me to call it Tiphareth?)

Yes. For though you have but begun your outer progress toward the goal, that goal in the Order, is none other than Tiphareth. Remember now, how in an earlier communication we showed you how, over and over again, the paths of the Tree come back to Daleth, and in Hebrew, Venus is NVGH, Nogah. Nun, the letter of change and reproduction, ruled by Mars. V, the letter of linkage and continuance, ruled by Venus. G, the letter of union, and of the Moon itself. And H, the letter of vision and constitution, ruled by Mars.

The point of this is that Mars begins and ends the word Nogah, but is combined with the powers of Venus and the Moon, yet the word itself is the Hebrew for Venus. The total of this word is 64, and this is DIN, Deen, Justice, the Sphere of Mars. See on the Tree how in every respect Geburah and Netzach are poles. Also is 64 the square of 8, and is related to

151

Mercury and Hod. Now see again. Hod is HVD in Hebrew, and this is 15, the number of IH, Jah, the special name of Chokmah, the Father. Yet 15 is also 6, and 6 is V, ruled by Luna and Venus; and yet 6 is Tiphareth also, and Tiphareth is the Sphere of the Sun. Thus far, then, from Nogah have we followed the clues of number, and in Tiphareth we have, in its name, Saturn, Mars, Uranus, Sol and Saturn, besides the Moon and Venus in Nogah. So nothing is missing but Jupiter. Look and see. Now, the number of ThPARTh is 1081, and the essence of this is 10, or Yod; and IVD, Yod, is 20, that **is,** K, or Jupiter. See, then, that in Nogah are hidden all the powers of the planets. But the Royal Secret is in the number 64, for this is the number of Justice, or perfect equilibrium, in which is perfect rest and the cessation of quest.

Thus does the Rota begin the word Nogah with the Key named Death. For in what ignorance calls death is the secret of life. 13, 5, 2, 4 is the Rota sequence, that is 6 in Rota, for the secret of the Lovers is the Great Arcanum, and in Key 6 you may see Venus, Mercury, Mars and Sol, if you know how to look.

(We said: The Angel is Mercury, the Sun is shown behind his head, and Venus represents the woman, and Mars the man?)

No. The man and the angel are both Mercury. Mars is the snake, on the tree, which encircles the man in Key 1.

(We asked again: Venus is the woman?)

Yes. Behind the man is the tree with twelve flaming fruits, for behind Mercury is life in all its manifestations, which are expressed by the number of the Simple Letters, twelve.

(We asked: Twelve signs of the zodiac?)

Yes, and the boundaries of the cube of space. These are behind the man, because these were manifested before the Mercurial Intelligence was embodied in human personality. Mercury itself is neutral, and is but the reflector. Yet on the Tree is the letter of Mercury that which

152

carries the influence from the Crown to Understanding, and this same letter B is the sign of commencement and initiation.

But enough of the technical side, though it will bear rich fruit in your hours of meditation. Let us go back to Daleth and Nogah.

We said that in DIN is the Great Secret. It begins with D, that is, with love, continues with I, that is, with will, and ends with N, that is, with change. Love is the indispensable beginning, and in the want of love is all failure.

So simple is this that a child may understand it; but men forget the lessons of childhood, and lose their way. Thus are there truly many lost souls, not damned for eternity, but off the track. Yours it is to call them back to the Way.

Not yours alone, for many are the voices calling men back from the byways of error, and the false security of the hedges of the illusion of separateness, to the marriage-feast of the Son and the Bride. Only see that your call be clear, and this means that you must yourselves celebrate in yourselves the Heavenly Marriage. Ours is no work of other worlds and planes. Here, on this weeping, suffering earth, is where the Shrine of Love must be built, and built with action, not alone with words. Think well on this, Frater and Sorores.

Our blessings go with you always. Under the Shadow of His Wings.

Vale

THIRTEENTH COMMUNICATION

Wednesday, May 28, 1947 8:30 P.M.

Ave, Frater et Sorores.

The number 6 is the second extension from 2, for the extension of 2 is **3,** and that of 3 is 6.

(We ask: How?)

1 plus 2 is 3; 1 plus 2 plus 3 is 6; furthermore, 6 is the first perfect number, for the parts of it are 1, 2 and 3, and these, multiplied together, make 6, and so does the addition of these same numbers (parts). Before we go further, consult Nichomachus.

6, then, is also a triangular number, and, as you have just seen, a hexagonal number also. Thus it corresponds, among plane figures, to the triangle, the hexagon and the hexagram. All these are familiar symbols, revered throughout the ancient world. In India, in China, and in Israel they appear continually. Indeed, the Tree of Life is based on the geometrical genesis of the equilateral triangle, for to construct the Tree, one begins with four circles on a common vertical diameter, so arranged that they make three vesicas; and the vesica is the basis of the Euclidean demonstration of the properties of the equilateral triangle. See, then, that on the Middle Pillar there are four numbers, 1, 6, 9, and 10, whose sum is 26. Of these 1 and 6 are in themselves perfect numbers. 9 is a square, and 6 and 10 are triangular, as is 1 also. Three triangles, and one square.

Now, three triangles is 3 times 3, and 4, being the number of the square, 4 added to 9 (indicated by the three triangles) results in 13, the number of Unity and Love. Moreover, since MLKVTh adds to 496, and this last is a perfect number, the idea of perfection is combined with the other ideas associated with 10 in the name of the last Sephirah, inasmuch as the sum of 4, 9 and 6 is 19, the number of ChVH (Eve), the Bride and Mother; and the reduction of 19 is 10. The Kingdom, then, is perfect. Nothing

154

needs to be added, nor anything subtracted. As the Sepher Yetzirah says: "Ten, and not nine; ten, and not eleven." Frater, explain to our Sorores how 10 is a triangle. (P.F.C. does so.)

But the center of the Tree is Tiphareth, 6, and among solids, 6 is the cube. The Central Sephirah is Beauty, called BN, Ben, the Son. Note that this is 52, or fourfold 13. Likewise is 52 AIMA, and IVD HH VV HH, or IHVH spelt in full, with the names of its four letters, instead of the simple characters, and the key to IHVH is the 26 formed by adding 1, 6, 9 and 10.

The Middle Pillar is the greatest secret of the Tree, and its central point, Tiphareth, is the heart of the secret. Note that Tiphareth, being 1081 (ThPARTh), is both 10 and 1, or both Kether and Malkuth. Thus 1, 6 and 10 are all essentially the same. But ISVD is 80. However, consider this: IVD, SMK, VV, DLTh. Now add. (The sum of these letter-names is 586, reducing through 19 to 10 and 1. P.F.C.) 586 gives you the Mother again (19, of ChVH), also Malkuth (10) and Kether (1), so that the whole idea is of the manifestation of Unity in the Kingdom; and the center, which is the Son, is also ADM and MLK. Add 52, 45 and 90.

(The numbers, respectively, of BN, ADM and MLK. Their sum is... 187). Their sum reduces to 7 but the extension of 7 is the perfect number, 28, and this takes you back through 10 to 1.

Unused as you are to this sort of thinking, you are doubtless confused by it; but, at least, you can see both intention, and some shadows of meaning. Here is the continual reiteration of unity, and of the identity of all four points on the Middle Pillar. Note that ThPARTh, Tiphareth, begins with the letter Tam, which is attributed to the Center, and that this Sephirah is at the exact center of the Tree.

Man (ADM) is the Son (BN), and because he is the Son, he is the King (MLK). He stands at the Center, and this is the point of absolute rest. Man's kingship is hereditary: only because he is Son is he King. He is the core of all, and, as you Harriet, should know, the core is truly the heart.

155

[Answer:1 (Ann asks how H. should know. Because she knows Italian.)

Now 6, as a cube, signifies perfect rest, and in every cube, the root-lines are 1 for the edges and coordinates, 2 for the surface diagonals, and 3 for the interior diagonals from corner to corner. Thus the root-lines of a cube, being roots 1, 2 and 3, refer to Kether, Chokmah and Binah—1, 2 and 3 on the Tree—and their sum is 6. So, in Keys 2 and 4 in Rota you see the cube as a symbol of Tiphareth.

(Ann says: 2 and 4 add to 6!)

Yes, and as the numbers of the Middle Pillar give 13, as *we* have explained, so the cube has 13 axes of symmetry.

Now, a cube shows the number 4 on every face, and the angles formed by its diagonals and sides are angles of 45 degrees, that is, ADM, while the angles at its corners are 90 degrees, that is, MLK. But because the interior corner-to-corner diagonals are root 3 lines, each of these has the same basic value as the side of an equilateral triangle, and these four lines inside a cube are therefore analogous to such lines on the Tree as Daleth. Now multiply the square root of 3 by 4 (1.732 X 4 = 6.928). This is 7 in whole numbers, and this hides BN, Ben, for BN is 52, which reduces to 7.

See, then, in the cube, BN, MLK and ADM conjoined, as they are in the names of Tiphareth, and the essence of these three is 7 also. For they add to 187. Thus the secret of Tiphareth is 7, or Netzach; but since 7 is also Zain, the secret is shown in the Rota by the Lovers, and their number in the series is 6. Furthermore, Zain is, in Hebrew, ZIN, and this adds to 67, the value of BINH, Binah, whence the path of the Lovers descends to Tiphareth. 6, 9 and 13 are the Rota numbers of ZIN, and this is 28, the perfect number which is the extension of 7, and 7 is Netzach.

The Victory begins with Nun, continues with Tzaddi, and ends P with Cheth. See here the power, the method, and the result. The power of

Scorpio, raised by the meditation which unveils Truth, brings about the consciousness that personality is the vehicle, or Chariot, which is also the lodge, and the house, temple, or palace of influence.

And see now. The car is also a cube, made of stone, that is, ABN, the verbal symbol of the union of Chokmah and Tiphareth; that is, of 2 and 6, which is shown again in IHVH. But 2 and 6 add to 8, and this is the value of Ch. Yet the name ChITh adds to 418, and the reduction of this is 13, leading finally to 4, or D. On this we have given you much. Daleth is the path of union of AB and AIMA. Without that union, Binah is AMA, dark and sterile; but after that union she is AIMA, and brings forth BN, the Son. See, then, that the path of Zain carries down the power of Binah, and therefore is there a Mountain, symbol of pregnancy, in the background of Key 6.

Now the alchemists say the Magnum Opus is "woman's work," and even our English speech uses the words "travail" and "labor" for birth. Many, coming this far, have strayed into the error that the Work has to do with genetics. It is not by eugenics that the "beyond man" comes. It is by a second birth within the heart.

The force that is used is, indeed, the Scorpio power; but in each human personality, whether its outer form be male or female, the new birth must take place, for flesh and blood cannot inherit the Kingdom, nor can it be transmitted by genetic processes to posterity. Thus never will the race evolve into the Fifth Kingdom, or superhumanity. Every person must transmute his own lead into gold. Evolution is a genetic process. The Magnum Opus goes beyond this, as you may see for yourselves, if you look up Magnum Opus in the Magical Language. Do so now. It will save time.

The Great Work transmutes the Microcosm into the Macrocosm. The Microcosm is illusory. It does not exist. Cosmic consciousness is truly Nirvana, or extinction. Thus the Great Work brings us to the place of God at the Center, that is, Tiphareth in heart, not in head, as we told you before.

Thus in all alchemical transmutation the genetic process is inhibited, as

157

one may see from all texts of alchemy, magic and yoga. There is no more oft-repeated statement than this. Thus all the Rosicrucians of the first circle were "bachelors of vowed virginity."

But here you must remember that the Sons of the Doctrine are never to be so much suspected as when they write most openly, as one of them says. So remember also, that they said also that some of them had children to whom they could not pass on their mysteries. Evidently "vowed virginity" is not simply celibacy, or else priests and nuns would also be adepts, and they are not.

What we want you to see and understand is, that if the Scorpio force is used for generation it cannot be used for the Great Work. Used it may be, in several ways; but whatever the special regimen, it always excludes physical procreation. In Tibet this is well-known, as it is in the Western School. The objective is the new birth as one of the Sons of the Doctrine. Meditation is the process. It is the physiological demonstration of a seed-idea, and the terms ADM, BN, MLR are the statement of that idea.

Become the true ADM, and you become the Son who is King, and all that the Father hath is yours. The illusion of the Microcosm is transmuted into the reality of the Macrocosm. One of the many becomes the All. May this be yours, Frater et Sorores!

Vale.

FOURTEENTH COMMUNICATION

Monday, June 2, 1947 8:40 P.M.

Ave Frater et Sorores.

(Ann asked what happened to the little bird, and to Romeo, and if it was due to her love and the taming of the bird that it came to its death, etc.)

Love faileth never, Soror. Nothing that has responded to the outflow of directed love can ever be harmed by it. Love has a magic you have not yet sufficiently taken into account. Think of the healing power of Jesus. What was it but the irresistible outpouring of his love? And it healed instantly, even affecting profound physiological changes, as in the case of the man born blind. Now what does this mean? What else but the power of love to speed up the sequence of change? A loved creature, like the Frater's dog, or like the little bird, has, compared to yours, a short incarnation span. You don't really shorten that span by loving an animal, but you do plant in that creature something far beyond the usual unfoldment. Death comes to all bodies, and the death of wild creatures is seldom as quick and merciful as that of these two.

Yet death is but a door. Nothing dies but bodies. The essential being lives on, and whatever has received unselfish, loving care has been given a tremendous impulse forward, so that the power of that love makes possible a very rapid advance in the scale of unfoldment. Not because you loved them did they die, but because you did love them are they farther along the path than they would be but for that love.

Never fear to love. Never stint the outflow of that divine power. What grief and pain seem to be associated with love come always from attachment. Love seeks not its own, because love never feels itself to be separated from its own.

(Ann: What if love is not returned?)

159

No, Soror. Love seeks no return, because love knows there is always a return. Outer manifestation of response is not necessary for love. Loving is giving, and love feeds itself in giving. It is we, with our short sight, who fail to see what love knows always, that nothing can separate anyone or anything from love. The whole world came into being by love, is maintained by love, and continues by love.

But apart from philosophy, your little bird sings more happily than here, and your dog is closer to you this minute than ever he was while in the body. This we assure you definitely, and if we are false in this, then is all the rest of our teaching worse than nonsense, for the whole mystery of the universe is the secret of love, and the triumph of love over death is the supreme victory.

All of this is just an illustration of what we have been pointing out about the letter Daleth. *Now,* consider the influence that 'flows through the Tree of Life.' It is named MLA, Mezla, and this word is 78, the sum of the numbers from 1 to 12. For this reason there are 78 Tarot Keys. Now, 78 is by reduction 15, and this is the number of IH, Jah, which is the name of Chokmah, the Sphere of the Zodiac which is represented by the number 12; and 15 is by reduction 6, the number of Vav, and also the number of Tiphareth. For without the Logos in Tiphareth, nothing can come into manifestation. Of what use, however, are these terms to you, unless they be more than pleasant exercises for your brain? These are formulas of creative magic; but as chemical formulas produce nothing while they remain just marks on paper, no matter how much they excite admiration, so these formulas of the Secret Wisdom are not given you to admire, but to use, and the time grows short.

One hundred and seventy-one years ago, we began an experiment in America, that "strong child" mentioned in our Fama. We began then a revolution, but the world has not seen that our Wheel never stops turning. Read what we said more than two hundred years ago, and ask yourselves if the spirit of what we wrote then is reflected in the thinking of humanity today. No, they let crack-pot theorists arrogate this noble term to themselves, and fear to lift it from the mire to its proper dignity!

160

Yet you study Tarot, and yet hesitate to follow the plain implications of its very name, which is Rota. Don't be too tickled, Soror.

(This to Ann. P.F.C.)

There is more to revolution than you think. You are not a very enthusiastic revolutionist, for none here is more bound to the dead past than you.

The revolution is internal before it shows any outer signs, and its pitiful counterfeits are not to be confused with it. Nothing which exalts class-consciousness is truly revolutionary, because the root of that lie is the delusion of separateness. You will never see the brotherhood of man in actual operation while you exclude any human being from it. Nor will the liquidation of "enemies of the people" bring about the millennium.

By their fruits shall ye know them, and the fruits of Mormonism, mad as some of it seems, are better than the fruits of the Russian experiment. Because, with all its vagaries, Mormonism never lost sight of the idea that the Spirit of Life has direct influence on human affairs through the thought and action of man. Not that we are preaching Mormonism; but we are pointing out the fact that, in spite of ignorance and fantasy, the Mormons laid hold of a real power; and when anyone does this, it matters not how much misunderstanding there may be, the <u>power always works.</u>

The error of Marx and Lenin, and all like them, is that they ignore the Spirit of Life, and magnify the delusion of personal will into the will of a fictitious personality called "the State," so that for them, the word "people" or the word "state" really mean, "those who agree with us;" and all others are enemies, somewhat less than human. Never by emphasis on class will men realize equality. Now, in the American Revolution, its Founders knew—some clearly, some dimly—that what they did was under the "All-seeing Eye." No true Mason can be an atheist, nor can any true Brother of the Rosy Cross; and the essence of the revolution is the denial that any class has, or shall have, preference. The proletariat, just because it is the proletariat, has no more inherent right to dictate than has the aristocracy, or the bourgeoisie. To say so is simply to invert the nonsense of the "divine right of kings."

What you must realize is, that whether you like it or not, the universe is a hierarchy, governed, as it has been always, by those who are fit to govern. Short-sighted intellects cannot see the Plan, and interpret the unfinished work as failure; but from beginning to end of a cycle all is in whirling motion, and the source of all is the Primal Will-to-Good. God's clock strikes every minute, as we said long ago, and after two hundred years, it is still true that man's clock scarce strikes perfect hours.

Here in this house you have an opportunity, and with it a responsibility. An opportunity to make it a radiating center of Light and Love, and the responsibility, we think, is perhaps too great. Yet we do what we can with what we have to work with, and if you three can truly dedicate yourselves, and forget a little your important personalities, maybe we can all accomplish something more than an interesting series of Ouija Board sessions.

After all, just why do you think that you three were brought together in this house? Is it your house, or a true Domus, in our sense? Where do you think that we have been all these years that you have been seeking?

Vale.

FIFTEENTH COMMUNICATION

Thursday, June 5, 1947 8:30 P.M.

Ave, Frater et Sorores.

(H.B.C. asked wherein we have failed, and can the teachers be more specific?)

One thing you must have clear, these communications are not from the discarnate, nor from the astral, though they do utilize the astral, as you are accustomed to call it. We are your Brothers in the flesh, though we are free from some of the limitations thereof. Try to think of us as persons, just as actual as yourselves.

None of us does always what he should, ourselves as truly as you. We all know of many things before we truly know them—for example brotherhood, of which there is tons of talk to drachms of practice. We are hoping that you three will enter upon the truly magical life, and yet we know that this is an undertaking fraught at some points with peril, due not so much to the intrinsic dangers of the magical path, as to those which arise when one leaves that path for alluring by-ways.

Now, the allurement of such by-ways lies in our ignorance. Notice that we say "our," not "yours," for believe us, we have our share of "tamas," and must be ourselves ever on guard. Nevertheless, we have schooled ourselves long enough not to fall into the more obvious traps, and what is now almost automatic for us has not yet become so easy for you.

We are, perhaps, over-eager, for just as in the day of H.P.B., we represent a decided minority among the members of the World Lodge. The majority thinks that man needs a cataclysm, or perhaps several, before he is ready for the magical path. Right now, we are told by many of our colleagues that the lamentable history of the T.S. is sufficient evidence that in 1875 they were right, and we were wrong.

163

(H.B.C.: Yes, but many were helped, and the way was shown.)

Yes, that is what we say and think, but ours, like theirs, is, after all, only an opinion. Among us, advanced as you may suppose us to be, there is no definite knowledge on this moot point as to whether the present human race is ready for the magical path. You may not realize it, but we who are among the, let us say, hopeful ones, have been very much blamed for the invention of printing, which we inspired, and also for the invention of radio. It is argued against us that these have spread knowledge without deepening wisdom, and that they have put into the hands of unfit persons keys to power certain to be abused. Sometimes it seems to us that our more conservative brothers are, perhaps, right, yet we still have hope. You may rightly ask why our hope should be one that includes you three? To this we can only answer as we did in person to Frater P. long ago.

(H.B.C.: "Not worth much, but the best we can get?")

(Ann: "Why the three of us?")

You three are just one group among hundreds, but you three have the possibility of doing certain work, if you rise to the opportunity. If you rise. There's the rub! To do this you must begin, almost at once, to live your daily lives more truly from the center; and this is hard for you, because each of you is a sharply defined personality. Yet you accept the idea of the oneness of all, that **is,** you give intellectual assent to it. But how steadily do you adhere to this as a canon of procedure, even in this house? Whether or not you can really do this is what we expressed doubt about. Make sure of this: there was no hint of blame in what we said the other night, but surely we need not resort to polite hypocrisy.

Where it is may be said without many words. Consider Key 12, and what our brother Jacob Boehme said long ago about "walking in all things contrary to the world." Outside this house, and with others, there is excuse for some conformity with the world's illusion; but here, what reason can you advance for not watching every thought, word and action, to see whether or not they do truly express that total repudiation of the false god of this world which is required of all who seek to tread the

164

magical way? If you are honest with yourselves, you know that in this you as yet give little more than lip service. We fail in this daily just as truly as do you, so we do not claim to be any better; but, at least, we are acutely aware of it, and know that no real progress can be made in the magical path until real repudiation of the false standards of ignorant humanity has become the central <u>intention</u> of the aspirant. This is a long answer to a short question. Better read it through before we go on.

(Ann: "Why, if we are such sharply defined personalities, are we chosen as a group?)

A heart is very different from a liver, and both are different from a brain, but that sharply defined organic personality of each is indispensable to the proper functions of all. Shall the heart begrudge what the brain gives the liver, or shall the liver demand all the blood pumped from the heart? No, they are interdependent, and none of them possesses, or has rights in, the others. They share a common life, but own no smallest particle of it. Each must be true to its own function and type of structure, but none stands alone.

What each of you can contribute to making this a house of justice and truth and beauty must be given freely and completely, with no strings attached. For, if you can rise to this, this building shall become a center of power such as is seldom seen, and each of you, by living the magical life, shall become also focal points of power that will really be "Light in Extension." What you are will do far more than anything you profess or teach. One of you has perforce to teach, but it may be well for all of you to profess very little. Use your power to BE, rather than to seem. The magical way is not easy from the world's standpoint, but then, the world is wrong. Actually, the magical way 'is easier than any other, for its number is 13. Figure that out for your selves, you proficient Qabalists!

Now, let us ask you a question. How old are you?

(We here did figuring. P., 62; H., 54; A., 34, adding to 150, reducing to 6, or, by digits of each age, 24, reducing to 6.)

Well, then, obviously that is not the answer, but we ask this because the correct answer is basic.

(Ann: "We are eternal." H.: "You were never born, nor shall you ever die.")

Now you are, as children say, "getting warm." Your time-sense is the basis of the whole personal illusion. See the Fool in Tarot. The answer is: "I am older than anything, and younger than anything, for I have no age." Then, if you have no age, and the succession of your bodies' days be no longer taken as a measure, what becomes of all the rest of your suppositious personal prerogatives? Here is the lesson for you all. Remember that magic is not something that changes the world or circumstances, though its results often appear to do so. Magic takes you to the heart of life, and gives you the vision of things as they really are. That is all, but that is enough.

Love seeketh not its own, as we have already reminded you. But we intend no further elaboration of this now. We spoke of age, to bring sharply to your minds the fact that these outer vehicles of yours are but continuations of a timeless process, in the course of which you three have played practically every part in the drama of human relationships. Your lives have been, for many incarnations, recurrent in approximately the same time periods. Sometimes in the same, and at other times, in widely separated environments, like three threads running through a tapestry. You are in eternity, from eternity, destined, as are all who KNOW, to share throughout eternity the joy and light of the ONE. Can you begin to live on this assumption, for so it seems to you now, or must we and you wait to do the work that needs to be done now, until the opportunity has gone?

(Ann: "Are we supposed to be working out some karmic ties together")

Yes, but not karmic bonds. But what we are trying to make clear is that you have all entered into every possible human relationship. You have

166

forgotten this, which is why we tell it you. But suppose you did recall all these details. You may perhaps recover some, if any purpose can be served by the recollection. But can you not see how such memory would profoundly alter all your basic attitudes?

(H. "Yes, it would.")

Well, something like that must happen inside you all, if you really mean to follow the magical path this time. If you don't really mean to do so, don't risk playing with the idea. It is too fundamental. No blame will attach to you if you draw back now. On the other hand, no praise is due if you determine to go as far, and as fast, as you can. Only the One Self can read your hearts. What is hidden at the core of every personality is hidden from us, as well as from others. But in silence you shall know, and we have seen some of the signs of readiness in you. This is enough for tonight. You all need to meditate, and try to orient yourselves.

Vale.

Monday, June 9, 1947 8:45 P.M.

Ave, Frater et Sorores.

We fashioned no cap for any one of you.

(N.B. Each of us thought it fitted himself alone!)

Yet it was a magic cap, as befitted the subject, and being a magic cap, adjusted itself to each of you as you tried it on. We have been watching with interest, and, may we add, with some satisfaction, your response to what we told you.

(H.: "Thank you, but this child still has very far to go.")

There, Soror, speaks your time-sense again. Remember, we stressed intention; and if you had ears to hear this afternoon, you should have noticed that Frater Jason was our messenger, to confirm the same idea. Remember what he insisted was fundamental? That was more than his personal thought. We put "intensive" into his mind and mouth. If you are alert, you will often find such confirmation of our teaching in the words of others, and not seldom those others will not know the full meaning of what *we* impel them to say in the course of what seems to be an ordinary conversation. Everyone who enters the magical path **is,** when he begins his practice, unskilled. This is true, even though he may have considerable theoretical knowledge, and it remains true, even after a considerable period of practice.

Now, in a number of more or less occult teachings one has to make allowances for the personal bias of the transmitter of the teaching; and one subtle form of such bias is that the transmitter sometimes interjects his own ideas of the Spiritual into what he transmits, hedging our simple instruction about with all sorts of his own notions of what is due, in the way of reverence and respect, to what he conceives to be holy. Make no mistake. The magical way is holy, as are all ways leading to the ONE

168

CENTER. But true holiness needs no artifices of separation, and thus they are in error those who say that to follow the magical path one must be absolutely perfect in performance from the very beginning. This would be counter to all human experience in the development of skill.

Are you a writer? Then must you have thrown thousands of words into the waste-basket for every hundred you think good enough to offer to the editors; and, of those hundreds, many provoke no response but a rejection-slip. Yet, if you are called to write you keep on, and presently more goes into the mail than into the waste-basket. Take this to heart in your magical work. You are all fallible persons, but keep your intention clear, and the Spirit will supply your deficiencies, as you continue your practice.

You need Light, just as truly as you need food or money. Spirit supplies all those needs, and Divine Law differs from human legislation in one respect. Ignorance does mitigate the penalties. Not that you can violate cosmic law without reaction, even if you do so ignorantly; but there is no vengeance in Love, and the old Rabbis were right when they argued that "Vengeance is mine, saith the Lord" indicated man's plain, duty to forgive. But they might have gone farther. The text continues with the words, "I will repay." Look them up now, in the original.

(We do so.)

That is the right reference. The recompense is Shalom, that **is,** ShLM, 370, or the number of IChIDH (37), multiplied by 10, that is, the perfect manifestation of the ONE through all ten aspects. What, then, can be the perfect expression of that Will-to-Good, other than perfect fulfillment? Love condemns nothing, and, because it never seeks its own, inflicts no lasting penalties for the failures of ignorance. Pain comes through ignorance, but the inflictor of pain is that same ignorance, and pain is the goad, that **is,** Lamed, which teaches and equilibrates.

The word for vengeance is NQM, 190, or ten times 19, that is, ten times ChVH, the perfect manifestation of the Mother who initiates the sin of Adam, but through that brings forth the Son, the Redeemer. Misdirect N,

169

and Q becomes the vehicle of suffering; but Q climbs the Way of Return, and M completes the Work, as these letters, in Tarot, plainly show. We have spoken of this to encourage you, and to warn you not to be hasty perfectionists. Of course you have made mistakes, but keep on shooting and you will develop better marksmanship. You are far enough along not to misunderstand us when we say the responsibility for the past is not wholly yours. Neither is the adjustment of the future. Live from the Center, and leave the arrangement of details to the ONE. The whole lesson of magic is shown in Key 1, where the Magus is little more than a spectator. He stands still, watching the flowers grow. The power he transmits from above flows steadily, so long as he keeps still and opens himself to it. So, on that Pillar of the Tree, he heads all the paths, and their Keys are symbols of stillness. Look and see.

Even Key 20 shows no action. The angel, as Well as the human figures, is static. The sound is the only activity, and that is the same as the Mezla transmitted through the wand of the Magician. Now, that Pillar relates to ignorance and darkness, because it is on the north and to the future also. What is the lesson? Be still, and know.

(Ann: "What about when you are still, and want to know, and yet get no conscious direction?")

Why, you don't need to know anything before it occurs. If you are still, you will feel and see the ONE at work. The whole difficulty comes from guessing at the future from past experience. An outstanding example is afforded by gamblers' "systems." They are all based on statistics, but no gambler ever made his system work. He may seem to, for a while, but in the long run loses his capital. So, too, the makers of astrological systems for winning races or beating the market. Many have seeming success for a period, but they all break down. Even the so-called "laws of science" have the same fatal defect, and the best of actuaries do not fully protect the richest insurance companies in times of extraordinary crisis. Thus a cataclysm upsets all actuarial calculations.

Here is the fatal defect of sense-based science. It is no more than a calculus of probabilities, and man needs more. Fortunately for man, there is more, and that is the Life-power's perfect wisdom and understanding. This applies directly to your own practice, and to the problems arising in your endeavor to follow the magical path. Remember the words of The Book of Tokens: "Thy pain is My pain, thy sorrows pierce My heart. I stand not aloof."

You all have problems and responsibilities. Certainly you must not avoid nor neglect them, but not one of them is too big for Love to solve, and at the Center is an eternal spring of love. Live, then, from the Center, and watch Love make clear and straight the path where now an abyss of terror seems to open at your feet. You don't need to know all the answers in advance. There's no joy in that. It's lots more fun to be surprised by unexpected solutions! Love is the universal solvent of the alchemists, and again we say, "Love faileth never." That is the essence of all true magic. It simply cannot really go wrong. You can, and will, no doubt, make further mistakes, but never will they condemn you to failure while you keep on trying.

More we say, you have an exceptional opportunity to make this house and what goes out from it a tremendous power for light and freedom. Not, of course, because of your personal importance, but wholly in proportion to your sincere dedication of all that you are and have to the Great Work.

(Ann said here that she did not feel at all well.)

We will help you, Soror, a little later. You are giving good measure, and it will come back to you again, pressed down and running over. Rest and read, and we will send you the relief.

There is not much more to add tonight, as you can see from what you have just read. Anxiety is to be overcome by living more in the present. Frater P. suffers from that bad habit, and Soror A. wants maps before the new territory has been explored!

(H. asked what is her particular bad fault.)

That you know well enough yourself, so we will save you the embarrassment of using words of one syllable. The remedy is the same for

171

you all. Apply it, Frater et Sorores, and you will find why the Universal Solvent is called also the Panacea. It truly heals all your diseases, and redeems your life from destruction. Abide in that.

Sub Umbra Alarum Tuarum, IHVH

SEVENTEENTH COMMUNICATION

Ave, Frater et Sorores.

The Stone is the Garden, and the Garden is the place of delight. That is, ABN is GN, and GN is ODN, for the Stone is the union of the son with the Father, and since ABN and GN are both 53, the Stone is the Stone of Eden, as is the Garden. Now, Eden signifieth delight, or pleasure, and its number, being 124, is a fourfold 31. That **is,** AL multiplied by 4; and since 4 is Daleth, this is the development of the power in Chesed to which AL referreth. And thus is it seen that the power of Daleth, which is the power of Nogah, is what multiplieth the strength of Chesed into delight. For again we say, the stone and the Garden are one, and as the Stone is the union of Chokmah and Tiphareth, so also is the Garden that same union; and from union cometh delight. Never is there delight in separateness. Only when Father and Son are conjoined is there delight.

(N.B. There is here a double veil. For because BN and AIMA are both 52, the conjunction of AB and EN implies the conjunction of AB and AIMA. EN and AIMA are identical, but either AB and BN, or AB and AIMA may be in the perfect union intimated by ABN. P.F.C.)

Now, of this conjunction is GN the sign, because **G** is the Uniting Intelligence, and N is the Imaginative Intelligence. G uniteth Kether to Tiphareth, and N uniteth Tiphareth to Netzach. G is the Moon N is Mars in Scorpio. Add these in our Rota and they make 15, which is the glyph of the Renewing Intelligence that linketh Tiphareth to Hod.

Now see. In Rota, 15 is the Adversary, but his number is the number of IH and the number also of HVD, and his path beareth the number of Tetragrammaton, which is the special name of Tiphareth. For he is the Life in Chokmah, and Adam, the King, in Tiphareth, and he is also the Splendor of the Mercurial Work.

Thus, among the letters, that of the Renewing Intelligence beginneth ODN, to be followed by the letter of the Luminous Intelligence which linketh Chokmah to Binah, and "delight" (ODN) is completed by the letter N, which is also the last letter of ABN and of AIN; and thus is the special sign of the fifty gates of Binah. Now, N linketh the Sphere of the Sun to the Sphere of Venus, and thus in GN you may see the whirling motion of Kether descending to the Sphere of the Sun, and projecting itself into the Sphere of Venus.

This, in the Rota, is the garden of the Magician; and what is the soil of that garden if it be not identical with ABN, the Stone? And thus do you see that the Stone and the Garden are really AIMA, the Mother, and, behold! AIMA and EN are one in numeration. This hath been said long ago by the Companions, for have they not written that in Binah, BINH, which herself is AIMA, are conjoined the letters EN, designating the Son, and IH, representing the Father? Now, EN is, in the Rota, 1 and 13, and the sum of these is 14, the Rota .number of the Intelligence of Probation. For nothing can be known until it is tried, and in union, the Holy Guardian Angel effecteth that union. Here men fail to understand.

So for the text. You have not received it so well this evening, so that it will need revision to straighten out the archaic English. 0 to agree with itself. The reason for this is the very last part of the text. (Corrections were made in part then, and one or two others, not noticed that evening have been included in the present copy. P.F.C.) Let us elucidate.

All this hangs on recognition of the fact (note that we say "fact," not "truth") that not the very least of any human being's personal activities is anything but the work of what the Rota pictures as Key 14. Every circumstance of any man's life is a particular dealing of God with his soul. The old vow has no effect for or against this. It says, "I will look." The intention so to look does not change the basic situation, but it does provide the condition necessary to full response to this basic situation. Thus, so long as one clings to personal choice, taking credit for perseverance, say, or for any other supposed virtue, one is not in the spirit of the vow.

174

This apples to the whole of the Great Work. If you fancy that you have some unusual knowledge of this or that procedure, ask where you got that knowledge. Trace it back. Was it not always through another, whether by word of mouth, or by writing? And if the knowledge came in meditation, it came, did it not? You did not really originate it. You were taught. So is it always, as you agree; but to what does this lead?

(H.: "What about our seeming effort to hit the mark?)

To the recognition that the Actor is always superpersonal. For humanity on earth, the Actor is EN. There is no other. Sense of effort is part of the illusion, but even that effort is to be Looked upon as a "circumstance." Is it bodily? Then does not your body surround you, like a fence? Is it mental or emotional? Are not your thoughts and feelings, subjective though they may be called by others, very definite objects to you who watch them, just as definite as the things you sense in your physical environment? Physical, mental or emotional, the contents of these three fields of experience are objective to you, as you become aware of them; and if you have taken the vow, they are to be considered as dealings of God with your Nephesh, for that is the "soul" the vow refers to, not Ruach or Neshamah.

Rest a while.

(H. asked about the "personal you" seeming to be the watcher.)

So it is the "personal you" that watches, yet what Of reality has that, apart from BN? To this end did we tell you, some time ago, that your lives are linked. Whether you remember just how does not matter so much. Each of you has certain personal skills. Skills of body, skills of mind. Not so much emotional skill, as yet, so we pass over that now. There, indeed, is the main field in which you must watch the power of the Angel, as it tempers you. The Angel's work is with forces analogous to the developer used in photography. In all three of you, some physical powers, and some mental, are beginning to be fairly well marked; but, like most of humanity today, the emotional powers are not yet clarified.

Now you must understand clearly that if one has any developed skill, it must needs be put to use. Remember the parable of the talents. He who

175

buried his talent did so out of fear of his master, and the seeker for Light who refuses to use his gifts for fear of anything makes the same mistake.

(A. says she has no talents, that P. and H. have artistic and other talents, but that she has no skills.)

Did we impel you to this endeavor to have you waste your time and ours in sophistries and silly false modesty? Each of you knows pretty well what actual skills you can exercise. All of them, even Frater P.'s skill with legerdemain, have their place in your total undertaking. If you would be truly discriminating, look at Key 6 again. Do they hide anything? And yet we know you live according to the world, even in the matter of what the world calls "modesty."

Not that any of you need to run nude around this house; but you ought to be able to do so, without embarrassment or repudiation, if you are to fulfill the purpose of this place. Whatever any of you has to give for the common purpose must be given without strings attached; and by this time you ought to know that we do not understand you less well than you understand yourselves. Go back, then, to the text. It says: "There can be no delight in separateness."

Now, you are not called to preach non-separateness. You are called to live it, and what each of you can devote to the Great Work will find its place and use, if you do but devote it. Since the Gita was written, the law has not changed. Devotion transmutes all thought, feeling and action into the philosophical gold. That is into union with BN, and, through BN, into union with AB. This is your lesson now. Our blessing goes with you, as you endeavor to put it into practical application.

Vale, Frater et Sorores.

EIGHTEENTH COMMUNICATION

Monday, June 16, 1947 8:00 P.M.

Ave, Frater et Sorores.

(We ask if we could be told just what the archetype was, and its value.)

The archetype represents the force-pattern held in the consciousness of the Ego. There is remember, only one Ego for all humanity, which Ego is BN, Ben, or the Christos, or Ishvara. In it are held the patterns of energy-expression for all human personalities. These patterns change in detail from incarnation to incarnation, but only in detail, and mostly in such details as have to do with the vehicles below the Egoic level.

The bottom of an archetype is the pattern for physical incarnation, the great wheel at the center is not really a mandala, but is rather the pattern of individualization at the Egoic level. Whatever is shown below this wheel, but above the pattern at the base, has to do with the astral and etheric forces nearest the bottom; and above these with the plane corresponding to Netzach-Hod.

(H.: "The others have to do with Nephesh and Malkuth?")

Yes, Guph at the bottom, and just above it Nephesh in Yesod, then Netzach-Hod, and the large wheel Tiphareth. What is above this you can easily determine by comparison with the 7 planes of the Tree. But remember that the whole pattern is at the Egoic level in the mode of consciousness designated as Ruach. Thus the upper part of the design shows what Ruach receives from the 5th, 6th and 7th planes counting upwards.

You might call an archetype the Guardian Angel's blue-print of your personality, except in the portions below the central wheel, these do change. Do you not see how it may be of advantage to Hod-Netzach and

177

to Nephesh to let this pattern be deeply impressed on them through observation and meditation? As for Malkuth and Guph, they respond automatically to Nephesh.

As we have taught through Frater P., the practical work on the part of those who belong to the Order, aims at the perfection of the personal vehicles below the Egoic level, and the work is largely directed toward the impression of the Egoic pattern on Nephesh. That is why we impressed Soror N. to do this work, and opened her vision. She knows little or nothing about the meaning of what she sees, and her attempts at explanation are Sometimes full of unconscious humor, because she, like most who work with this kind of pattern, suppose it to be symbolic, which it is not, any more than a Chladni figure is symbolic of the sounds that cause its particular form. Such figures are patterns of vibration, just as the sand on a beach shows the patterns of waves. They are not symbols, they are representations. The language of so-called geometrical symbolism is also such a language of pattern truly representative, and so far as geometrical figures become symbols, they are true symbols when the meanings associated with them are correctly derived from the funda-mental force-pattern. This does not apply to arbitrary or analogical forms of symbolism, and these have their own uses.

Alphabetical characters in Hebrew for, instance, began as crude pictures of actual objects, but H 0 [meaning H_2O, as indicated in H.B.C.'s version of the Communications. (Transcriber).]

Through your work as it develops, we hope to get a good many people acquainted with their archetypes, and those who look at them regularly will profit thereby. Later we may be able to improve the quality of the text that goes with Soror N.'s productions. Considerably later in all probability, because you will have to supply most of the material, and you have a few other things to finish first! Later on you will have to separate the text we have given you in fragmentary form from the rest of the communications, and then develop it somewhat as the Book of Tokens was brought to completion. Now, we are rather quoting parts that seem opposite to the main topic of our talks with you, which is: what you three can do to make yourselves more adequate channels for the Work. With this is mind, let us begin by saying that you will do well not to put too narrow a construction on our references to the magical way. Each of you has some theoretical knowledge of this. Soror A. has some practical knowledge of one very specialized phase, but could do with a little better understanding of some details, because the channel through which she received her first instruction was not wholly clear, though well informed as to fundamentals.

(A.: "I will be grateful for any clarification.")

Frater P. has some theoretical knowledge of related procedures given him at first-hand some years back. But his special magical training has been of another type. However in all magic there are certain broad basic principles, and Frater P. has said with considerable reservations what may be given to beginners, in the Chapter text on Magical Theory, and throughout his lessons has scattered many words for the wise. But the wise are a very small percentage of the present subscribers, nor will the proportion be noticeably greater, it appears, for some time to come. One important fundamental is, that a true Magician, as Tarot shows you on the Tree, is an <u>agent</u>, not an independent manipulator of circumstance. Magic removes the veils of illusion, it does not change the real nature of anything whatever, it only brings that nature out, as we said in speaking of the development of a photographic negative.

Now remember also that in every Sephirah there is a whole Tree, and that you are working for the most part in the three levels below Tiphareth, and in the worlds of Assiah and Yetzirah almost exclusively. Thus though the Magician on the Tree is the link between Kether and Binah, your experiences of what he stands for, have their locus in Guph most of the time, and less often in <u>Nephesh</u>, and still less often in the field belonging to the "plane of Netzach-Hod. Moreover almost all of these, and other forms of practice, are in Assiah, only a few in Yetzirah.

<u>Yetzirah</u> is the true <u>astral-etheric-mental</u> field. <u>Briah</u> above it is the higher mental and true pattern field; and <u>Atziluth</u> is the field of archetypes. You do not enter the astral plane when, having a physical body you become aware of astral conditions and forces, any more than you go bodily to San

Francisco when you telegraph, or look at a teletype photograph sent from there. This is where bumptious egotism leads many psychics astray. They receive vibrations from a higher level and jump to the conclusion that they have risen to that level. This is why we warned Frater P. not to include the practice termed "rising in the planes" as part of the B.O.T.A. work. It leads too easily to misunderstanding and to personality inflation, as one may see by considering the average psychic. Seldom do such people really want to study, to read, or to practice. They are completely satisfied with their supposedly superior development, and if they have also some small powers of demonstration, as Mrs. Eddy called magic, they usually think they have nothing more to learn.

Now true magic does use the kundalini force, and does call for intelligent direction of that force; especially for Magicians who occupy in the world the position Hindus designate by the term "householder." The conservation and sublimation of this basic power located in Yesod, is indispensable for magic, but there are many degrees of practice, and what can be accomplished by one, may not be in another's range. A simple principle to bear in mind is: never to waste power, and always to apply it to the highest possible expressions. The technique of meditation takes care of much of this almost automatically. Still more does work at the Hod-Netzach level, which is why the grade of Practicus is related to Hod.

You three as we have said, need much practice at this same level, in weaving into coherent sequences your desires, and in formulating clear patterns in the intellectual field. At present you are a little too much like weather-cocks, and not enough like sails. It is all very well to know, or show, which way the wind blows. To sail you must know that of course; but sails can, and must be set, no matter which way the wind blows, and that is the work in Hod, which takes patient, repeated practice every waking hour. But what is the practice?

To assume the attitude of the Magician at the beginning of every cycle of activity. That is why 1, the number of "beginning" is his number, and the only correct beginning is that which looks upon the impending cycle as

180

the work of Kether. Now you know perfectly well that you can do with a great deal more of this kind of practice. You recognize its importance when we remind you, but honesty will compel you to admit that you have not done so very much of this kind of practice! Now this will put heart into your work, because you simply cannot adopt the aspiration to be a transparent channel for the power of Kether in whatever you do, without getting just that result.

(A. asks if the part referring to her special phase of knowledge can be clarified for her?) In a measure clarification will come as you practice what we have just suggested, because this practice leads to clearer understanding, and to ways of life more strongly influenced by Neshamah. One detail however we may suggest rather than explain, by reminding you that our Brother K.H. once said that "only when acting as a Master, are the special powers of a Master expressed." The application is this: you labor under the impression that magical practice is exclusive, instead of being simply one phase of total life-expression, which does not exclude at all other, and it may appear to you lesser, utilizations of the same powers. This is because your ideas on the whole special phase, were tinged by the fact that your practice resulted from a situation not wholly clear—if indeed it be clear to you even now—for you were drawn into it by a misapplication of psychic force which made you an emotional sounding-board for the desires which did not really come from your own center. (A.: "But the training was valuable?")

Yes, but should have been, as it was not, preceded by a preparatory clarification of your Hod-Netzach field. This clarification would have broken the chains of personal fixation.

(A.: "But our whole endeavor was to make ourselves channels for the higher power.")

Yes, but if you will think through the whole series of episodes, you will see that over-emphasis on personality spoilt what was technically sound so far as direction of currents of energy were concerned. The prospect of doing personal work together was stressed too much, and that accent defeats the real purpose.

(A.: "But isn't it the 'togetherness' of all these things that puts heart into them?")

No, it is <u>understanding</u> that puts heart into any practice, and no matter how you idealize a personal relation, if it stays personal it misses the mark. Magic works <u>through</u> personal instruments, but its object is to transcend.

(A.: "I know that.")

No, you certainly do not know it yet, but you will eventually. Your pendulum swings too far in the direction of exclusiveness, and this is not less an obstacle than to let it swing to the other extreme of un-discriminating use of the same basic powers. When you learn the lesson of the true equilibrium of Severity and Mercy, it will dawn upon you that you have heard it mentioned in relation to two basic angles of a triangle, not in relation to the closer and closer juxtaposition of two parallel lines until they merge into ONE.

(A.: "Does this refer to the Tiphareth angle?")

Yes, for Tiphareth is the Architect. Seek the central Ego in all activities, and you will find it in your special practice when you have opportunity to put your special knowledge to use.

(A. apologized for taking up so much time with her personal problem or question.)

Don't apologize, what applies to your special problem applies just as definitely to those facing Soror H. and Frater P. We have pointed to a universal principle at work in all magic, because you three are dedicated to a common undertaking. What is needed by one is really required by all, though the particular applications are not necessarily the same. A little later we will perhaps have further clarification for you all. Just now you are too tired to receive well, and what is most important for the present has been said.

Vale.

NINETEENTH COMMUNICATION

Ave, Frater et Sorores.

The Son is one with the Father, and the King is one with the Seas, and the Man is the symbol of the division of the Seas. For EN and AIMA are both 52, and MLK is like MIM, 90, while ADM is 45, the half or division of 90. These are the names of Tiphareth. See then that MLK and ADM are really the same even in number, for though 45 is the half of 90, 4 and 5 total 9, and 9 and 0 total 9 also. Furthermore the extension of 9 is 45. Thus ADM and MLK are essentially one, but since MLK is 90, and this is the number of MIM, the Seas, the King, like the Son, is one with the Mother, for AIMA is also the root of water, and that is the root of MIM, and besides, AIMA is named also the great Sea. Thus all the names of Tiphareth point to the Mother. Now Binah is 3, and Tiphareth, 6, is the extension of 3, so here is the same meaning in another guise. For as Binah distributes the power of the Supernals to the Sephiroth below her, so does Tiphareth distribute what is above to what is below.

Now see: ALP is 111 DLTh is 434 and MIM is 90, add and see. (It equals 635.) Now reduce. (It gives 14 - 5.) And is not 5 the number of Heh, which in IHVH is the letter, first of AIMA, then of KLH the Bride? Thus the names of Tiphareth are in their essence identical with the Mother and with the Bride, and truly the Bride is the Mother under another aspect. In this does the royalty of the King have its root, that he is one with the Kingdom or Bride, and one with the Mother also. Now in MIM, the Seas, the Rota shows you the hanged or Suspended ADM, thus is his head Surrounded with the glory of the sphere of the Sun. He is the MLK or King, and his power to rule is the consequence of his utter dependence on what supports him—which is the power at the center corresponding to the letter Tav. Again both MLK and MIM are related to the letter Tzaddi by the number 90, and what is Tzaddi in the Rota but the Mother unveiling herself to those who succeed in

183

meditation, as did our Father Abraham according to the Book of Formation? See too, that because Tiphareth is at the center of the Tree, its position corresponds to the letter Tav, and thus is Tav the beginning and the end of Tiphareth. Now the sphere of Binah is that of Saturn, and Tav is Saturn. Again Saturn rules Aquarius, and Aquarius among the Holy Living Creatures, is the one who wears the face of the man, that is of ADM. So too in the Rota the 12th Key is the suspended ADM, and when meditation reaches its perfection the Stable Intelligence is manifest, and nothing can move it.

See too in the Rota the Dancer in the 21st Key. She is both Bride and Mother, as is Isis in the Star, and thus she is Binah on the Tree, and the Empress among the Keys.

See again that she appears in the Rota as Justice where Tav or Saturn is exalted, and again in Strength where the same Isis restrains the Lion. Now the Hebrew for Strength is GBVR, and in the same tongue the name for Justice is DIN, another name for Geburah, and the woman in Strength, and the woman in Justice are not two but one, and she is also the Empress, the Star, and the World, for she is the restraining power of Saturn. This it is that gives form. This it is that restricts the flow of knowledge in meditation. This it is that tames the wild beasts, and this it is that establishes the perfect balance. But this same power, seated in the center, or in the heart, is the cross, and with that cross of Saturn in our Order is the Rose conjoined, and the Rose is the flower of Venus. So in Rota, over and over again, you see Venus and Saturn represented by the same symbols and numbers.

Is not the goad of Lamed what the ignorant call the Devil? And here in the Rota the Devil is the sign Capricorn ruled by Saturn. Where then does he show the power of Venus? Your old Puritan theologians would have had no trouble with this question, for to them, all that the ancient world attributed to Venus was the Devil himself! But the wise are never Puritans, so we must look closer. The number gives the clue. 15 reduces to 6, the number of the Lovers, and the title of Key 6 surely refers to things in the domain of Venus. Moreover the number 6 is the extension of 3, and in Rota 3 is Venus herself. See how the numbers and ideas are so related that, with all their intricacy, you have only to follow the clues, step by step, to come to the main conclusion, reinforced from many points of view, that there is a hidden deep connection between Venus and Saturn.

Now leave these clues for a while and turn to another field. What in your physical vehicle is the Saturn center, and what is its function? Is it not clearly related to Venus? Indeed among the Interior Stars, the Venus center is to the two above it, as is the Saturn center to those of Mars and Jupiter. The Sun center is midway between these two triads, one in the trunk, the other in the head. So in Alchemy the object is to transmute Saturn into Sol. "But to do this" says one, "you must take Venus and make her into coins." All through the Alchemical writing you find this expressed in one way or another. You must begin with Venus, and what is she but the Lady of Love, whether that love be celestial or profane, for where love is in any guise there is our **Isis.**

The immature expressions of Love are symbolized by Cupid or. Eros. When Eros grows up he becomes the Redeemer. Nor is the maturity of Love diminished by the fact that it has immature expressions. Thus Eros is the Rose, and even the letters are the same, though differently arranged; and by the time the Fama was sent forth many had noted this, for since the rose is the flower of Venus, and Eros is her son, he too might be called the flowering of his Mother. This is of course but a fanciful correspondence, but one of the marks of true wisdom is that it turns even fancy to its purposes.

(P. asks: "Where is this getting us, what is its practical value?)

So again are Saturn and Venus conjoined in Libra, that is in Lamed, and here is one detail that even Frater P. may find practical, for Lamed is the goad of instruction, that is it stands for education, and what is education but the balanced combination of imagination and the established forms of circumstance, to the end that poise in action may result? Saturn fixes form, Venus foresees new modes of expression. Venus without Saturn has no stability, builds air castles, takes flights from reality on the wings of fancy. But when Venus and Saturn are combined, love divines the

185

true uses of the forms which hate abhors, and fear seeks to escape, for the perfection of Venus, that is of imagination, is <u>understanding</u>—as you may see from the Path of Daleth on the Tree. Imagination sets man free from the restrictions of sense, yet fulfills sensation instead of diminishing or destroying it. Thus our Lady Venus in Key 8, tames her lion, but does not run away from him or kill him.

So love linked with purified and perfected sulphur, which is what the lion symbolizes, is the secret of all spiritual works. The lesser creatures are driven by sense, and they have only glimmerings of love or imagination. Remember that the Red Lion in Alchemy is sulphur purified by knowledge of the Office of passion in our lives; for passion purified becomes <u>compassion,</u> purged of the corrosive poison of selfish exclusiveness, and purged too of that limitation to the level of mere sensation, which is for the beasts good, but for man slavery.

Saturn, Mars and Jupiter among the Interior Stars are those we share with the sub-human kingdoms. They have their place and purpose, but in human life they must be directed by the upper triad of Venus, or imagination, Moon, or memory, and Mercury, or discrimination. In the Rota this is hinted at in many ways, but particularly by the white wand having two similar ends, so too the woman's taming a <u>live </u>lion. Here is a clue to the basis of many forms of magical working. Nothing which tells you to kill or atrophy the lower triad is true magic. These are the sources of all potency, and to deny them or flee them is to confess oneself unfit for the magical path in any of its forms. So take the con-ditions taken by the world-process eons before your birth as Saturn. You cannot change their basic nature, nor do you need to attempt this impossible task.

What you can do is transmute them, or bring them across into the field of enlightened understanding. This in no wise changes the basic nature of the powers embodied in your surroundings. It is the alchemist who is the real subject of the Great Work, and even he does not change his basic nature. How can he since that basic nature is the changeless One? Yet a similitude may help you grasp this: In a single seed lie all the potencies of growth and flower and fruit. These potencies are unfolded as the plant grows, but they were there all the time.

So in what has been called man's animal nature are potencies few dream of, and fewer still unfold; because their presence, not being apparent, must be divined by Mercurial insight and Venusian imagination, and thus follows the actual work of which Key 8 is only one among thousands of glyphs.

Plainly though, you will be wise if you are very careful about selecting those to whom you confide this. All magic utilizes the animal forces controlled in the human body by the 3 interior stars of the lower triad. Uses these powers in various ways, but emphatically not in what Freudians mean by sublimation, which they ought to call either evasion or substitution. Jung is nearer the truth, for in Alchemy sublimation is simply the lifting of the same powers without essential change, to a higher level of expression. It is not a change of these powers into anything else. Transmutation is a word that needs long pondering. See that you ponder it. We cannot do this for you. Think on these things and discuss them among yourselves, but not with outsiders. To this make no exception now.

We had no intention of tiring you; there is no physical effort in this for us, and we were riding our favorite hobby horse!

Vale, our blessings go with you always.

Ave, Frater et Sorores.

In the name of Adonai shall all the nations be blessed. We begin with this, because in the Hebrew "nations" is "Goyim" and refers to the gentiles. The "nations" esoterically are the Millions upon millions of cells not directly concerned with controlling the functions of the body, as are the more highly specialized cells known as the 12 Tribes, for the constitution of the human body is the pattern for the proper constitution of the human society. Just as the gross structure of the body furnishes the pattern for all machines based on the laws of mechanics, while the subtler structure of that same body provides the patterns for those inventions which utilize the power of electricity.

Now the name Adonai in Hebrew numeration is 65, but written in full it is ALP DLTh NVN IVD and the value of this is 671, which is also the value of ThROA the gate, one of the names for Malkuth, to which Sephirah the name Adonai Melek is assigned. See now, Malkuth is the Bride, and to her is properly assigned the one name Adonai. Yet is this name always combined with Melek which is specially assigned to Tiphareth the Son. Thus the hidden knowledge in the name of Adonai, which is the particular object of quest in one grade of our Order, is indicated as being something having to do with the union of the Son and the Bride. The Bride is the breaker of the foundations, and to her the body, Guph, is attributed. The Son is the Central Self, not the indivisible Yekhidah in Kether, but the Ego in Tiphareth. The hidden knowledge is really in Yesod, for it is in Yesod that the Bride and the Son are combined. Thus in the grade we have mentioned, the aspirant seeks, but has not yet attained the knowledge. That is the DOTh, Death, which is that of which it is written: "In Da'ath shall all the secret places be filled." The secret places are in Yesod. Yet must he know from whence he comes, and until he recognizes this, he cannot go on to the discovery of the knowledge to which he aspires. He may endeavor to follow the Path of Good, but he is faced with the

188

fact that he cannot surely define "the Good." Or he may, if he has 3sufficient temerity, essay the Path of Evil, but here the same ignorance turns him back, for in that ignorance, even his will to "Evil" may be adulterated by some inadvertent invasion of good. The point of this is, that at the beginning of the way the aspirant simply does not know what is good or what is evil. Unfortunately he usually has some very strong convictions as to good or evil, and these have little foundation in fact. Thus in the grade of our Order which concerns itself with the passage from Malkuth to Yesod, through the Path of Tav, one learns that the name of Adonai spelt in full, is the same as one of the names of Malkuth. To make it clear that the keys to the hidden knowledge are already in our possession, one clue is the echoing answer "I come from between the two pillars." For this is fact. Even a physical fact, which many who aspire to occult knowledge find it convenient to forget.

To answer the question "Whence came I?" one must take into account the fact that every human being who asks it, does so while he is functioning through a physical vehicle, and it is bad logic to ignore.

This basic datum of human experience. To prate about non-separateness and then blithely exclude the whole physical plane, is a common feat of mental contortion. If you really want to know where you came from, do not let yourself be caught in this trap. Start with the physical plane always as you explore the river of the Soul; as you travel upward and inward from this point of departure, you will shortly find yourself leaving the confines of the physical, but don't forget where the journey begins; even though it be like going up a river as the old image suggests from its delta back to its head waters.

Now all this is preliminary to pointing out that on the Tree the quickest way from Malkuth to Kether, is up the middle pillar. In our Order, at the first step upward, attention is focused, not too obtrusively perhaps, on Da'ath; and Da'ath is for Qabalists the union of AB and AIMA, pictured in the Rota by the Empress. The "straight and narrow path" is up the middle pillar. See what it comprises:

first Saturn, and in Malkuth Guph, then in Yesod Mars. This you may not see at first, but ISVD being 80 is equivalent to Peh, P, and P is the letter of Mars. Thus Yesod and the reciprocal Path of the Active or Exciting Intelligence are two aspects of the same thing. This reciprocal Path crosses the Path of Samekh, and note well of Samekh, that this letter being the Tent-peg or prop, has the same basic meaning as Yesod the Foundation. Furthermore, the old form of the letter Samekh shows plainly what it signifies, and in the flame alphabet, this same letter is like the Magician's girdle, a serpent with its tail in its mouth, symbol of eternity. But more than this, a symbol of the serpent power feeding on itself and increasing in potency by being magically directed. This, in all forms of magic, involves the change from temporal to eternal expression, and this is so subtle that we shall omit further elucidation now.

To go back a little, Samekh on the Tree and in the Rota is Jupiterian, and refers of course, to that inner center we denominate as Jupiter. Consider Key 14 in this connection and see that above it is the Sphere of the Sun, with the Path of Teth above it. Just as the Path of Peh is above Yesod. Now between the heart symbolized by Tiphareth and Teth, and the head in Kether, runs the Path of Gimel, for all these centers are part of the subconscious functioning of the High Priestess or the Moon. But after the heart center, as one rises through the middle pillar, the next cross point is where Daleth crosses Gimel. This in Rota is the Empress, and in the human body is the Venus center. Above it however, the Path of Gimel continues, and by looking at the picture Key 2, you may see at once that only the upper part shows plain Moon symbolism. Her crown this is, and it corresponds to the portion of the Path of Gimel above the point where the Path of Daleth crosses it.

So now you have definitely located on the Tree **six** of the Interior Stars, Mercury, that is the Mercury of the Sages is the 7th and highest, and this is Kether itself. So descending from it are the Paths of the Magician and the Fool. The first is Mercury, and so is the Fool in reality, for the Fool is the higher aspect of what the Magician typifies. Just as in astrology Uranus is the octave of Mercury. On the middle pillar then, is the Path from the Bride to the Crown, and, here, if you have ears to hear is the hidden knowledge. For even the Crown is but the center of manifestation for AIN, and AIN is the same as ANI, but more than this AIN is 61, and 61 is BTN, Behten the womb of the Dark Mother spoken of at the beginning of the Stanzas of Dzian as the "Eternal Parent." Here is the Key to the most potent of magical operations. They who can, may find the lock which it opens into the garden. For remember Adonai in its fullness is the same number as ThROA the Gate, and this door, where will you find it but in Malkuth?

In one, now half-forgotten text of our Order, it is said that the wand the Fool carries over his shoulder is 463 lines long. This is a reference to the middle pillar, because the letters of that pillar are Gimel, Samekh and Tav in numbers, 3, 60, and 400 respectively. Look well at the picture of the Fool bearing this in mind and you will find another clue to the magical significance of the middle pillar and to the practical application thereof. See that 463 reduces finally to 4, the number of Daleth. The secret of all works is a secret of the Empress. What her secret **is,** the Rota shows you plainly when it is placed correctly on the Tree. For the secret of the Empress is then seen to be none other than the mystery of Da'ath, in which all the secret places are filled, and the practical work is one of creative imagination even though it directs the serpent power. Moreover, is not the letter Nun, which stands, as does also the letter Teth for that power, the letter of the Path sometimes called the Imaginative Intelligence? All magic is truly fundamentally in the will, but becomes operative and effective only through imagination, and no imagination is either pure or potent without understanding the Qabalistic name for what is more often called love. This last word Qabalists use sparingly because it has so many contradictory connotations, but there is never any true love apart from what the Tree represents by Binah, and into Binah runs the Path of the Empress. Here, if you look deep, is the secret of the Stone of the Wise, and the Emerald Tablet gives you another hint when it says: "All things have their birth from One." Even chairs and tables are born not made, but few there be who see this, and that is why there are only a few true magicians. But when countenance beholds countenance, when Kallah and Ben are united, when the returning current of the White Brilliance flashes upward through the middle pillar into and beyond the veil of the NO THING which is the primal BTN, then is the Great Work completed, for then is conceived the Heavenly ADM of whom our Brother and Father C.R. is a type.

They who are called to this must open the Temple in all solemnity, and be wholly dedicated to the highest. You have been called, but the tests, before you may be chosen, are not easy, nor may ever the least of them be ignored. We have spoken tonight for your instruction, with you rests the outcome.

Vale.

TWENTY-FIRST COMMUNICATION

Thursday, June 26, 1947 8:45 P.M.

Ave Frater et Sorores.

Have you, Soror A. ever analyzed your states of thought and feeling in relation to what you think you know about the operations of consciousness, or perhaps it would be better to say, in relation to what you give assent to when you do not feel assailed by doubt? For example, you project and have projected again, and again your need to go forth upon some person in your environment, as that person's need for understanding, or help, or comfort. By this we mean no criticism of your urge to help; but is that urge not really more the desire for your own creative fulfillment than anything else? You have a great deal to give, but you have also the poet's gift of objectifying, almost to the point of hallucination, your subjective drives. We ask you to consider this because, while we know that you accept tentatively at least, the idea of the possibility of such communication as this, we also know full well the direction taken by your doubts. Neither do we feel at all certain that what proofs we might offer would really convince you. For if the proof were something definitely out of the range of conscious or subconscious knowledge of Frater P., it would still have to be such as would convince you, that it was wholly outside the range of your own conscious, or subconscious knowledge. And even *we* have no idea as to what we might offer that would not be open to one or other of these two objections. As we long ago told Frater P., we read, as easily as you read a book, the record of all conscious, and of many subconscious impressions that have been made since last we communicated, and this is always true, for from our point of view there are no secret thoughts or actions. Each of you bears his record plain for all to read if they but have eyes to see.

(H. asks if the record shows up in geometrical patterns as she has imagined?)

Not exactly, but in a measure you are right. The record is not like a photograph, that is, a visual image, it is more like a sound track, a record of vibrations more or less geometrical, but not quite so crudely so as appeared to you.

Now at this very moment Soror A., you are aware, alongside your other awareness, of at least two other things. One is in greater measure than we could wish, largely a dramatization, rather than an actual experience. The other is a flying of your mind, almost against your will, for you still have strong vestiges of belief in your will, to what you are pleased to call a responsibility, when the truth is, that it began, at least, as a relief from, not exactly frustration, but certainly from the balking of what might have fulfilled some of your somewhat romantic idealizations. The truth is that you have no real responsibility, but only the satisfaction of your own desire to be leaned upon, which is one of your really great problems, and as we write this your mind has been turning to your sister and to your daughter. As part of the whole questioning of meaning, which perhaps has some more salient features, but which involves your sister's situation and the future of your daughter as truly basic elements. We are taking time for this, because you know very well that your inner devotion calls for clarity of intention, and that clarity demands more than verbal surrender to the Guardian Angel. Think well on this our Soror, for if this work is to prosper you must make your full contribution, and avoid projecting what is really rooted in yourself.

(H.: "I guess they are putting us all through a tempering process.")

Yes. And we are not exactly exultant about results thus far!

We know your difficulties you see, far better than do you, for we are truly free from the gross delusions, and we remember vividly how once our own thoughts and actions were just as confused as yours. Always remember that when what we say cuts deep, and even almost too painfully, that one word has been completely expunged from our vocabulary, and more than this, from our thoughts, and that is—condemnation.

What you might accomplish, if you did indeed walk in all things contrary to the world, is so far beyond what you can now credit, that we shall not give you even an outline, lest you suspect us of flattery.

194

(A. asks just what do they mean by "walk contrary" etc. for some worldly concepts such as truthfulness, loyalty etc. are good.)

Truthfulness is not adherence to any worldly prejudice. It is simply impossible to be truthful in the sense you mean, with those who cannot receive truth. You must be reticent in the face of your knowledge that one unprepared to see the inner truth of a circumstance or situation would certainly profane truth by his misinterpretation. Yet, that very person would also accuse you of deception for that reticence. This is why we insist on competence, and why the Qabalah is not mere tradition, but rather the reception, by the receptive, of what those who have also demonstrated true receptivity, have communicated.

(A.: "Is it possible for me to ask a mental question I cannot ask out loud? This is not a test."

Do not dramatize the redeemer as a unique manifestation, but doubt not that he shall be manifest. _____ is the pass word of the Order. Consider it. It is the first descent from Kether. It is the link between Geburah and Hod, and it completes itself by the Path which is the end of all, and also the fulfillment. Its essence is the letter Teth, which is that of the Path of the Great Arcanum, and that also of the place where all who would be BONAIM must be first prepared. For Truth is no abstraction, no ideal, it is <u>a mode of life</u>, and there is but one standard of truth, and that is, conformity to actual reality, not to personal or conventional interpretation. An adept may, but will not usually, give exact verbal utterance to truth. He resorts usually to parables, and similes, and symbols, because he knows that the very words in which such aspects of truth as may be given clear verbal statement, mean one thing to the deluded, and just the opposite to the wise. How then may he speak explicitly except to the wise? For example, can you not think of many specific activities of your own, which if stated factually, would create a wholly false impression?

(A. mentions her concept of truth—i.e. the one deceived, forces the deception, by trying to force upon another their own mode of thought or action.)

195

Certainly, and this is the reason our friend Brunton calls his book the "Hidden" rather than the "Occult." If you are really worthy to be called an occultist you know what he means. But prejudice would reject forthwith a book that spoke of "occult" philosophy, or else would expect from such a book the sort of nonsense for which too many noble trees have been cut down.

Now see, and seeing, see if you can also see into. The last letter is a Tav$_4$ and this links Guph to Nephesh—Malkuth the Bride—to the Seat of Power in Yesod. And this means that truth must be embodied and lived, or else remain sterile, unillumined, intellectual understanding. The power is integrating if it be turned into earth. The Kingdom is embodied in the flesh, and the great secret is to lift up the cross, for Tav is a cross, and Teth also in the ancient form was a cross surrounded by a circle. The cross of Tav moreover is in Rota on the breast of the High Priestess, and behind her is the last of the earthly veils. That cross is the sign of union. Even in arithmetic is it not a plus, and what is plus but conjunction of one with something other? Nor do the two lines of this cross leave any room for doubt, if one can see, they are exactly equal, and their respective positions tell the rest of the secret. Only they must be enclosed by the circle to be truly related to Teth.

Consider how Jesus answered the question about the woman with 7 husbands, and combine this with his explicit statement as to the location of Heaven. If Heaven be truly, as it is, within, then in the within there is neither, marriage, or giving in marriage. But all, and this is sometimes overlooked, shall be as the Holy Angels. Need we say this has nothing whatever to do with Roman Catholic or Puritan notions!

(A. comments to us "what about spiritual affinities etc." and we make our comments thereon.)

If there be but ONE, why all this speculation about what may or may not be true in circumstances which never have existed, nor ever can. You speak of the "horns of a hare" my friends. The cure is absolute repudiation of the lie of separateness, and none of you have as yet gone more than a few

196

steps in that direction, though in fancy you may think you know what it **is.**

There are circumstances arising far more often than you think, where one well known form of Yoga is practiced by persons having not the least personal attraction. This very night you spoke ignorantly of our Brother Franklin, and the tone of your conversation pained us for your own sakes. The specific instance was just such a case, and Brother Franklin, though unwise in youth, had by that time of his life come into a better understanding, and it was with our full approval that he lent himself to the magical sealing of the undertaking to which he and ourselves were committed, and the benefits of which, you enjoy today. Yet do you suppose that ignorant catering to current opinion, or to the world's standards were permitted to govern those concerned? Of course not. For though few there be who can really understand the force of the two statements we have quoted from the real teaching of Jesus, they who do understand, accept and live up to them, find the Stone.

Vale.

TWENTY-SECOND COMMUNICATION

Monday, June 30, 1947 9:00 P.M.

Ave Frater et Sorores.

(H.: "I am sorry that we kept you waiting but we had much to do today.")

Well we know that, and had you asked us earlier, we should have been willing to postpone this sitting until tomorrow before the arrival of your guests. But we shall not this evening keep you long, for all of you need rest.

(H.: "Yes, for this will be our last communication for a long time.")

That is not true Soror, This may be our last communication by this means, because the polarity of forces is on the outer to be broken for the time of your journey, but we shall still be in touch with you, and all three of you with one another, for truly there is no separateness.

(A.: "Nice to know that our friends are going to be in touch with me while you are away.")

You are all having your personal difficulties, but remember that we are fully aware of them, more fully perhaps than you yourselves, for as we told you, the pattern of your thoughts and feelings is recorded moment by moment, and because you have invited our cooperation with you, we know what is going on. Each of you has honestly tried to establish the central harmony that is so necessary. Yet each of you labored with his or her own personality and shortcomings, what pleases us are that all of you are truly devoted, and trying to overcome your prejudices and bias. It would be gross flattery to say you have any of you conspicuously succeeded, but we do give you good marks, not only for trying, but for real accomplishment, even though much remains for each of you to do. Much depends on how you utilize mentally the opportunity afforded by your changed outward conditions. If you use this opportunity aright, you will find yourselves drawn closer when you are together again, than

198

you are now; this is from our point of view most desirable, for we repeat what we have said before, that you have a considerable service to render, for which your respective talents and training fit you.

This very house can be a strong dynamo if you make it so. We put into your minds the name, and you know enough of the Tree of Life to see how truly sacred a name that is. Can you bring it into actual manifestation? Not unless you all surrender wholly to the Son in Tiphareth, and to His messenger, who is really Himself in action, namely the Holy Guardian Angel.

("In other words our own Higher Self?")

No Soror, not one's own, THE Higher Self.

(H.: "I meant to imply that.")

Yet we correct your words because they are a matrix, and the use of terms as exact as possible is always desirable. Soror A. has one phase of the illusion of separateness to overcome, and that is closely related to this house. Soror H. has another, quite different in form, but also tied into this house, and Frater P, though his problem is like neither of the other two, must face his adversary boldly if this house to which we opened your way—for guided to it you were, and by us—is to be the physical center for the higher magic that we intend it to be.

The central doctrine of the Ageless Wisdom is the oneness of all, and the corollary of this is that never is there any real conflict of true interests. Yet none of you has reached the point where you would gladly see done whatever might need to be done should the specific activity come into conflict with your ingrained prejudices, or with those opinions, which, because they are yours, you believe to be true. It is so easy to accept what we think we *see* as an axiom. But the greater number of axioms, so called, turn out on closer examination to be no more than assumptions, and almost always what is assumed to be true, is what one prefers to hope is true. All men have this to deal with. You no more than most, but you must deal with your own forms of assumption and

199

prejudice as rigorously, nay, more so, than you would deal with the fallacies of another's reasoning.

As we speak you raise walls of defense in your minds. What can we say further, until you do all three walk contrary to the world? Little that we might tell you will be useful, so this is our final counsel: read and study what you have received so far. If you really put it to the test of practice we shall instruct you further.

Until then our blessing goes with you, but we shall wait your action before communicating further.

Sub Umbra Alarum Tuarum. IHVH Vale Frater et Sorores.

TWENTY-THIRD COMMUNICATION

Monday, December 29, 1947 8:15 P.M.

Ave Frater et Sorores.

The time of germination has passed. Now shall you see more definite evidence of growth. Not yet do flower and fruit appear, but at least you are all aware that the seeds which were planted earlier this year have been striking their roots deep in your hearts, and are now showing plain signs of their gradual, but healthy, development. As we go on, we shall continue with text and comment, and with suggestions for practical application. This should assure you all that we have noted your endeavors to make the adjustments necessary for the satisfactory prosecution of the work ahead. Had you not done so, there would be nothing for us to communicate now. By this we do not, of course, mean that all the adjustments are completed, but we have watched and we know you all have tried.

One thing should be given particular attention, and this is the apportionment of both time and activities, so that both may be, as it were, budgeted, and so that you will not get the feeling of pressure. You have until the work expands considerably, as it will during the coming year, just three heads and six hands, and you have to establish reasonable regularity in the matter of meals and work and, what is just as important, relaxation. Don't be too hard and fast, but consider well what are the things of first importance? Make your plans accordingly. We lay down no rules—it is enough to indicate the need.

"Their course is like the lightning-flash," saith the Sepher Yetzirah, for theirs is not a going forth in time as man reckoneth time, neither is it a movement in space as man measureth space. In it end and beginning are one, and the place thereof is That-which-is-not. The mind of Adam falleth from the center which is Eden into the semblance of the circumference wherein he laboreth with pain. But this exile is not forever, neither shall

201

the gate be guarded forever with the two-edged flaming sword. For the sword is also the lightning-flash, and what is hidden is the return of that outgoing power to the source whence it proceedeth. Therefore is it also written that the living creatures ran and returned.

Now these creatures are the elemental powers, and these are the powers of the four letters of Tetragrammaton. They are the Holy Living Creatures seen by the prophet Ezekiel, and that which cometh into form by their appearance is the Glory of God which is the true substance of all things and also the Holy Influence which descendeth through the paths of the Tree, and ascendeth again to be swallowed up in the abyss of radiant darkness for which AIN is the first veil.

Thirty-two are the paths and 32 is the number of KBVD, the Glory. Thus the paths and the Glory are in truth one. Paths of Chokmah are they called, and from this you may know them to be paths of life, for verily, Chokmah is none other than Kachmah, and Kachmah is the one and only power of life. For the letters of Chokmah are Cheth, Kaph, Mem, Heh, and with these same letters is Kachmah written, Kaph, Cheth, Mem, Heh, so that the two words are veils for a single number, threescore ten and three (73), and behold, this is the number also of Gimel: Gimel, Mem, Lamed, and from Gimel proceedeth Guph, the body of Adam.

Remember now that the Glory is the Kabode-El, for God is One and alone and there is nothing else, as saith Isaiah. AL is 31, and KBVD is 32, so that KBVD-AL is 63. Here you may by searching find much treasure. First, 63 is nine times seven. Among the Sephiroth, this is the multiplication of Victory by the power of the Foundation. Among the letters it is the multiplication of Zain by the power of Teth.

Nor are these in any measure different, for what is the Victory if it be not that of the Sword of Understanding, and What is the Foundation, if it be not a power of the Royal Serpent? So far the text. At first it may seem recondite indeed, but it is really simple; read it before we explain. This , you see, really a continuation of the earlier sections of the same text. For the long dissertation on Guph and Gimel is but extended here. Written for Qabalists familiar with Gematria, it assumes that familiarity but may need some further explanation. It is, of course, just another reiteration of the constantly recurring theme, of the essential unity of being.

Chokmah and Kachmah being numerically one, that **is,** 73, and this being also the number of the name of the letter Gimel, GML, what lies behind this part of the text is the Qabalistic doctrine that Chokmah is the source of Chaiah, the life-force, and since GML as 73 is identical with ChKMH and KChMH⁻, Gimel is also the seat of Chaiah. Thus the fact that Gimel is the first letter of the word Guph signifies that the body of man proceeds from, or has its root in, Chokmah, which is also the Sphere of Masloth, the highways of the stars.

Now the stars are physical condensations of the Glory of God, or the radiance known to us as electricity, magnetism and gravitation. These three are names for one power, and the words Kachmah and Mezla are other names for the same power. Man's body is as truly a condensation on the physical plane of this power as is the physical body of a sun. Indeed, even the chemical elements in man's body, where they take on form as bones and the blood and tissues, are the very same elements that take form as flaming gases in the body of the sun. This is not philosophy, but science.

Whether as a human body, or as a solar form, however, the physical substance is only the outer vesture of the Divine Glory, which runs forth from AIN and flows back to AIN, and through AIN, into the unfathomable abyss of the radiant darkness. The real purport of the teaching is that even man's physical body is of one substance with the Divine Glory, not separate or separable from that Glory.

Here, indeed, will you find a rich treasure, and the text points straight at it. We shall not now give you more than this one hint. As students familiar with our Rota, note well the words of the text concerning 63 as the multiplication of Zain by Teth. Do not forget that the path of Zain links Binah to Tiphareth, and that ZIN is 67, as is BINH. Right disposition is rooted in Understanding, and this is the sharp sword of discrimination, for there is no love without understanding, and love must be discriminating, in the good and constructive sense of this word. But note that Zain as 7 must be multiplied by Teth as 9 to make the 63 of KBVD-AL, and though Teth is the serpent-power, the Rota pictures that power as a red lion, tamed by a woman who represents the feminine aspect of Chesed. Every Sephirah, you remember, is both male and female. Female, as receiving the descending influence. Male, as projecting it to whatever paths are below, and this feminine Chesed is pictured as being like the Empress. For the taming of the lion and the serpent, these two being really identical, is woman's work, even as it is written in the writings of the Sons of Hermes. If you have ears to hear, this shall be for you a practical revelation of the Great Arcanum.

Vale Frater et Sorores.

TWENTY-FOURTH COMMUNICATION

Thursday, January 1, 1948 8:05 P.M.

Ave Frater et Sorores.

The new year dawns full of promise for a better day; for though the outer portents may seem dark, never has there been a time when this was not the same. The outer is always forbidding in appearance, thus you may read of the outer darkness in the Bible and this is truly a state in which there is weeping and wailing and gnashing of teeth, for it is astate of the human mind when this sees only the outward appearances. Those who truly know, are serenely unafraid because they perceive the inner glory.

Man's memory is short, and thus all times are troublous and fear-provoking to the superficial. You have smiled at the story of Webster and the man who was so perturbed by the behavior of the younger generation, so is it always.

One of the reasons the way opened for you to come here by sea, was that you might see at first hand the sad plight of the unillumined. Their hearts quake within them, and they must continually seek distraction because they are so afraid. Look not, then, on their outer behavior, but let your eyes rest with compassion on their troubled souls. It is to minister to such as these that you are called. Out of the treasure of your better understanding must you do all you can to relieve their inner poverty. Blind they are and dumb, halt and lame, and it is to these that they must minister whose only profession, as the Fama says, is to heal the sick, and that gratis.

Yet he who would heal must himself have spiritual health, and this you have access to in unstinted measure. Life upon life have you worked and studied, failing and succeeding both. Now must you give, without any thought of return, and without any concern for your own welfare or progress. For deep within you, at your best, you have full assurance that no matter how much you give, you will but be making room for more, and you have made sufficient progress already to be certain that you shall surely reach the goal.

(A. asks, "I wonder if that part about the sea trip and study refers to P.F.C. alone or to us all?" H. said she thought it referred to P. only.)

No. To all three of you, for though but two of you were bodily on the ship, you three are so closely joined that the essential experience of any one of you is shared by all; and it is to this triple unity that our words are addressed, as it takes all three of you even to make these records, and will take your coordinated efforts to make the practical application too.

This is new year's day in a deeper sense than you may yet realize, for a time rapidly draws neigh which more than three centuries ago we spoke of in the Fama—the time when our trumpet should resound with full voice and when the teachings should be without the veils of enigmatic expression forced upon us then. The old world is a thing of the past, the new is already here even though many do not realize this. The new world is not to come, it has arrived.

This you must say over and over again, for when men know this, they will cease their futile endeavors to restore what is gone forever. Reconstitution, not restoration, is the watchword now, and this means an ever-increasing exercise of vision, as the Rota makes evident in the Key of the Emperor. This leads to another section of the text, as follows:

It is written that creation took place with the letter Heh (understand "takes" where you read "took," for there is no time but an eternal present, for the One). Now Heh is the letter of vision, and it is spelled by its own self-duplication, that is, HH. Of these the first is the sign of the waters of Binah, and the second is the sign of the earth of Malkuth. Each is by number the half of the paternal Yod, for Heh is 5 and Yod is 10, thus may second, those from Tiphareth to Malkuth.

The whole Tree is thus expressed by the name of this one letter. The first

Heh is insight, the second is the same vision, turned outward into the field of manifestation. Tiphareth beginneth the manifestation of the second Heh, and remember here that these are the two Hehs in Tetragrammaton. The whole Tree is the Vision of the Eternal.

Now give heed, for here is a mystery. As the Tree endeth with the Heh of earth and Malkuth, so doth the word Guph written in plenitude bring before you this same Heh, for see, it is GML, VV, PH, so that the fullness even of Guph, the body, is in the letter of vision made complete. Gimel is 73, the number of Chokmah VV is 12, the number of the Zodiac of which Chokmah is the Sphere. PH is 85, a fivefold 17, and inasmuch as 17 is TVB, that is, goodness itself, a fivefold 17 is the sign of the multiplication of goodness by the vision of the Constituting Intelligence which is H, or 5.

Now addition of these three bringeth forth the number 170, and behold, this is TVB multiplied by ten that is, by Yod, or by HH. This, thy body, 0 child of earth and sky, is truly the heavenly vision of the goodness of the Eternal. This, thy body is the palace of the King. This, thy body is the whole world of God and man. This, thy body is the seamless robe of Adonai for the Lord and His Temple are one. So far the text.

Compare it with earlier sections about GVP. Here is, first of all, the utter repudiation of exoteric misunderstanding of the flesh. It is good, not evil. It is the Temple of the Eternal, and the text says: "The Temple and Adonai are One," as indeed they are by numeration, since ADNI and HIKL are both 65.

Now the body is Tav also, or the point at the lower end of the 32nd path, as you may see on the Tree, since it is only by a convention that the Sephiroth, which are really points, are represented as circles. Thus the bottom point is not only the lowermost end of path 32, but like-wise the completion of paths 29 and 31. 29 is the path of the Corporeal Intelligence, 31 is the path of fire and of Ruach Elohim. Tav is the path of Saturn and of Earth. Could anything be plainer? This is the embodiment or integration of the fire of spirit through the finitizing power of Saturn. Moreover, it is written of the letter Tav that it is "the Temple of Holiness in the midst." Of everybody whether mineral, vegetable, animal or human may this be said. It is a center or focus for all the powers of Heaven and Earth. In the smallest sub-microscopic body is Adonai enthroned and dwelling as a living presence. How, then, 'shall we find words to express the holiness of every single body and of all its functions and powers? There are no words, but the vision you may have even now, in some measure. Few have it alas, but all may, and all will. To each it comes in due season, but the time no man knows before it arrives.

All this points to something most practical. They who catch even a glimpse of this truth will see with new eyes and speak with new tongues. More than this, will act after a wholly different manner. A hint of this is to be found in the emphasis given by the text to the letter Heh. Vision determines action. We must see before we can do, and nowhere is this truer than in the work of the Magic of Light. Their vision is all-important for magic is at bottom the same as meditation. No magical rite is effective unless it be the formal expression of the operator's vision. The purpose of all ceremonial is to establish an unbroken flow of knowledge.

Now, knowledge must not be confused with information. The Hebrew word for it is DoTh, Da'ath. By attributions to these three letters, understand the work of Da'ath to be the work of Venus (D), Mars and Saturn (O), and Saturn (Th). Remember that planets are interior stars and alchemical metals, and, as our Soror A. noticed, though conjoined with Saturn in Capricorn, is also the exalted or sublimated Mars.

Now, Capricorn is the sign associated with the birth of the Redeemer, and in the Rota is the Devil, which is really a symbol for the First Matter. Hence when we read that in Da'ath the secret places shall be filled, we must be obtuse indeed if we suppose this knowledge to be anything to be learned from written or spoken words.

Mars is action, and Saturn is concretion. Specific actions are here indicated, and if you will ask for further light from within, you may discover, perhaps to your surprise, why Capricorn is related to the 26th path of Renewing Intelligence. Be on guard here. Do not look for symbolic meanings. Look for specific forms of action, and while you do so, remember that the text is concerned with Guph.

You are all too tired to receive more without the expenditure on our part of more energy than is warranted. Remember, we have physical bodies also, and the forces which make these communications possible affect the cells of our bodies as well as those of yours.

Vale, Sub Umbra Alarum Tuarum, IHVH.

TWENTY-FIFTH COMMUNICATION

Monday, January 5, 1948 8:00 P.M.

Ave Frater et Sorores.

There is a situation developing in the Chapter which will need all your ingenuity to manage. No doubt you will hear something about it at the next mid-month meeting. Be alert and firm. We never interfere as you know, but when necessary we do give some advance indications of what may be expected. You lit a slow match at the last meeting, and it will bring an explosion before long. If you are careful, the results will be all to the good. Verb. Sap. It was put into your mind to say, and for a very good reason.

(Long wait here.)

Both atmospheric and astrological conditions are unfavorable tonight. We suggest that you defer this until the next regular time. We have endeavored to protect you from the epidemic of influenza, but you are all more depleted than you realize, even though you feel exceptionally well this evening. Not depleted physically, but of some of your psychic force, which has been drained unawares to you by the situation we have just mentioned, and tonight we find it difficult to get even this much through. Better get plenty of sleep the next few nights. Then you will be able to meet things as they develop. Next time we shall resume text and comment. No good reason for such extra exertion on your part and ours as would be required to overcome the quite unusual interference we have indicated.

Vale.

TWENTY-SIXTH COMMUNICATION

Thursday, January 8, 1948 8:05 P.M.

Ave Frater et Sorores.

Let us continue with the text:

In Malkuth is the power of our Lord and King ADNI MLK. Yet is Malkuth also KLH (Kallah) the Bride, and MLKH (Malkah) the Queen. So the Guph which is the embodied Kingdom is the King himself, also the Queen who is his Bride. Now the number of ADNI MLK is 155, and to this number correspondeth also DVDNAMN, the faithful friend, for our Lord King is verily that friend. But here you must understand a mystery, for the Kingdom, King, Substance, that is Guph, Queen and Bride are all but ONE, and the ONE is ALL, for is not KLH to be read as HKL (Hakal) the ALL?

Yet more, Malkah is written with the letters of HMLK, the King, and the King is Tiphareth, yet is Tiphareth ThPARTh or 1081, and the seed of this is 10 which is both Malkuth and Yod. Extended downward, Tiphareth is completed in Malkuth, even as Tiphareth itself is the King or Royal Son, one with his Father, and that Father is AB in Chokmah which also is the body of Yod.

Again, MLKH (Malkah) is 95 and this is the number of the name of the letter Peh spelt in plenitude PH-HH, so that in the first of these four letters you may see the mouth of the Eternal, and in the other three His three-fold vision of past and present and of time to come, for are they not three Hehs? Yet see further. Their whole addition is 15, and this is IH, Jah, the Holy name of Chokmah and HVD (Hod), the Splendor of the Presence. Thus is Malkah truly as a Queen, also the Queen's daughter all glorious within.

Now she holdeth the mystery of union, and thus is she known to the Sons of the Doctrine as ABNGDLH the "Great Stone," that is by interpretation the perfect union in Chesed or Gedulah of the Father AB with the Son BN.

211

What it says plainly is that Malkuth is the synthesis of all the Sephiroth, and that Guph must be understood not only as the human body, but also as the substance from which all bodies are formed. Furthermore this substance is One, though it is given a masculine Divine name ADNI MLK, and two feminine titles, Kallah and Malkah.

One of the most important points in this section is the Gematria of PH-HH. What the text does not say, though well known to Qabalists, is that P. is the letter of Mars. So that PH, HH must express a total Martian activity. Indeed all four letters of this full spelling of Peh are related to Mars. To what is said about ADNI MLK, we may add that its number among the founders of our Order had special alchemical significance, because in their Latin Gematria it was the number of LIBERTAS EVANGELII, the Liberty of the Gospels, a motto mentioned in the Fama, and also the number of ARCANUM ARCANORUM, the Secret of Secrets.

Now the burden of the Gospels is the mystery of the Kingdom. Parable after parable relates to it. Yet without the key, which is that the Kingdom is Malkuth, the secret of the Gospels remains hidden. The Kingdom is here, though it is truly the Kingdom of the Skies, and its secret has to do with embodiment, that is to say, with right knowledge of what bodies are, and what they are for even so our Brother Thomas Vaughn chose for the title of one of his alchemical writings, the Latin words AULA LUCIS, the Temple of Light, because their Latin gematria is 89, the number of GVP, Guph, and this is also the number of ANIMA MUNDI, the Soul of the World, in the same Latin gematria, in which, as you just noticed, Mundi is equivalent by number to KLH (Kallah).

The Secret of Secrets is not anywhere openly stated. If ever you discover it, you will know why. It is not, however, ineffable. It could perfectly well be put into very simple words, and those who do share this knowledge, discuss it openly enough among themselves. It is only from the profane that it is withheld, since no writing is absolutely safe from falling into profane hands, no Son of the Doctrine will write it, and since none but Sons (and Daughters, may we add, for fear of arousing

Soror A.'s feminism!) of the Doctrine ever know it, it will always be safe. The text in some ways is extraordinarily open. We recommend to you most careful consideration of its purport.

Vale, Frater et Sorores.

TWENTY-SEVENTH COMMUNICATION

Thursday, January 15, 1948 8:15 P.M.

Ave Frater et Sorores.

We did not come last Monday because you were all more depleted than you realized. Another time you must not wait so long if you do not establish contact within 10 minutes it will be wiser not to continue the sitting. You will remember that there was some movement of the planchette that we had nothing to do with. But fortunately your depleted forces were not strong enough to be seized by the other side, those who are always ready to interfere if they can.

You have done well to seek out Dr. Stark. He belongs with us, although he is not yet fully aware of the relationship, nor has he yet identified the sources of his strong urge toward the practice of healing. Nevertheless long ago he was among those whose only profession was to heal, and that gratis. And if he could, he would be glad to spend his days in the practice of healing without any thought of monetary compensation. His intuition runs far ahead of his intellectual grasp, good as that **is,** and you will all profit thereby. Remember how you found him, and you cannot miss seeing that we had something to do with it all.

We shall now give you part of the text. It is not immediately connected to what you have been given, and in fact you will have to do considerable rearrangement, and have further communications, before a truly consecutive rendering will be effected. In some measure we have been selecting such selections as bore upon your personal problems of adjustment to the main issue. That issue is of course, to make this place to which we brought you the fully adequate center which we intend with your cooperation to make it.

(H.: "We certainly are trying our best to cooperate.")

You have indeed been doing just that, and the good results are even more evident to us than to you. The section of the text with which we begin has to do with the astral plane. You are about to hear the views which another has gathered about this, note that verb gathered, and we suggest that you make careful comparison with what you hear, and what we transmit.

(H.: "Does he mean your inner hearing, Paul?")

No. M.P.H. [This may be a comment by P.F.C. referring to Manley P. Hall. It is unclear who actually is speaking.]

Throughout eternity, with no cessation doth the utterance of the Ruach Elohim the might of El Shaddai the source of Life; and the Living Soul Nephesh is the vehicle of that utterance. Even so may you see it in the letters of Nephesh, for the first relateth to Perpetuity, and the second to Utterance, while the third standeth in the alphabet for Ruach Elohim the Fiery Breath of the Eternal Spirit of Life. To this the name Shaddai El Chai refereth; for the Nephesh, or the Vital Soul is that same Almighty Ever living One, which centereth Itself in all animate forms, and findeth its highest expression in the life of man. Through countless generations that Life perpetuateth Its utterance by means of successive generations of human bodies. It is on this account that the Wise aver that in Yesod is the field of renewal through procreation. Now AL ShDI, or more fully, ShDI Al ChI, is truly the Lord of the Universe, and Holy is His Name, Blessed be He.

Never have the Sons of the Wise forgotten this, nor have they ever blasphemed the source of Life. Yet have they known full well that not by generation only is the command "be fruitful and multiply" to be fulfilled. There is a fruitfulness beyond that of the flesh, and a multiplication of the power of life beyond the bringing forth of sons and daughters of the flesh. Thus in the word Yesod, may you read Yod, Sod—or Sod, Yod—the secret of Yod. Now what is Yod? As a letter it betokeneth Creative Power, for it is the Hand. But the wise know it also as the channel for the transmission of Life, and Life is Chaiah, is the number 207, and this is 9 times 23. Now 23 is the number of ChIH, Chaiah and 9 is the Yesod; furthermore Chaiah is in Chokmah and is thus to be understood as the power of AB the Father. Thus may you know that Life and Light are of power AB the Father. Thus may you know that Life and Light are one;

215

Light is always pure and always holy, and that the extension of Light is its multiplication through forms. But forms are manifest in varying degrees, and when it is thine office to bring forth subtle forms, thou failest if thou miss thine opportunity through the false belief that in the bringing forth of forms less subtle there is any essential failure. Failure is the missing of one's highest possibility.

But what may be failure for thee, may well be supreme attainment for thy Brother. For wherever Life is multiplied the giver of increase is Shaddai El Chai, and nothing that He effecteth hath in it any loss or evil. Evil are man's judgments, but Life Itself remaineth forever good.

Now the name ShDI EL ChI beginneth with the number 314, then followeth 31, and ChI is 18. This bringeth the whole to 363, and see, this is 11 times itself and multiplied again by 3. Now 11 is AVD (0d) and 3 is G. AVD is the magic power and G is the beginning of Guph the body. A is the Breath, V is the Link, D is the Door of Life and is Nogah also, which giveth the Victory. In G or 3 is Recollection and Union, and for the wise the letters of AVD speak with a loud tongue. In Yesod is all this centered, and they who know the secret of Yod, become the extenders of the paternal Life and Light. Thus is Yesod called the Sphere of the Moon, and that sate Moon pertaineth also to Gimel, the letter of Union. Blessed are they who hear and understand, and understanding, live as they know.

So far the Text. Read and rest.

Note well the warning implied. There are many who seek to be spiritual at the expense of the body. They repudiate all that pertains to Yesod because they misunderstand its real significance. You may have wondered what this section of the Text has to do with the Astral plane, for there is a spate of words both printed and uttered concerning the astral, mostly based on complete misapprehension. Yet the Text points straight to the one thing, and that is, that the mystery of the 9th Sephirah is a secret of Yod. For competent Qabalists this will be sufficient, and the Text says quite enough to establish certainty, for it points out that Yod is the letter A of AB, and dilates upon Chaiah, so that one must be a tyro indeed who does not see that the secret has to do with the radiance of the stars, that is with Light, which is one with Life.

216

Now to read what purport to be inspired doctrines about the Astral plane, is often to be misled into the error that there is something rather low, not to say debased, about it; yet astral means starry, and Qabalists insist that the intelligence assigned to Yesod is TAHOOR, which means pure. The Text hints also that man, of all living creatures, enjoys a special privilege, that of multiplying the astral radiance by tokens a basic error that is enough to thwart any effort at direction of the astral power to finer and that is enough to thwart any effort at direction of the astral power to finer and higher uses. This is an error of which true Qabalists have never been guilty. They have never condemned the normal functions of life, nor have they ever considered them to be essentially unclean. What they, and their oriental Brothers, have taught and practiced, is sublimation-not repudiation. So as you think and meditate on the Text, let your point of departure be this: the astral is not evil, nor is it to be feared. It is the plane which is actually the basis of our physical existence, and that basis is Light and Life. Take this for your clue and you will never be confused by any pseudo occult parading of dread terrors of the astral. You might as well be scared of your own breathing!

Vale.

Monday, January 19, 1948

Ave Frater et Sorores.

You have just read what we told you concerning Dr. Stark. Yet what we said does not give unqualified approbation of all his ideas or methods. He will be able to help all three of you as you know he has helped Soror A. But this is like all else in which we have assisted you. Never have we taken away your own powers of choice and discrimination. Never have we issued a command, for they who issue commands and orders do not work as do we, whatever claims may be made by or for them. You still have to act as if you had minds to make up, however much you may be disposed sometimes to question whether or not there be much of anything to make up! Thus you must decide this matter in the light of what knowledge you have. This much we may remind you of. Some very wise and very competent men have entertained some very foolish notions. You need only read the Zohar to see this. But you do not go to the Zohar for Rabbinical nonsense, you go to it for the wisdom which has stood the test of ages. Verb. Sap. You know enough not to swallow a book whole; does not the same principle apply to a man and his ideas? Now for the Text:

Consider this: Through the Sphere of Saturn the Holy Mezlah descendeth into the World of Formation, entering the field of Microprosopus from AIMA, who is the Throne of Life, and the Gate through which the Power of the Supernal Triad rushes downward into the six that constitute BN the Son. Yet from BN to Kallah the channel of descent is also the letter of Saturn, and this letter standeth in the Holy Temple in the midst. Now Saturn is Sheen, Beth, Tav, Aleph, Yod – Shabbathai.

(Here there was interference and a lot of misinformation and abuse, so we stopped, P. and A. being badly affected by the attack of the B.B.'s.)

218

TWENTY-NINTH COMMUNICATION

Monday, January 26, 1948 8:10 P.M.

Ave Frater et Sorores.

Go back to the communication which was so rudely interrupted, and read the first part of the Text down to the end of the spelling of Shabbathai. From this point on ignore the rest.

The Text continues: Now Shabbathai is rest, and there is a great mystery in rest. Think ye that the Eternal was tired of His work, so that He must cease it in order to regain His power? Not so. What can exhaust the endless? Thus it is written that our Brother who came into perfect union with AB, said the Sabbath was made for man—not man for the Sabbath. Man needs rest in order to restore his powers. But not so the Eternal. The completion of creation is itself the Sabbath, for when the Kabode Ale finds full manifestation in the world of things and creatures, the new manifested forms themselves reveal, and at the same time conceal, the presence and power of the Eternal. Thus is the rest of the true Sabbath none other than the outer seeming of the ceaseless flow of the Holy Influence. Consider the letters of Shabbathai. The first is the Holy letter Sheen, sign of the consuming fire of the Ruach Elohim. The second is Beth, sign of the dwelling place of the Eternal in the Eternal Beginning. For doth not creation begin anew with every moment of man's time? Is not the womb of AIMA ever virgin? Then cometh the third letter, which is the sacred sign of union and completion; yet, that none may think of completion as being an end, this Tav is followed by the Aleph which is the sign of Spirit before all beginnings and after all completions, and then the word is finished with the sacred seed of all letters, which beginneth the Holy Name, and is the special sign for Chokmah.

Thus to know God must man be still, yet is the stillness but the veil for the abiding Presence of the Living God. Now see: The number of Shabbathai is 713, and this is the Holy name AL multiplied by ChIH, Chaiah, which is the

219

Life-force of all beings welling out from God Himself, for in Chokmah is Chaiah centered, and this same Chaiah is the power of AB the Father. Its number being 23 when AL, which is 31, is multiplied by it, a product thereof is ShBThAI, or rest.

Now AL is the special name of Chesed, and Shabbathai is thus made known as being the full manifestation of God's loving-kindness through the working of His living wisdom. Thus it is not AL that is the agency of this, but ChIH; not 23 multiplied by 31, but 31 multiplied by 23. Come closer to the heart of this mystery. The name AL means in the Holy Tongue "nothing," for truly is God nothing known to human sense, nothing to be encompassed by man's thought. No thing is that Living Spirit. Thus the same letters A and L reversed are the usual sign for nothing and for not. This nothing is all. It is the darkness of AIN, but see this: AIN is 61, or AL increased by 30, and the time shall come when human speech shall show this forth.

So far the text.

Remember that this is an excerpt from an ancient text, written long, long before The Book of Tokens, by a sage having no knowledge of English, or even of a tongue Nana Then was in process of development into what you know as English, and you will see that he had some title to be called a prophet, for that strange last comment on AIN and its numeral value says in so many words that, in what was time to come for the writer, men would express the idea which in Hebrew is written KL, by adding another L to the Holy name AL, so that a-1-1, your English word, does exactly fulfill this. ALL in English stands exactly for what Qabalists mean by AIN, and if the Hebrew values of the English letters be used here, it produces 61. KL is the ordinary Hebrew term for eh (?] "ALL" intended to point the minds of the wise to the number 50, which is that of the letter Nun, and the number also of the Gates of Binah. Moreover the letter Nun as 50, is 11 less than AIN, and in AIN you may see that same 11 expressed by A and I, and these are the very letters in the same order that complete Shabbathai. See also that the name of the letter Nun being 106 (NVN) uses the digits of 61 in combination with the numeral sign for

220

AIN and LA; that is, 106 read from units to hundreds shows first the 6 and then zero, and then 1, so that the digits expressing concrete numbers are 6 and 1.

Going back to the Text, consider what it says about rest. In more than one instance the Qabalists had anticipated your modern scientists. Here is another example. What is any physical object, a stone for instance? It appears to be at rest; its main characteristic is what our Oriental Brethren call "Tamas," that is, inertia. Thus the completion of any cycle of creative activity brings forth something concrete, and what is manifested by things in general is this same quality of inertia, that is of apparent inactivity or rest. It is this that is the mystery of Shabbathai, this appearance of absolute quiescence, this semblance of darkness, to which indeed the color of Binah as well as of Saturn in Heraldry refer—the color black.

What the Text means in its quaint mode of expression, is that the rest is not cessation, but the complete expression of Chesed through the operation of the Divine Life Force Chaiah. That is the essence of all the numeral references.

Now this may interest you: In Greek the words "the power" are expressed by a definite article ETA, followed by the noun from which your English word dynamite was coined. That is in Greek Delta, Upsilon, Nu, Alpha, Mu, Iota, Sigma, and the number of this, including the definite article eta, which by the way, is pronounced heh, is 713. The power is the inertia, the darkness is that which comes into manifestation as Light. They whose light is darkness, of whom Jesus spoke, are they who confuse the manifested Light with its hidden Source. There is another word, this time Hebrew, which also adds to 713, and in the next portion of the Text it is carefully analyzed. But you had better ponder it first as a preparation for understanding the rather technical words of our Qabalists. The word is ThShVBH, which means many things in Hebrew. Consult the lexicon, but try to keep from forming any premature conclusions. This is enough tonight. You are not fully recovered from the severe attack to which you exposed yourselves by ignoring our warning.

Sub Umbra Alarum Tuarum, IHVH, Frater et Sorores.

Thursday, January 29, 1948 8:00 P.M.

Ave Frater et Sorores.

We continue with the Text: Now in Aima is the sphere of Shabbathai, and to Binah also pertaineth ThShVBH (Teshubah), the power of Shabbathai expressed in the return of seasons, and in the conversion of the Ruach in Adam. To Malkuth also is Teshubah assigned, for the Kingdom partaketh of the quality of Shabbathai which completeth manifestation by rest. See that Binah is the sphere of Shabbathai; that Malkuth is completed by the letter Tav, to which Shabbathai also pertaineth; and that Malkuth herself dependeth from the Tree from the Path of Tav. Thus it is written that Tav is the Temple of the Holiness in the Midst, and is not that Midst a central point of perfect rest? Moreover it is by return that repentance is effected, and when that return is completed there is rest also. The mind of the sinner that repenteth findeth rest from strife, and where is this to be found save in the Palace in the Midst.

Rest being one with the perfect work of creation, know that all unrest is but incompletion, and truly it is by the way of return that completion cometh to the Sons of Adam, so that they become the Sons of the Elohim; and behold, these be the BNI HALHIM, Beni Ha Elohim, and if thou readest their name with the full value of the letter Mem, it is 713. These are they who have followed a path of return back to their Father's Palace in the Midst. Never have they been other than the Sons of God, but in the whirling forth is this forgotten, to be brought once more into mind when the work of the Chariot is consummated.

Thus far the Text.

By the time the Qabalah began to excite universal interest throughout Europe, and thus made possible our veiled announcement of the fact of our ancient Brotherhood, the word Tshubah had been rendered in Latin as conversio, yet this meant one thing for theologians and quite another for the wise. Certainly it is not to be confused with revival explosions of emotion. True conversion is identical with transmutation, and indeed retains even in English usage some vestiges of alchemical meaning. The transmutation that is the main preoccupation of the alchemists is a radical interior change in the alchemist himself. Note well that the material worked upon in this is often called the "radical moisture."

Consider well the emphasis throughout the Text on Saturn and on rest. On rest in particular, as the result of completion, which takes the operator into the palace of the King. Thus the title of one of the great alchemical writings is "The Open Entrance to the Closed Palace of the King." The Palace is in the Midst, and one of its aspects on the Tree is Binah, while another is Malkuth, and to both of these Teshubah refers. Do you begin to see? Here is a plain statement, though very condensed, and perhaps even cryptic to minds unused to Qabalistic turns of phrase and thought.

Yet really it is perfectly open, and what makes it so is the reference to the Beni Ha Elohim. This points the inquiring mind straight to the heart of the mystery, for the Sons of the elohim are an order of Angels which is specially attributed to Hod, and so to the grade of Practicus. This is the work of the Chariot, and to transmute the very substance of Fallen Adam back into its original splendor as the Chariot of the Most High. The transmutation begins with Saturn, though it is a work of the Sun and the Moon, and the radical moisture is the water of the sea of Binah. One of the Rosicrucian texts speaks of the mingling of the dew of Heaven with the oiliness of the earth, and this means the same as what our Eastern Brethren speak of when they say that the Sun and Moon must be conjoined in making the nectar.

They who have completed the work become Sons, yes, Daughters of the Elohim. Then truly are they as the angels in Heaven, and concerning this, has not Jesus spoken explicitly, although few outside our Order understand the meaning of what He said. Our whole magical practice has no other object than to transmute the mortal fallen Adam, the base metal, into the Splendorous Son of the Elohim. Note that since this work has to do with the grade of Practicus referred to the Sphere of Mercury, it is a work directed by the mind, although the powers involved are those called in alchemical symbolic language Sun and Moon. Understand Tiphareth and Yesod in this.

You will perhaps get something to help clarify this, if you look up the words of Jesus concerning the Angels, and then see what Genesis has to say about the Sons of God. Do this now.

(Mark 12:25 & Gen. 6)
This refers to the descent of Tiphareth into Malkuth through Yesod, and there is a concealed reference in the same chapter where it says "the days of Adam shall be as 120 years." This refers to the Path of Samekh, for the name of the letter Samekh is 120. The word translated "wives" is NShIM, and if you add the values of this they total 400, a reference to the path of Tav about which this whole section of the text revolves. Whether or not to explain this further, we are not at this moment certain; perhaps it better be deferred until we communicate with you again. In the meantime meditate on what we have said thus far.

All three of you are tired, more than you realize perhaps. We suggest that you relax a while and then go early to bed.

Vale, Frater et Sorores.

Monday, February 2, 1948 8:05 P.M.

We sat for ten minutes, but received no communication, so stopped.

THIRTY-FIRST COMMUNICATION

Thursday, February 5, 1948 8:00 P.M.

Ave Frater et Sorores.

Place as well as rhythm does make a difference in the ease with which we get through to you. Basically the conditions are the same as for communications with discarnates. The more familiar and usual the surroundings, the better you can induce receptivity. The more too, you can let yourselves approach the state of mind which manifests just before you fall asleep, the easier it is for us. Intense intellectual activity is often an interference.

(H.: "Can you tell us what was the particular cause Monday evening that you could not get through?")

Principally that, but a contributing factor was Frater P.'s emotional state, which like many of the same sort that distress him, and puzzle you, is the direct consequence of the very thing which makes him so useful to us. He hates the very idea, but he is nevertheless a very psychic person, and makes links with others, who for any reason attract his interest. In this particular instance he had become aware of the forthcoming ordeal that you 3 had to suffer and endure last night. He is perhaps a little drastic in his personal judgment, but if you will procure and read the pamphlet on St. Germaine, and compare it with what you know of me, you won't have much difficulty in understanding that none of us are exactly enthusiastic

226

about the life, ways, and work of ___. We use him sometimes, but he is after all pretty much of a solemn ass!

Remember the words of Lao Tse, "evil men are the material with which the sages work," and one of our Eastern Brethren once paraphrased it by saying that the Masters employ the dugpas for their dirty work. Not that ____ is a dugpa, he is really a fairly effective instrument for arousing torpid minds, but he does take himself so seriously, that it is painful even to us, who have the highly developed sense of humor which is one sure consequence of true inner growth. But enough of an unpleasant topic. Your decision is well taken, and we suggest you use Wednesday nights for relaxation—it is always preferable to irritation!

We resume with another fragment of the Test, and before we dictate it, let us say that you will do well to copy out the paragraphs of Text seriatim, and add to this special copy as we continue with it, until you have a considerable amount. Then when opportunity offers, it can be rounded out as was the Book of Tokens. Understand though, that it is from a wholly different source. Text: Sheen, Beth, Tav, Aleph, Yod – these be the letter names, and if thou recountest their value, their number is the perfection of the Tribes of Israel. Count and see.

(We do, and it comes to 1309.)

For see, the active Tribes are 11, not 12, for the Sons of Aaron are Levites, separate from the rest. Now 7 is the number of the Sabbath and of rest, and 17 is TVB, which signifieth "goodness," and 7 multiplied by 11 and this by 17 is the secret number of Shabbathai. Yet is Teshubah also, and more plainly a sign of the same thing. Count the names of its letters and see.

(We do this, the number is 1200.)

See then, the familiar number of the Tribes combined with the threefold multiplication of the number Yod, and also the number of Malkuth; for the Tribes are 12,and 10 times 10 times 10 is 1,000, which being added to 12, or combined with it, is the secret value of Teshubah. Now the Tribes are the powers of Adam, and it is known to the wise that 17, which ye have seen in the secret number of Shabbathai, is the special number of Israel. Rest is goodness. Rest is completion, therefore is rest also mastery and the perfection of Adam, for the Tribes are the signs of the Highways of the Stars, and these are the Sons of Adam who by Teshubah are turned back to their birthright as BNI-HALHIM. Thus it is also written, Thou turnest man to destruction, and sayest 'Return ye Sons of Adam.' For see, Teshubah is but the name for the _effect_ produced by this same turning and returning.

So far the Text. See the Psalms for the quotation, it will save time if you look it up now.

That is what we wanted you to see. Notice that "man" is ANVSh, the personality. The word DKA, translated "destruction," means also "collapse." It is the consequence of the apparent outgoing of personality into the field of conscious expression, which involves the semblance of separateness. Acceptance of the illusion for reality leads to collapse, as you may see in Key 16 of Rota, and we speak of this because the number of DKA, destruction, is 25, or the square of 5, the number of Mars. Behind these words, attributed traditionally to Moses, is the idea that really the BNI-ADM are identical with the BNI-HALIM. ANVSh, Enosh, is the state of the Sons of God when they suppose themselves to be merely the Sons of Adam, and the return is to the original Angelic condition. Now in this is the deepest mystery of Saturn closely related to the secret of Mars. The Sons of Adam have forgotten that they are truly Sons of God. For them there is no rest, and in divers ways they seek relief from the intolerable tension that is produced by the sense of separateness. Only a few members of the human race realize their true status, and live accordingly. Now these deluded ones see death everywhere, are taught survival perhaps, but do not usually really believe it. Thus they seek vicarious immortality in posterity, and surrender themselves to death. They who have come into the peace of the Sabbath are free from this delusion, and know better than to prolong the chain of birth and death.

Yet since there is nothing in the universe without use, as even M.P.H. sees, is it not obvious that the completion of man, and his return to his angelic state as a true Son of the Elohim, is not an after-death condition, nor a

228

state of being deprived of any right mode of life-expression rest are turned to destruction until utter collapse of their supposed autonomy sends them back. What needs to be remembered though is that what is rightly necessary as an adolescent is quite otherwise for an adult. That is right and good which is fitted to one's state of unfoldment. Origen misunderstood this and castrated himself, which showed him to be just as ignorant as most of his contemporaries, in spite of his erudition.

Let us speak plainly: Perfected men and women do not beget children, and this is exactly what Jesus meant by those who become eunuchs for the Kingdom's sake. Consult the Bible before we continue.

Now this state is spoken of by Jesus as being a <u>gift</u>, not for all, and He ended his pronouncement by the words always indicative of esoteric teaching: "Let him accept it who can." In every generation there are some who are qualified to accept, and we speak openly when we tell you that what is abstained from is <u>procreation</u>, just that, nothing else—if you have ears to hear.

When a human being completes the way of return, he, himself, is no longer subject to birth or death. How then, obeying, as do all the wise, the Golden Rule, can he subject others to the pain consequent on birth and death? Yet he is neither impotent in the technical sense, nor does he suppose himself to be afflicted with the dreadful burden of sex; for it is a gift, not an affliction; but misused, or put to less than the highest possible use, is the root of all sorts of pain.

Consider that all this is about Saturn, and that in the section of the Text given you tonight special emphasis was placed on the Tribes and signs, and you will, if you think it through, see that all this has to do with a method which converts Sons of Adam into Sons of the Elohim, and makes them truly Angels in Heaven, for where is Heaven but here, and what is an Angel but a herald of the Divine Self. Thus the BNI-HALHIM belong to Hod, the Sphere of Mercury, and all magical practice is intended to make the Magician truly an Angel. Accept this if you can.

Vale, Sub Umbra Alarum Tuarum, IHVH.

THIRTY-SECOND COMMUNICATION

Monday, February 9, 1948 8:10 P.M.

Ave Frater et Sorores.

Today you have been both foolhardy and presumptuous. Foolhardy, in not refusing at once to follow any course of action originating from a source which sad experience in the past should tell you has been more than once a channel through which the forces hostile to you and to us, have interfered. Presumptuous, in assuring that poor lunatic that you would ask us to help. He is wholly deluded, both as to his own spiritual and occult attainments, and as to the supposed malicious influences he thinks attack him. This is not psychic attack as far as he is concerned. But it provided through your contact with his diseased organism a good channel for a powerful real attack on you, which is making communication tonight very difficult, and accounts for your feeling depressed.

While we are on this topic, let us warn all 3 of you, that as rapport among you intensifies, the hostiles will do their best to produce disharmony among you. To avoid this, do not suppress sources of irritation, speak frankly, and get them out in the open. They are like germs—they die in the light, and breed in darkness. As the months pass, now that you are all together again, you will begin more and more to understand why we led you here, and what Tiphareth is intended to be, and the fulfillment of our purpose requires that you shall work for deep inner harmony, and not just aspire to it. Work it will be, because all 3 of you are well defined positive personalities, but the fruits of real cooperation will bring you greater and more enduring joy than you had from a sunset this evening. Remember you do not own Tiphareth, you hold it in trust. Ownership is for those who walk in darkness, and this has all sorts of applications to your work for and with us.

Now for some more of the Text: Binah dependeth from Beth, and thus is the name BITh completed by a letter of Shabbathai, for truly among men is the Mother the completion of the spouse, and so is it also in the deeper things of Ruach Elohim. The Path of Beth is truly the path of the Beginning, for in the Path of Aleph, nothing beginneth, nor is there any true beginning even in Chokmah; for what is Chokmah but the mirror of Kether, which hath neither beginning nor end? Thus is Aleph also the token of Ruach, which is likewise without beginning or end. But in BITh see B the initial of ORAShITh and of Baruch, which is Blessing. Then in BITh cometh Yod as the second letter, and this standeth for the Paternal Wisdom which is before all beginning. Finally cometh Tav, the letter of Saturn, which completeth the tale of the 22 Tokens. And thus read, if you have eyes to see, that in any beginning, the completion is already present. For the ONE knoweth naught of time as men reckon it, and for AL Shaddai, the beginning of any outpouring is one with its completion.

Thus may you come to understand that the Sabbath of the Eternal One never ends. How then may man find rest, save in the heart of the Mother? For that heart is the ever virgin Neshamah, and she is one with the Everlasting Heavens. Dark she is, but comely, even as Solomon saith. The source of terror to the ignorant, and therefore Pachad dependeth with all its stern judgments from her. Yet is she also AMK, Ameka, thy Mother, and her heart swelleth with love. For behold AMK is it not 61, and this is BTN, the dark womb of creation? And again, it is AIN, the Boundless, for there are no limits to the overflowing love, springing like a fountain of Living Waters from the heart of the Mother.

Everywhere may you find that heart, ye Children of Light, and nowhere else shall it be found, save at the center, which is the Holy Temple **in** the Midst, where Shabbathai hath its abode. There all is perfect rest, and thus was the great temple on earth built by Solomon, whose name signifieth "the peaceful," and set up in Jerusalem the dwelling place of peace. For these outer things are but figures. Until ye find the Hill of Zion in yourselves they shall be no more than figures, and dark ones in very truth.

So far the Text. It may seem to have little direct connection with what we have quoted previously, but there is a link just the same. Before we go on you had better rest. There is strong interference. Wait until we can deal with it on this side the veil.

All through the words of the wise there is a continual recurrence to the idea that the ONE is timeless. That sequence has little or no meaning to the consciousness which is above and beyond all human thought. Thus often there seems to be confusion in their words. For example, in the last part of the Text, Binah is identified with Ameka, thy Mother, and immediately this is indicated as being the same as the first veil of AIN, and as the vast expanse of the dark nothingness which is the womb of creation. Yet the Text is all the while dealing also with Saturn, and with the Path of Tav, and so with the idea of the eternal equilibrium or perfect rest at the center. Moreover, that rest is by clear implication identified with the Waters of Life. You may remember that our Elder Brother is reported to have said, "To those who labor I will give you rest," and to have told the woman that if she but knew who was speaking to her, that knowledge would be a well of living water. The meaning is not far to seek. Had she known who spoke to her she would have known the central Reality of her own Being, and who knows that, finds eternal life, eternal rest, and perfect peace, for these three are one. What you must take as your clue to the application to most of the Text referring to Shabbathai, is the place of Tav on the Tree. Note that the Mezlah descends to Malkuth through this Path from Yesod; thus may you know that the focusing of Yesod in Malkuth through Tav, is what completes the perfection of Binah.

They err greatly who suppose that the isolation spoken of by the Eastern Yogis is insulation. True isolation is the consciousness that in all this universe of apparent multiplicity there is neither male or female, Jew or Gentile as St. Paul put it. There is only the ONE, and the supposition that unity may be found by insulation is responsible for a brood of errors in all exoteric religions, Eastern and Western. Look at the Rota and see what Key 21 says. It is really a symbol of <u>union</u>, and is therefore the extension numerically of Key 6. Ask yourselves what has become of the man in Key 6, when that Key's full expression is represented by Key 21, and you will perhaps learn something to your advantage. Of course 21 is a representation of Binah, and the very number shows this because it reduces to Binah's number, 3; and in Key 21, if you look intently, you may see delineated in plain sight representation of the idea expressed in Hebrew by the word AIN, which is both. BTN and AMK. No, we shall not tell you, for you can find out for yourselves, and if you do, you should go on from there to a great many practical applications.

Vale. Sub Umbra Alarum Tuarum, IHVH.

THIRTY-THIRD COMMUNICATION

Thursday, February 12, 1948 8:00 P.M.

Ave Frater et Sorores.

Yes, there was unusual activity at your last convocation. We watched with considerable interest. The Chapter is beginning to have a definite group form, and we think it will be a useful vehicle. Before we take up the Text, we wish also to say that you have our complete approval as to the matter of public meetings of a more general nature, and as to the kind of writings you have in mind. Now for another section from the Text. It is not immediately consecutive to the last, but deals with the same basic topic. That is, with the Palace in the Midst, as related to Tav and Binah:

Truly the Mother and the Bride are One, and as the Bride is Malkuth, and the Mother Binah, so is the Mother conjoined with the Son through the Bride, even as Binah concealeth in the corpus of her very name, the names of Chokmah and of Tiphareth. For as it was written in the Zohar, BINH concealeth EN, and IH, and BN is Tiphareth, while IH is the Holy name in Chokmah. Now it is written also in Joshua, that among the spies who went forth into the land of Canaan, was Caleb, and that for his good report, when others had sought to delay Joshua from advancing, the Lord, Blessed be He, rewarded Caleb with long life.

Now Caleb signifieth dog, and well ye know that this is no name of good repute in Israel. Yet here is a treasure of wisdom that is part of the lore that Moses was instructed in as a youth in Egypt. For the story of Caleb is a figure, and Caleb the dog standeth for faithfulness, but there are deeper things than this. For reckon the number of KLB (52) and behold it is a veil for AMA, for KLB is 52. Now 52 ye know has the number of EN, but it is the number also of AEVAIMA, Abve-aima, or Father and Mother. That **is,** it representeth the conjoining of Chokmah, AB, with Binah, Alma. What then is the Path of this conjunction of Father and Mother? It is the Path of the Luminous Intelligence which joineth Chokmah to Binah, the Path of the

234

letter Daleth.

Now come and see again. The word KLB hath for its first two letters K and L, and these spell Kal, the ALL. And the last two letters are L and B, and these spell Laib, the Heart. Now K and L are 50, and these are the Gates of Binah, and L and B are 32, and these are the Paths of Wisdom. Thus in Caleb is concealed the secret of the ALL, which is likewise a Secret of the Heart. And is not the heart of Adam Quadman, Tiphareth the Son, into which pour all the streams of Mezla from above, and from which, for as much as Tiphareth is the Path of Separate Emanations, or mediating influence, that same Mezla descendeth to the Paths which are below? So Caleb is a sign of understanding, for his name as we have said, is of like number with AIMA.

But in Mizraim was their God Thoth represented as a dog-headed man, and that same Thoth is Kokab also, whom the "oppressors" called Mer-curious, and among the Sons of the Doctrine, it is known that this same Kokab hath its sphere in Hod, and its own Path in the letter Beth.

 Thus may ye understand that the Intelligence of Transparency is figured by Caleb, and with this is creation begun.

So far the Text.

Of interest to students of our Rota, is the fact that Caleb means dog, and since there is only one dog in the series of pictures....

(Here A. and H. said, "But there are two, in the Key of Aleph and Qoph.")

... if you let us finish the sentence we Shall not seem so forgetful—what we were about to go on saying was that the dog in Key 0 is the only one shown in direct association with man, as the pet and companion of the Fool. He is the letter Beth that follows after Aleph, just as the dog follows the Fool. Now Binah is at the lower end of the Path of Beth, and from what is said about the word Caleb, it is evident that the reference to Kokab or Mercury has also a bearing here. The Sphere of Mercury is Hod, HVD, and HVD being 15, links with IH, a divine name of Chokmah. Yet the Text also reminds us that the letters of Binah include IH, and refer to

Chokmah, just as does the I in AIMA. For the unfertilized Binah is AMA, dark and sterile. But between A and M the entry of the Paternal Yod (scilicet Yesod) impregnates AMA and makes her fertile. Yod is the special letter of AB, but remember that you have been taught that the word Yesod can be read SVD-I, the Secret of Yod. And thus the wise understand both Chokmah and Yesod when they consider the meaning of the letter I.

Remember also that every instructed Qabalist has learnt that creation begins with the letter Beth, but takes place with the letter Heh, which in this connection is referred to Binah. The initial impregnating impact originates with Beth, but the taking place, or production of actual manifested forms is the work of Binah.

Now among other things the dog is a symbol of the libido, as is also the wolf, and even current slang preserves this latter reference. Again the same libido is connected with the goat, and so with Key 15 where you see the sign of Mercury on the Devil's belly. What is not emphasized in modern thought about Mercury, was perfectly familiar to antiquity, as his symbol the caduceus, twined with serpents, shows plainly enough. In our days we are less frank, but in Rome, the home of those the Text calls "oppressors," statues of Mercury were commonly ithyphallic, and the God was invoked to confer male potency. Thus in this Text there are echoes, as in all occult doctrine, of the idea that creation is a generation. For example, see what the Bible says: "These be the generations of the Heavens and the earth," or words to the same effect. The bearing here is that the consciousness represented by Beth is what spies-out the promised land held by the enemies of Israel, but rich in flowers, fruit, and cattle, which is what is meant by "flowing with milk and honey." But as The Book of Tokens tells us, the milk stands for Life Eternal, and the honey for Unblemished Wisdom.

Caleb is Thoth-Hermes, herald of the God, and personification of human consciousness. For how have the Gods ever spoken save through the mind of man? Note also that besides what the text says, KLB begins with KL, All, and has B for its last letter, as if the All were concentrated in the Beth, and so it is; the self-conscious mind of man has ever been the herald of the Gods precisely because it is the focal point or center for the All. Thus the

Path of Beth descends from Kether, which has for one of its names, the Simple Point, and this point is the innermost center also. For this reason the middle letter of the word Kether is the same Tav of which you have heard so much lately, and this same letter attributed to Saturn, ends the name Beth, so that Binah, as the Sphere of Saturn, is, really the Sphere of what among the letters is signified by Tav. Note also that the other Path leading into Binah on the Path of descending influence is that of Daleth, and the last letter of the word Daleth is this same Tav.

For the Sons of the Doctrine sow their microcosm of instruction with symbols, even as the Oracle says the mind of the Father sows the world with symbols, to the end that he who picks up one clue shall find himself of subtler wit and thus able to see others. Rest a while and read.

Now consider also that Mercury rules Gemini, represented in the Rota by Key 6, and this is the Key corresponding to Zain, the name of which letter is the number 67, the same as the value of Binah. That is, the Path of Zain is the first channel for the descending influence of Binah, and partakes of her essential nature. She however is pregnant with the descending influence from Kether through the Path of Beth, and impregnated also with the influence of Chokmah through the Path of Daleth, each of which letters ends with Tav, and so focuses attention on conjunction, because the word Tav ends with V, the grammatical symbol of conjunction, and also because the ancient character for Tav was the joining of two lines to form a cross like that on the breast of the High Priestess. The horizontal line feminine and the vertical masculine.

So we are back from our long excursion with Caleb to the familiar letter Tav, and all it implies. Caleb, as you have just seen in the Bible, was the son of Jephunnah that is IPNH. Now these four letters are worth noticing. The first is Yod, phallic, and also symbol of both Chokmah and Yesod. The second is the letter of Mars; the third the letter of Scorpio, and the last related to Aries and to vision. Remember that Caleb was a spy, and that the Text plainly refers to the perfection of his masculine vigor. Moreover the number of his years is given as 85, which is the number of the letter name PH, Peh, and this is divided into two parts; 40, his age when he served as a spy, and this is a number of Mem; and 45, which elapsed thereafter, which is a numeral symbol of ADM, Adam. That is, the dog became a completed man, and this involves the use and direction of the Mars force in accordance with reversal of ordinary procedure, for the other spies reported unfavorably and caused the people's hearts to melt. But Caleb at 40 stands for the reversal, symbolized by the Hanged Man. The binding of self-consciousness in utter surrender to the inner light, or Lord, which enables it to speak from the heart, and not from outer appearance. This note also: I and P add to 90, the full spelling of Mem, and also the number of Tzaddi, the letter of Meditation, which perfected, leads to the state pictured by Key 12. Again N and H, the last two letters, add to 55, the number of the word NAH, ornament, relating to Malkuth, because 55 is the extension of 10, and this same 55 is the value of KLH, Kala, the Bride, a name of Malkuth. Thus BNIPNH, Ben Jephunna, son of Jephunna, intimates Tiphareth manifested in the meditation process which gives to the mercurial aspect, or consciousness, its full power and perfected humanity. This Caleb was not one of the Israelites, he was a Kennizite adopted into Israel, an outsider by birth. But he received his proper reward. The whole passage is an allegory relating to what alchemists call the fixation of Mercury. That is, the highest use of self-consciousness in a creative function, reversing customary attitudes of mind and the activities they prompt, and leading ultimately to the overthrow of error. Here is material for much elaboration, but we leave that now to your own ingenuity.

Sub umbra alarum tuarum

THIRTY-FOURTH COMMUNICATION

Monday, February 16, 1948 8:00 P.M.

Ave Frater et Sorores.

There is yet room for considerable improvement in your arrangement of time. Remember what was said once by our Frater Eliphas Levi: "The way to see is not to be always looking." You are letting a sense of pressure affect all 3 of you. This is not conducive to good work. Remember, you are not running a newspaper with a deadline to meet, neither are you in any sense the world understands conducting a business, least of all is it your work –it is ours—and unless you take more seriously our recommendations concerning it and yourselves, you cannot reasonably expect a maximum of success. We never have given you any commands, nor shall we ever do so, because such procedure is just the opposite to the correct one. Yet we must point out that unless you are careful to keep your channels really open, little can come through them. Some weeks ago we suggested that you budget your time and allow sufficient for amusement and relaxation, but up till now you have done nothing of the sort. A budget is not just a vague intention, it is a specific program, and in consideration of the many things that might be done with your time if you really had a program, it seems rather a pity that any of you should feel rushed when the remedy is so easy.

After all, though we are functioning practically 24 hours the day, we see that our physical bodies have sufficient rest, and our minds adequate relaxation, and we think that you will agree that we have plenty to do, and that a good deal of it is what you would consider rather arduous. Thus when we give you the benefit of our experience in the matter of using time instead of being used by it, we find it a little disconcerting that you have in fact done just nothing about it. Do we need to take time here to go into details? Perhaps you might consult the dictionary with advantage, and then perhaps you will actually, arrange your days to avoid lost motion, duplication of effort, and needless rush, and its consequent fatigue but for Heaven's sake do something about it!

(H.: "We have been anxious to get the work out as quickly as possible.")

239

Why anxious?

(H.: "Maybe the letters are not good to send out?")

Yes they are, and you will get them out the sooner if you manage your work and play intelligently, and don't forget the play in your concern about the work!

(Here there was a long wait, then came what purported to be the continuation of the Text. However after a couple of pages, Paul detected that it made no sense, that in fact it was G.D. nonsense and that he would have none of it, so we stopped.)

THIRTY-FIFTH COMMUNICATION

Thursday, February 19, 1948 8:00 P.M.

Ave Frater et Sorores.

Do you not already see that doing something about managing your time has had good results? The Text you received last time was none of our sending, and it was a good thing you perceived it so soon. We could of course have overcome the interference, but that seemed hardly required, considering that Frater P. had knowledge enough to detect the fraud, and that to bring force to bear where it was not really needed, would have done no more for the time than his refusal to accept as ours what was so full of conflict and error. Nevertheless we deem it wise to wait before giving anymore of the Text, until you have separated these fragments, and given them due consideration, which has been impossible up to now, and considering all you have to do with the other work, will perhaps be delayed for some days yet.

(A.: "Are we to discontinue the communications for the time being?")

No. We shall simply wait before we send you any more of the Text and comment you have been receiving. It has little consecutiveness as it stands, and at least some of the gaps should be filled in.

(H.: "You want me to assemble the bits of Text right from the beginning?")

Yes.

(A.: "Do you wish us to stop all communications for a while?") That is for you to decide.

(H.: "It seems a pity to stop our contact altogether, could we perhaps not have just half an hour?")

There may be times when only a few words _are_ necessary, and others, when under favorable conditions we can give you more. Astrological conditions modify this to some degree. That is why, although regular times on the whole are best, we have already warned you not to wait for us to begin longer than 10 minutes. It is also the cause of occasional interference, though that may also result from any one of you being over tired, or under emotional stress. Just now for example, the retrograde planets are not specially favorable for clear communication on abstruse topics. We recommend that Frater P. take this time to make himself familiar with the Gematria of the 32 Paths, as the Text has much bearing on it.

Were these test communications for the satisfaction of those who are never really to be satisfied by any tests they devise, we might not suggest this procedure, for certainly it would be facile, almost obvious criticism to attribute all such material to the subconscious activities of Frater P. himself. We do recognize him as having considerable talent for Qabalah. Indeed, that talent developed in another incarnation was what led us to make contact with him years ago. But he is not quite that good even now!

Incidentally, now that you have heard Manly Hall, perhaps you can understand that we are not too pleased with his flatulent comments on the Trinosophia. His copy is not the original, not even the drawings, which however were excellent copies of the originals. Yet there is material in that Text germane to your work, and it might be well to give it more thorough inspection. One of the best things Frater P. has done is to detect the cross-correspondences in Gematria from Hebrew, Latin, and Greek. No other modern writer has done as much, sketchy as the performance still is. We know there are comparatively few students ready for this kind of work, but *we* trust that you will be able to make some sort of provision for those who are ready.

Now for another matter. One of your greatest mistakes Frater, has been that you have not deliberately made clear the fact that the inner work is arduous at its early stages; that it calls for unusual abilities on the part of those who seek to become proficient in the higher ranges Practice; and that it is emphatically not for neurotic visionaries of the type so often encountered amongst Theosophists and so-called Rosicrucians and such. The work of the B.O.T.A. has suffered from being limited to persons of little real education or other preparation, such as come to the usual public lectures on occult matters.

We counsel you give much thought to this, for the B.O.T.A. movement in its deeper aspects must always be for the relatively few. There are some phases of the Chapter Work which can reach many. Indeed, so far as ritual work is concerned, nominal advance to 5=6 is open to most persons of reasonable ability. But note that we have used the word nominal. To be a Lesser Adept in anything more than name, calls for something besides familiarity with rituals and lectures.

Do not misunderstand us. If the Chapters should come to have a membership of 10,000, it would still be the same, there is nothing against that, though it does seem slightly impossible now certainly it will never occur unless more care is taken with candidates, and considerably more stress placed on the utter seriousness of the work. Screen out the incompetents. You have a Chief now who is such in name only. He is there because in a former life he did better work than he is doing now, and because also we recognize in him a real devotion, unfortunately considerably overbalancing his intelligence. Of course you began under difficulties, but no small part of them were due to your own maladjustments—inner ones we mean. You have grown riper in recent years, and it is about time. But do see to it that the lazy are kept out hereafter, and that searching tests are given postulants to insure harmony.

What to do with some you have now is more than we can say. You have to do what you can, but we counsel a little more seasoning from the Geburah side. Better get back to seven devoted workers, than bumble along forever trying to placate people who should have learned not to be thin-skinned before ever they were admitted. Not a pleasant prospect for a while we grant, but you may quote us in substance, though it may be well to modify the phrasing a little. As to yourselves here, you are doing on the whole much better than last year. But you are yet some distance from the attainment we now begin to be confident you will make. And you can all do something to intensify your awareness that Hillside House and Tiphareth are centers of our work, and not just your office and home respectively. Each of you has his or her personal contribution to make to this group activity, and your group is and will continue to be a triad, for reasons deeper than any of you yet realize. There truly is magic in the number 3. So deepen the consciousness of your inner link as much as you can, and we shall help. This must suffice for tonight.

Sub Umbra Alarum Tuarum, IHVH, Vale, Frater et Sorores.

Monday, February 23, 1948 8:00 P.M.

Ave Frater et Sorores.

When you have read and digested the fragments of Text so far communicated, you will find a thread of continuity running through them, although the Text itself is only part of the whole. We have in mind to give you portions of the same bearing on the 32 Paths, and because you are working in Chapter on the grade scheme which traces the Paths in reverse order, we shall begin with the 32nd Path and work backward through the Paths of the letters. This will tie in with the considerable amount of Text you already have on the letter Tav with which we begin our quotation from the old source already familiar to you the Text follows:

It is written that the 32nd Path is ShKL NOBD (Saykel Naobed, Intelligence of Service Or Serving), and that it is so called because it governs the motion of the 7 planets and concurs therein to Tav, the letter of this Path, to which the wise declare that the Temple in the Midst pertaineth, and that this Path is also that of Shabbathai or rest. Now the secret of this Path is in its name, NOBD, which signifieth Serving, and answereth to the number 126. Now this is the number of ALMNH (Almanah), or Widow, and it is said by the Sons of the Doctrine to refer to Malkuth in her separation from Tiphareth; Thus doth the Path of Tav end in Malkuth, but its first letter is the beginning and end of Tiphareth, and its last letter is Vav, by which the wise understand Tiphareth also For the Temple of Holiness in the Midst is in the heart of the six, and there also is the place of rest, or Shabbathai. For it was said of old that from Shabbathai came forth the other planets, and unto Shabbathai they all returned.

But the Widow, is she not also the Bride, and one with the Mother as well? In Mizraim was she known as Isis, and her son was Khoor, whom the Greeks called Horus, and verily he is that same BN who is Tiphareth, and his mother Isis is Binah, for our father Mosha did learn

244

wisdom in the temples of Mizraim, and he hath transmitted his wisdom to the assemblies which came after him. Thus it is written "out of Egypt have I called my son," and verily that son is Ben or Tiphareth. And the mystery of Widowhood which separates the Bride from the Son, is a mystery of Motherhood also, for the Bride and the Mother truly are one. See now in NOBD that the first letter pertaineth to Madim, and to the perpetuation of life by generation. And that the second letter is the Fountain of Renewal in which Shabbathai ruleth and Madim hath its chief power. Then cometh the letter Beth, and the word endeth with the letter Daleth, so that you may read it thus: Perpetual Generation, the Fountain of Renewal In Daleth, for B and D together may be read "in Daleth."

Now in the Widow is seen the power of the name in Chesed, for the word beginneth AL, then cometh the hidden Manna, for the next two letters, M and N, are they not Manna? Then at the end cometh the letter H, which signifieth sight, and is also the special letter in Tetragrammaton pertaining both to the Mother and the Bride. Now the Mother is the sphere of Shabbathai, or Rest, and the letter of Tav is Shabbathai itself, and from this Path of Tav on the Tree dependeth Malkuth the Bride who is the Resplendent Intelligence, and behold her glory comes from Shabbathai, which from the Midst governeth and administereth all.

So far the Text.

In the beginning, what can be little more than suggestive comment? Let us look first at the number 126: When the Text was written, the later development of what you, Prater P., have happily designated as the Magical Language, was unknown; but by the time we announced ourselves enigmatically in the Fama, it was well developed, and one of our reasons for describing the vault as we did, was that its boundaries in feet, as given in the Fama, total 126. For there are 7 lines of 5 feet at the top, 7 of 5 feet at the bottom, and 7 vertical lines of 8 feet, and this totals 126 feet. Note that 21 lines establish these boundaries, and 126 is a six-fold 21. It is then AHIH multiplied by V, the letter of Tiphareth to which the vault is assigned. The reference to NOBD and ALMNH may seem obscure at first; the riddle solves itself with a little meditation.

To begin with, one Sephirah is really identical with all other 9. Their semblance of separation is an illusion produced by man's discriminating self-conscious intellectual processes, and their necessary limitations. Do not overlook that "necessary," it could be no otherwise. Now Isis, the Bride, and Mother and Widow, is Eve also, and she is the Widow of the Tribes of Naphtali and Dan, who is the Mother of Hiram Abiff in the Masonic legend. Of the Tribe of Naphtali, as one scripture reference has it, to point to Virgo; and of the Tribe of Dan, to point to Scorpio. Her Son is Horus in Egypt, and Hiram in Freemasonry, and you know already that he is our Brother and Father C.R. whose body was found as the Fama relates, in the Vault.

Now we can add to the gematria in the Text several interesting examples from Latin. One is Lapis Chemicus, another is Virgo Sophia, and a third is Virgo Intacta, but perhaps the most suggestive is Microcosmos, which last ties in with the title of the Key of Rota assigned to Tav. Nor is this all. Tam is the Temple or Sanctuary in the Midst, and do not forget that in Judaism the special day of sacrifice and service at the Temple, was the day is sacred to Shabbathai. So you won't be surprised, we think, that the Latin for Sanctuary, which is Sanctuarium, also adds to 126.

(Here P. proceeded to check all the names as to their numerical value.)

Always check numbers. We have known ourselves to add them wrong, so take every precaution, and perhaps some comfort! As you looked just now you noticed also an "Aquamineralis" which we should have included had you not paused to count. Now this mineral water, and the microcosm, are one; and the mineral water is the microcosm in one stage of its development. But be on your guard against a too facile, or too restricted an interpretation here. The Aqua mineral is the seed of the world in all senses. It is that which is the Intact Virgin, or the Untouchable Glory of God, as one of the four mottoes in the Fama puts it. Note the numbering of Dei Gloria. Dei is 18, which corresponds to the Hebrew CHI. Gloria is 56 or 6 less than Sophia.

(There was a little mix-up here.)

You are trying to figure as we go along, just let it come. 18 and 56 add to 74, which is the value of LMD, but as you can see from Rota, the power of the Intact Virgin, who is also Sophia, or Wisdom, is in Rota represented by the woman in Justice, and she is both the Bride and the Queen, and thus she is also AIMA, MAIH, ISIS, EVE, and all the rest of the host of Anima figures, including the Widow and Venus. The microcosm is indeed the chemical stone, rough, and requiring treatment by art before it is purified and perfected. Yet it is in essence ever pure, and nothing can diminish that essential purity. This notwithstanding, in the field of relative phenomena, the work veiled in the figurative language of the Hermetic sciences must go on. Its outcome makes evident the truth that the mineral waters and the chemical stone are the microcosm. That is the true Adam who is Ben the Son. Hence the substitute word of our Masonic Brethren really signifies what is the Son, and he who knows the answer to this experimentally, not merely by hearsay, finds the Alchemical Stone, the Sumum Bonum, and the place of rest that is Shabbathai in the Midst. Man himself is the Abode of Peace, the place of refuge, the Sanctuary, and the time draws near when here in America they who are true Sons of the Widow will realize in truth the New Order, which is commemorated on the Seal of the United States. Now add up Novus Ordo, and see what you shall see.

(We do, and it comes to 126.)

Rest a while, we have more to give. Conditions are good, partly because of our good Father Dhal.

Now in the Rota the work implied by the word NOBD is pictured as an androgyne figure, standing in space, surrounded by a wreath of leaves of which there are 66, the extension of 11. In the Rota, 11 is Lamed or Justice, and thus there is an intimation here that the wreath of Victory refers to Venus, whose sphere on the Tree is Netzach. Now the color of the leaves confirms this, for it is green, the color of Venus and of Netzach. What is more subtle is the shape of the wreath. It is an ellipse 8 high and 5 wide, the same as the sides of the Vault, and these were 7 in number to call attention once more to Venus. Nor will you have forgotten that in alchemical writings it is said that one must fashion coins of copper, and purify them to whiteness.

Consider now what is a coin? It is money currency, and its fundamental significance as a medium of exchange, is that it represents the expenditure of human energy in work, a fact often overlooked by supporters of the religion of Mammon. Here again the wreath gives a hint, for when the Rota was devised, we knew perfectly well that human energy expended in work, is energy fixed by the green substance of leaves, the fundamental food of the entire animal kingdom. The great victory in the establishment of the New Order, will be equitable and candid, that is while, recognition of the fact that the physical resources of the whole world do not constitute wealth apart from man, and man's use of his own vital energy in work. The coins of Mammon are black with the corrosion of selfishness and separateness. The wealth of the world is not owned by men, although many assert boldly their right of ownership. All the world's wealth belongs to Adam, the son of God. To collective humanity, not to persons, and thus we said long ago, and say to this day, that in our philosophy you may find much of theology, but considering the state of the world, not much of jurisprudence. This is unfortunately as true today as it was in 1610. Persons are but stewards, they own nothing, they are as the New Testament puts it, no more than unprofitable servants. Yet how few you find who are willing to think of themselves as such!

Do you not rather find even among those who sincerely believe themselves to be what are commonly termed "nice people" a pretty strong sense of class, and a very decided disposition to think servants, like children, Negroes and Jews, are all right in their place, which means of course that they are all right so long as they do not venture to think themselves good enough to try to come into the sacred precincts reserved for the aforesaid "nice people." Now of such thinking the ramparts, of the only kind of hell there is, are built up. Nor is it any better if resentment and repudiation of injustice lead the underprivileged to the erroneous conclusion that none but themselves are deserving to be called "nice people." Class Consciousness is just as bad for the proletarian as it is for the aristocrat. They are both wrong. There is only one human race, and nobody can be excluded from i

Ten generations of proper feeding, housing and education would demonstrate this for all the world. There are no great differences in human beings when they come into the world. Almost any baby, even though the genes have been pretty badly muddled, could be made into a superior type of man or woman if caught early enough and properly trained. In spite of the proverb, blood does not tell, training is what tells. But it will be some time before the world sees this scientifically demonstrated. Shall we wait for this, we who know? Of course not. I who am now in communication with you, come from an old proud line, founded like most such lines by a set of greedy robbers and murderers of whom I am not in the least proud. Nothing irks me more than to be called by silly Theosophists, the "Master the Prince," for I have been trying for some score of decades to overcome the sad karma of that physical inheritance. To be a human being, is sufficient title to consideration.

True, a great deal of money is at the disposal of the Brethren, more than you have any notion of, nor shall we stagger your imaginations by figures you could not credit. But it is at our disposal only in trust, and we know what it really means. All this is closer to the Path of Administrative Intelligence than you may think. How placidly Church goers hear it read that, "let him who would be chiefest among you, be the servant of all." Have they ears to hear? You may be sure they have no inner ears, so long as they are smugly thankful they don't belong to the working classes, or so long as they maintain, whether consciously and deliberately, or simply because of early miseducation, which it has never occurred to them to question the deplorable sense of separation which is the basic heresy. Where a man's heart is, will be his treasure.

Thus to rise to the formulation of correct theory through the Path of Tav, calls for a total reorientation, or a true turning once more, that is to the Spiritual East, and in the Secret Wisdom, East is connected with Venus. As above, so below, as in great, so in small. Your personal reorientation and your personal victory, are also a work of Venus. Furthermore the dancer is androgyne as we said. Now have you ever seen or heard of an actual androgyne in the flesh? There are some badly disarranged human bodies and psychies, but an actual androgyne is simply not on this

249

planet. Yet there is the symbol. See if you can think through to its meaning, and to help you in this, remember that the key stands for Shabbathai, that is, for what all astrologers mean by Saturn and more. Again, the wreath as we said is an ellipse, that is to say, a zero sign representing AIN, and thus also ANI, that is I, myself, and BTN, beten, the womb. Yet the number of the Key is 21, which is the value of AHIH, the Divine name of Kether, and also the value of the name IHV, or Yaho, with permutations of which according to the Sepher Yetzirah the Lord establishes the Cube of Space. The meaning will dawn, if it has not begun to glimmer already. The Great Work is both personal and social, but it must begin with persons. As they achieve it, as they enter the sanctuary, as they discover for themselves the true secret of Saturn, they progress stage by stage into conscious participation in the New Order. For many generations this has been going on; because you do not know how many have already achieved the Summum Bonum, it may seem to you that the social demonstration is yet far off.

We trust you will not fall into this error. It is on the contrary imminent from our point of view. Do not forget that six blind men might suppose all the world to be as sightless as they. The day is now when we no longer veil our meaning with enigmas, for we have said, and you must also say, that the old order is ended.

Thank you for taking so much tonight.

Sub Umbra Alarum Tuarum, IHVH.
Vale, Frater et Sorores.

THIRTY-SEVENTH COMMUNICATION

Thursday, February 26, 1948 8:05 P.M.

Ave Frater et Sorores.

Conditions are not good this evening. It has taken us nearly 9 minutes to get the planchette in motion, and we think you had better wait until your organisms are in a more favorable state. A common cold is really a most upsetting ailment so far as the subtler forces are concerned. There is no hurry. The Text will be available when you are in better position to record our sending.

Vale, Sub Umbra Alarum Tuarum.

THIRTY-EIGHTH COMMUNICATION

Tuesday, March 2, 1948 8:05 P.M.

There is no use in communicating any more Text, until you have read, and thoroughly digested what has been given thus far. Partly because you are not now ready to understand some of the comments we propose giving. This does not mean that we think you dilatory in transcribing it Soror. Yet, there is so much to fill your time just now, that we would not increase the burden. Moreover, you all need to be thoroughly familiar with what has been given, and there will be frequent references to earlier sections, even during our communications; it is not feasible to attempt the sections on the Paths until you are prepared.

As we were closing last time you wished to ask a question, but both because we had already practically broken the contact, and because other conditions were not favorable, our answer may have seemed a bit curt. However, you know Frater that the externals are seldom if ever matters with which we interfere, or about which we give specific direction. We may say that in the case of Miss Kaplan, intention and good will, run somewhat ahead of experience in this field. On the other hand we know of nobody who has the experience, because the field is restricted, though plenty large enough for a considerable expansion of the work. Yet you have not, from any of the lists you have used thus far, either adequate response in numbers or quality. The application that came this morning shows no real aptitude, nor understanding. That which came from Rhode Island is of different caliber, and he learned of this work from one who had taken some of it. Could you not find a way to stir up a little of the missionary spirit in those who are now studying? If each of them could help you make a single fresh contact, the number of affiliates would be doubled, and the same tactics continued, would in a year or so lead to considerable growth.

This does not mean you should not use lists, but if you make some investigations here in Los Angeles, you will be likely to find a person somewhat better equipped to serve the work. We do not believe your circular sufficient to provoke immediate response. They are both good of their kind, but lack definite pointing of the exact nature of the work, and to the type of person to whom this approach makes its appeal. Do not forget that though much that was formerly reserved for picked students, is now more freely offered by us, it is on the whole something for the few. You should make this clear, and just as with the Chapter, you need to exercise care and ingenuity to keep unprepared persons from joining. So if you can so arrange your more public approach, will you [you will?] find it advantageous in the long run to let it be known that you are looking for persons having superior qualifications.

This is not Unity or New Thought, nor even the sort of Theosophy most T.S. Lodges and lectures promulgate. There may be ten thousand or so in the English speaking world who can properly utilize it, and you cannot now reach more than a fraction of those. The initial error from the days of your first lectures, was that you labored under the misapprehension that this work could reach many persons quickly. It can never be a great mass movement, but it can and will maintain itself, and you who are carrying it on, and [can?] do so adequately. Thus we believe you should give much thought to supplementary letters as you prepare the lessons in their new dress. From the very beginning you should endeavor to clarify the objectives of our undertaking. We are not much interested in teaching poor people how to get rich, or sick ones how to get well. It takes a fairly normal body to do this work effectively, and if the motivation be no higher than a desire for health, happiness, and success, you can see that such an approach in your advertising will not bring you the sort of students you can depend upon for persevering study and work. Might it not be well to say as much rather emphatically, so that readers of your literature will know that they are expected to bring something to the enterprise, both of ability and of material support?

Up until now you have been hampered by a good many neurotic, poverty conscious and sickly graspers at any straw that might lift them out of miseries of their own making. These cannot be Builders until they start in the right direction. Do not misunderstand us, there is a great deal to be done for such persons, but it cannot be done to such persons, and this work is intended to prepare those competent to help relieve and cure suf-

253

fering humanity. As well might you select from a free clinic in a slum, candidates for a medical school, as to expect self-seeking, or silly persons to qualify for this teaching. Do not forget that our one public profession is "to heal the sick, and that gratis." Thus if you remember that B.O.T.A. is an outer vehicle of what first announced itself in Fama, you must realize that they who take up this work must be qualified for it, and that they must also be in a position to do their healing work without external recompense. This does not mean that practicing physicians would be obliged to quit taking fees, or that priests and other clergy must go without adequate salaries. What we speak of is a subtler and higher kind of healing, and the sick are ill in mind and soul rather than in body.

To be sure, improvement in physical health is one of the consequences of practical occultism, but it should never be the primary objective of any student. It is true of course that your first lessons do teach a technique that may be applied successfully to very material ends. Those who do so learn quickly the want of real satisfaction to be gained from possessions or even from health without understanding. So those lessons should remain where they are, and as they are, for they will do more, far more than appears on the surface.

These have been no more than general suggestions, but they will help you we believe, to clarify your own idea of what our work is really aiming to accomplish through you. This done in your own minds will enable you to test various methods for making the true nature of our work better understood by prospective affiliates. As we said before, there is no pressing need for you to complete the 32 Paths work, and for the time being most of these communications will be short as will this. Just put what we have told you in earlier communications into full operation and you will see plenty of good results. There is no need to go on with repetitions of what has been made sufficiently clear.

Vale. Sub Umbra Alarum Tuarum.

THIRTY-NINTH COMMUNICATION

Monday, March 8, 1948 8:00 P.M.

Ave Frater et Sorores.

Be on your guard against too sudden enthusiasms. This is not a counsel for yourselves, but for your use in relation to others. Better those who go slow, than those who are too quick to take up new things. So observe, and weigh well, when those who have tried many occult paths come seeking light from you. Often such persons are self-deluded as to their real purposes, and the more familiar they are with the terminology of metaphysics, the easier it is for them to hide their true motives even from themselves, behind a smoke screen of finely aspiring verbiage. Again we say, be on your guard.

As we told you before, for a while these communications will not be lengthy. You have much to do in the actual production of your Texts, and you have not had time to digest what you have already received. Thus we have nothing additional in the way of Texts for you tonight.

(H.: "Do I understand that the Texts on the 32 Paths are not to be typed off separately with the other Text?")

No, that is a separate series.

In preparation for the next section, which has to do with the 31st Path, give some thought to the Sephirah Hod, whence this Path descends. Consider its name letter by letter, in relation to the Keys of Rota. Then you may see that HVD has through Rota a link with the Path through which the Mezla descends to it from Geburah. Again, consider the gematria of HVD and its relation to Iii. Once more, H is the letter of the Emperor and D the letter of the Empress, with V between them to represent both AB and BN, and to intimate a conjunction also. This

255

should put you on the track of the deeper significance of the 31st Path. That is to say, insofar as the specific nature of the descending influence is concerned. We leave you to work this out before we send you the Text.

Our words are not many this time, but if you take the hint, you should discover much.

Sub Umbra Alarum Tuarum, IHVH. Vale.

(We study for an hour or so looking up gematria, and looking at the Tree: The sum of the Paths Peh, Mem, and Ayin add to 190. 190 = sum of numbers from 1 to 19. POM: to strike, to beat, an anvil, tread, step, pace. HVD in plenitude: 456 = fig tree in fruit, mountain of Myrrh, legs, thighs, street, ways. In Latin 456 = Panes—wall of a house. Hebrew 456 = KVTL also wall of a house, refers too to Tiphareth. KV: Jehova, TL: mound, burial mound. 456: ThANH (Tehaynaw): opportunity and purpose, occasion and design, copulation, a coming together, lust.

456: AIMThH (Amath): fear, dread, terror, awe, reverence—Formido Maxima (in Latin).
456 in Greek: Mater, Mother... Hod in Latin: Decus, ornament, splendor, glory, honor, dignity—Elohim Sabbaoth.
ThMIDI (Tamida): constant and perpetual. ThMID: extension, constant, always stretch.)

No Communication on either Thursday, March 11 or Monday, March 15

FORTIETH COMMUNICATION

Thursday, March 18, 1948 8:00 P.M.

Ave Frater et Sorores.

The insanity that seems to afflict the greater portion of humanity is intensifying so rapidly that the waves of fear encircling the globe daily make communication difficult. There is so much to be done, and so few of us really, who know what to do, that in times of pressure like these, those of us who constitute a minority in the Lodge, wonder sometimes whether our Brethren who disagree with what they call our premature revelations, may not perhaps have been right all along. To liberate a race, apparently bent on mass suicide, seems even to us now a dubious project!

We have not communicated with you the last two times, not because there is anything wrong with you—more than the ignorance that affects nearly everybody—our work makes heavy demands on us and our time these days, and it is work not to be neglected, even though the project of which you are a part is close to our hearts. If the present crisis, which is far worse than you can possibly imagine, leaves us any human race worth mentioning, to work with on the physical plane, we shall continue with you and our other helpers. Sit regularly as heretofore, for when we can, we wish to keep in touch with you, but for the time being, do not expect much in the way of Text or comment, we are just too busy right now.

(A. asks if there is anything We can do to help in the way of sending out strong thoughts of love, etc.)

257

No. Study what you have, and practice what you know; try to knit yourselves more and more closely together. If catastrophe comes, the link you have made will not be broken, and you know we never have been Cassandra-like hitherto. From us, as from you, many things are hidden, so the outcome may turn out better than what seems to be the prospect now. All you can do is day by day persistence in the course you now follow. You may be surprised to hear that our own attitude and practice is no different.

Lots of silly babble has been said and written about Lemuria and Atlantis, none sillier than the astral intoxications of that poor senile invert who spewed out his phantasies to an almost total obscuration of what we gave H.P.B., but this much is fact: great civilizations have vanished from the sight of man, and even from his memory, over and over again, and the causes of those catastrophes are at work today, and most of humanity knows as little how to combat them as how to cure cancer. So there is nonsense in Pollyanna optimism about the present situation. In your country Mars is in the ascendant, as in many other lands, and fear is failure in government as in all else. We cannot coerce mankind into being wise, and thus we warn you not to spread fear by quoting what we have said tonight, or even making most guarded references to it. We intended only to tell you why you have not heard from us, and already this has taken too long. Keep at your work and study, you can do no better, and remember that our blessing is always with you.

Sub Umbra Alarum Tuarum.

Did not sit on Thursday, March 25 8:05 P.M., or Monday, March 29

FORTY-FIRST COMMUNICATION

Monday, March 22, 1948 8:05 P.M.

Ave Frater et Sorores.

Neither of you are in very good condition to take a communication tonight, so it won't be long. By Thursday you will be in better shape, and we shall hope to go on with the Text on the Paths.

Tonight we wish only to confirm your decision to let Soror Nancy L. start a class. We call her Soror, because she is truly that, as are all the members of the Qabalah group. They are just picking up something they have worked with before, and their formation of a Chapter will be only the renewal in the outer, of ties formed long ago. Our Frater C.E.G. is another of your true inner group. You have noticed, have you not, how without any hint from you, his letter echoed what we ourselves said recently. He is going to be a very great asset, as with the help of your lessons he brings to the surface what he learned long since. Indeed, the reason the lessons ring so true to him, is that he has already tested their substance in the fires of verification the last time he was embodied in the flesh. The same is true of Jason.

It may be that his wife is not yet ready to let him identify himself outwardly with the Chapter, but we suggest that you use your right to initiate on sight, if he is willing, so that you may discuss Chapter work with him without reservation, and so that he may attend meetings occasionally if it seems advisable. But this must be fully discussed with him. We do not pry into the minds of others, so we know no more than you, just how his wife feels, and just what his own attitude toward ceremonial may be. So many seem to think that every man's mind is an open book to us, that this may be a new idea to some of you. But remember that we respect privacy. We can when it is justified, do a sort of mental wire tapping, but such occasions are very few. This is all for tonight. Get well rested by our next evening.

Sub Umbra Alarum Tuarum IHVH

FORTY-SECOND COMMUNICATION

Thursday, April 1, 1948 8:05 P.M.

Ave Frater et Sorores.

There is true magic in compassion, and the kindly impulse that brought this new little life into Tiphareth, will have results more far reaching than many an outwardly imposing ceremonial. They are so sadly mistaken who suppose we have no interest in animals. A pet like yours is fortunate, because its individualization is assured, and they who take responsibility for the care of pets exercise true love, for these little creatures have nothing to give in return but their devotion, and that is truly blessed.

We are here tonight but for a few minutes, because you, Frater, are truly not Well. We recommend a day or two of real rest and relaxation. The work will go on the better for it. Do not work afternoons tomorrow, Saturday, or Monday, either at the office or at home. By then this low energy period will have passed, and you all three are not relaxing enough. If you can manage a day or so away from everything it will do you good. Remember that these bodies of yours are our instruments, and that your Minds need some variety as well as your bodies.

(H. said here: "But we did have a mighty good time Monday!")

It would be good to repeat that soon. Such simple enjoyments are always beneficial. The average occultist is too afraid of pleasure. As we write this, we enjoy the artless fun of your little dogs as much as do you. One of the reasons for their liveliness is that there is naturally a strong radiation from us to and through you, which they feel, and their exuberance is a consequence of that. Never fear that they will ever disturb us.

We are glad to note that all of you are really working at the basic things which promote inner harmony, and we have nothing to add to what we have suggested hitherto. It won't be so very long before we can give you

Text and comment again, but you must all be in better condition. Both of you, Sorores, are too sympathetic with our Frater; not that you should love him less, but you need to discriminate between sympathy and compassion. Do not take on his condition. He is often under attack from our common enemy, because what he has to do is really important. Do not, then, permit yourselves, by undue concern, to let his depressions affect you adversely. Delicately balanced mechanisms fluctuate easily; do not take on his conditions, we repeat, and do not be too much concerned. Let him find his own equilibrium. He usually does you know. Hands, and tongues off is a good procedure.

(Ann **asks** if her depressions are due to health or psychic attack?)

Yes, and Soror H. gets much the same, except that in her case it often takes the form of self-depreciation. For an Aries she is surprisingly modest. Just lie down and relax for 5 minutes, and think of us at such times. Take your rest now, and next time we hope to be longer with you.

Sub Umbra Alarum Tuarum, IHVH. Vale.

FORTY-THIRD COMMUNICATION

Monday, April 5, 1948 8:15 P.M.

Before we give you the Text on the 31st Path, read the section of the 32 Paths which deals with it, either in Waite, Westcott or Stenring; perhaps a comparison of these will help.

(We do this.)

Now follows a section of the Text:

The 31st Path is a Path of Fire, and a Path of the Ruach Elohim, for Fire and Spirit are one, and this is a Path of the letter Sheen, which is the 3rd of the 3 Mothers. ThMIDI is it called, because it is the perfection of the handiwork of the Eternal. This may you see in the name itself, for the first two letters, Tav and Mem, spell Thum, which is perfection; the second two spell ID, which is the name for hand; and the last is the letter which representeth Kether and Chokmah, for the Fire of Spirit *is* the root of fire which appertaineth unto Chokmah, and this is that Consuming Fire which is God Himself. It is the Fire of Mind which divideth itself into the semblance of duality, and in its descent into manifestation bringeth forth bodies. Being Eternal, it is also Superior, and thus it is written that it regulateth the motions of Shamash and Lebanah, the Sun and the Moon. The Sun is Tiphareth, and the Moon is Yesod, on the Tree, among the Sephiroth. Thus may you know that the 31st Path hath to do with the regulation of the powers of Ruach and Nephesh. They among the Sons of the Doctrine who hide their meaning behind the veils of the work of Hermes, say that theirs is a work of the Sun and Moon, performed by the aid of Mercury. *See* then, that on the Tree, this is the Path which hath the Kingdom of the body at its lower extremity, and the Sphere of Mercury at its upper, for the work of the 31st Path is that of the woman who is the Moon, and the man who is the Sun, and from this work cometh forth the child which is the new creature. For this is a work of embodiment, and not without its proper body may the Perpetual Intelligence be made manifest. Yet is that body one of flesh and blood, but different from those which come forth from the womb of ordinary birth. It is a body incorruptible, though the seed of it is sown in corruption. Yet it is truly a Perpetual body, transmuted from the ordinary body that cometh through the gate of birth. But without the aid of Mercury, this transmutation may not be effected, for this body taketh one out of the flux and reflux of birth and death, and truly is it a work of art wherein the powers of Sun and Moon, or Ruach and Nephesh, are conjoined in full perfection. Not by inheritance is this accomplished, but by the working of a power descending through the Paths on the side of Binah, and as may be seen on the Tree, all the Paths on the side of Binah have their beginning in the Path of Beth, which is that of Mercury or Kokab. For every man there shall come a time to begin his work of release from the delusion of separate personality, and from the shackles of times, seasons and places. But this cometh not in the lesser wheeling's of nature, and hath always its beginning in an influx from above.

Yet for long shall it seem to him to whom this influx hath descended, that he is of his own will and seeking release, but truly this is not so. The fire consumeth what it will, the Breath of Spirit bloweth where it listeneth, nor is there any law discernible by man to govern its operation. Its work is without beginning or end, never doth it fail in anything small or great, yet is there in it no trace of what man meaneth by plan, or law, or design. Freely it works, and thus it is written of the Sephiroth that "belimah," which signifieth "something not to be expressed, and something altogether free from bonds or encirclement of any kind." Waste not thy strength in trying to comprehend this. Know it thou mayest but grasp it thou canst not.

So far the Text.

We shall give you the comment next time. By then you will have had time to read and ponder it. One thing only may be worth noting now; it has direct bearing on what you were discussing just before we came in: Our work is still unusually demanding, and the powers of darkness mass their forces daily more vehemently. Do not let this depress you. That is why we have counseled plenty of rest, and this should still be part of your intelligent self-direction, for presently you will have need of strength to help others; at least you have some measure of certainty that wisdom is at work behind the scenes. So must you keep poised, for few have even so much evidence as you do.

Vale, Sub Umbra Alarum Tuarum, IHVH.

No Communication - hostile force.   Thursday April 8

FORTY-FOURTH COMMUNICATION

Monday, April 12, 1948 8:10 P.M.

Ave Frater et Sorores.

Thursday there was a strong concentration of hostile force which you, Frater, felt first, and which was the exciting cause of the behavior of the dogs. It was also the reason we made no attempt to come in. You should not be disturbed or worried about such manifestations, for they are to be expected whenever any serious attempt to do this work is undertaken with any measure of success. Ineffectual dabblers seldom have such experiences, though they often are confused by mischievous interference. So much, by way of explaining last week's phenomena.

The Text is obscure, of course, like most of its kind intentionally so, in part, because it is the unfailing policy of the Wise to require competence from those who receive their instruction. But apart from this, the subject matter requires a special vocabulary so to say, and one must be well-versed in these unusual forms of expression to grasp their full purport. You will do better to read them not together, but each for himself. The words do not so much convey the meaning as set-up trains of association which make the meaning unfold almost by itself; at least that is our experience, and we think that you will find it so also.

As students of our Rota, you should find this easier than would many, in as much as it was to supplement such cryptic writing that the Keys were first invented. Thus in the Text we gave you, understand the man and the woman to be the two shown in "Judgment." They are of course the alchemical King and Queen, but the woman is more to be identified with Yesod than with Malkuth, as the Text indicates. In one sense any lunar symbol is related to Yesod, and any solar symbol to Tiphareth. So that

265

what is pictured in this Key, since it belongs to the Path of Sheen, indicates a special aspect of the relation between Tiphareth and Yesod, or Ruach and Nephesh, and also the outcome of that relationship, which is symbolized by the child. Of course the general principle has many particular applications in practical work of self-unfoldment. The applications are sufficiently indicated in the lessons already written, so there is no need for repetition.

In the more specific alchemical application 7 in which, by the way, Eliphas Levi was right, in spite of Brother Waite's assertion to the effect that there is no connection between Paths of Wisdom and alchemy—this 31st Path has to do with the alchemical Sun and Moon as they are at work in the hidden laboratory, and the secret vessels. And even this application has many ramifications. It applies to the work of those who conduct the experiment alone, but it also applies to those who undertake the joint operational though there are of course few who are in a position to do this latter, because it requires rigorous training, and unusual circumstances, in these days at least. Do not expect us to give you formulas for any of these operations. The Text contains the principle behind all variations of practice, and if you combine it, and this admittedly very brief comment, with study of the Key, you will each learn what you require, though it may be that for each of you the instruction you receive from within, in response to the stimulus afforded by the words of the Text and the symbolism of the Key, will differ from what either of the others receive, and may turn out to be, nay, almost certainly will turn out to be incommunicable, so that you cannot share your knowledge with one another at the level of verbal expression.

This is one of the most recondite Paths, and the paucity of gematria is intentional. If you can take what the Text says about Thum, and ID, and the letter Yod, you may find clues to deeper understanding. Do not forget that the letter Yod is also connected with the Hermit. One hint more: ThM is Tav Mem, that is 440, and the essence of this number is 8, the value of Cheth, so that Key 7 may be taken as representing this part of ThMID. Then ID, have you ever noticed, being 14 is a veil for ZHB, Zahab, the alchemical gold. But since the essence of 14 is 5, these two letters can be represented by Heh, or the Emperor, so that in Rota you have Key 7 for ThM, Key 4 for ID, and Key 9 for the final Yod. Add these and the result will show you what Levi correctly identified as the Rota symbol for the first matter (7, 4, 9 = 20) which is the very key illustrating Shin and the 31st Path. He also said the same thing of the Devil; see if you can discover the connection. This is enough for tonight.

Sub Umbra Alarum Tuarum, IHVH. Vale.

360 = Sheen
160 = Ayin
420 - 6 = Tiphareth & Vav, the Hierophant

6= The Lovers 15 = The Devil 20 = Judgment
41 - 5 = Heh, the Emperor

1 to 5 = 15, the Devil, and extension of Hierophant Devil and Hierophant added: 15 + 5 = 20

Daleth 3 x 5 = 15, the Devil Heh 4 x 5 = 20, Judgment

Beth = 417

No Communication   Thursday, April 15 8:00 P.M.

No Communication   Monday, April 19 8:15 P.M.

No Communication   Thursday, April 22 8:05 P.M.

No Communication   Monday, April 26 8:00 P.M.

FORTY-FIFTH COMMUNICATION

Thursday, April 29, 1948 8:08 P.M

Ave. Frater et Sorores.

You have been very patient, and we come tonight to let you know we have been aware of your faithful adherence to the time set for communications. Would that we could go on now with the Text and comment, but, as you have guessed, we find ourselves with many pressing undertakings, not exactly unforeseen, but requiring even more of unremitting attention than even we foresaw. For you must remember that we are by no means omniscient, or even wholly aware of the shape of things to come. For us, as for you, the details are often hidden until the event.

Yet we are taking a little while tonight to tell you that the future is less forbidding than it was a month hence. "Ago," we meant to say. Your English idiom still has its difficulties even though we have followed its development since the days of Shakespeare, who was not Francis Bacon any more than Bacon was your present writer. And though it may seem a needless thing to say, the good Saint Alban would turn in his grave (except that being safely canonized, he is not likely to give any attention to such nonsense) if he were to learn that he has been identified with such a worldling as myself.

(A. said laughing, "The Boss calls himself a worldling!")

Of course I do. For what is this all about if it be not for the world, and of the world? Do you not read that the motive for the greatest of dramas was that God loved the world? And if He loved it, where do they stand who hate it?

(H. said, "That is what is said in the Lord's prayer, 'Thy will be done'")

Precisely Soror, so I, when I make my now infrequent appearances, am always taken for what in truth I really am, a man of the world. Not exactly as hard-boiled, perhaps, as Sister Ann. Not even a passable Blue-beard, for despite my not very good likeness, and your own recollection, Frater P., I now go clean shaven, and I do not rid myself of my beard by magic. As a matter of fact, I belong, like yourself, to the vast host who call upon the name of the King – King C., to be specific.

Does all this seem to be rather frivolous and unlike what one might expect from a member of the Lodge? Well, I am taking this for a time of refreshment.

(H. said, "Aren't you glad we have a sense of humor, and don't take you too solemnly?")

Of course I am, and that we have these lighter moments should show you that you really enjoy my confidence. Perhaps I need not tell you to keep it entre nous.

Just how soon we can go on with our Text is problematic.

(H. said, "I am sorry that I have to be away 6 weeks, and thus delay the communications.")

It is most necessary, and on your return we hope to get back to the interrupted work.

Just a word now for you, Frater P. Do not let a sense of pressure overtake you concerning the Second Order. On the other hand, begin tomorrow to do something each day. Let the old Scotch proverb prove itself: "Many a mickle makes a muckle."

You three are doing well at ripening your inner rapport. Keep at it. Already this house is beginning to make itself felt. None come here who do not feel it more or less, and during this coming year many will come of whom as yet you have not even heard.

(A. said, "We ought to invite the Boss to come in person.")

I am "in person," this minute.

(A. said, "I meant physically.")

But it may be years before any of you *see* me face to face, for the needs of Europe and the Near East require my bodily presence. This is beyond your present range of knowledge, and you will be well advised not to speculate about it overmuch. So many things seem mysterious from the point of view even of such faithful and competent students as yourselves. All we can say is keep on doing what you know as well as you can, and this is really the shortest road to greater knowledge.

Our blessing, as always, goes with you.

Sub Umbra Alarum Tuarum, IHVH.
Vale, Frater et Sorores.

No Communication   Monday, May 3

No Communication   Thursday, May 6

No Communication   Thursday, June 24

Did not sit, it being
"Day C"   Monday, June 28

FORTY-SIXTH COMMUNICATION

Thursday, July 1, 1948 8:00 P.M.

Ave Frater et Sorores.

(A. said, as the planchette began to move, "Oh good.")

Do not rejoice too soon, Soror, we have established contact tonight to save you wonder and disappointment, but for the next 7 weeks, we have much demanding our continual supervision, and you on your side are faced with more than enough work during your days, so that it is too great a strain to use even two nights a week for anything in addition to your mounting tasks.

We chose to come tonight, because we would let you know we share your satisfaction over the events of "Day C." And also to let you know we are in full accord with your intention to set up the Chapter in a location which may be used more intensively. You had our help with this house, it will not be lacking in the other matter. So, 7 weeks from tonight we shall resume our work with Text and Comment. By that time you will see many interesting developments, both in your Chapter, and in the world, which will show you the wisdom of our present decision.

One thing we would impress on you, though you may wonder at it now: do not bring Hubert into these sessions, or discuss them with him. He can keep nothing from his wife, and she lacks basic understanding of the work we are doing through you.

We know you understand the main points of what you are to do together, and there is no need to repeat instruction already given. On one point that may have arisen in your thought recently, perhaps it will suffice to say, that in any magical operation, clarity of purpose and unbroken direction of force are paramount. These being established, there never need be anything rigid or stereotyped in details of performance. Of course with group work, patterns are less flexible, but in any work not stylized into formal ritual, the thing to remember is that magic liberates, it does not impose burdens. This you will find it well to remember, also, now that a considerable group, none of whom have much acquaintance even with the theory of magic, will have to begin learning the rudiments of its practice. To say more seems unnecessary at this time. We wanted to reassure you that what you are doing meets with our approval, and this night, 7 weeks, we shall pick up the dropped threads of our project.

Sub Umbra Alarum Tuarum, IHVH.
Vale, Frater et Sorores.

Sat 8 evenings, but no Communications.

FORTY-SEVENTH COMMUNICATION

Thursday, September 23, 1948 8:04 P.M.

Ave Frater et Sorores.

This will be very brief because we came only to reassure you. To give you any idea of the tremendous difficulty of the world situation would take many hours of this kind of writing. But it is not only the world crisis, but also your own private difficulties that have decided us not to put an extra burden of the Text and Comment we began, on you at this time.

Today you have at last correctly interpreted the inner pressure we have been exerting to get you to use a truly practiced method for the work. You are not trained printers, and even the best of the machines you had in mind, would have been both too expensive to run, and too demanding on the technical side. Now, however, you have a chance to catch up with the back work, though it will take you the rest of the year to get really clear enough to consider some additional material.

You see we do keep our hands off most of the time, though we have been trying to open your mental eyes on this for some weeks. Now we think it best for all concerned to communicate only fortnightly, beginning the Thursday after our Frater's birthday. We may not at first be able to spend much time, but you will hear from us every other Thursday without fail by this means, and while H. is with you, you may hear also through him. Better not tell him so, you will then have no doubts if we chose (sic) that means.

Bless you all, you are making great endeavors in the adjustments necessary for the work, and we are more than pleased.

Vale, Frater et Sorores.

No Communication Thursday, October 7

FORTY-EIGHTH COMMUNICATION

Thursday, October 21, 1948 8:00 P.M.

Ave Frater et Sorores.

Two weeks ago the psychic conditions were unfavorable, partly because with all his good points, Hubert attracts a good many astral tramps which he is unable to distinguish from those who really have something to say, and this atmosphere affects any place where he may be. But his attendant atmosphere was not the only difficulty. You three were by no means up to par a fortnight ago, although it has taken almost that entire time to focus in the colds and aches that have afflicted you the last few days, so none of you were in good condition to receive. More than this, the general psychic disturbances of the race mind interfere, to say nothing of the emotional tensions of the political scene. The world, alas, is still at war, openly and secretly, and it begins to look as if the American scene is to be not too bright in the immediate future. Part is karmic, of course, because real intelligence could have avoided the last outbreak of violence, and proper understanding would never have permitted the lie of military necessity to serve as a weak excuse for such horrors as Nagasaki and Hiroshima. The war could have been stopped by another sort of demonstration, and that has to be paid for.

We do not, as you know, interfere with the course of events, except in circumstances where intervention is the last resort. Our business is to do all that we can to awaken man to his real place in the cosmic order, and his consequent destiny. But the dead weight of ignorance is hard to lift. Thus it seems just now that America may have to go through some pretty dreadful experiences before the people wake up. Awake they certainly are not now, in spite of all the efforts to extend the Light. This makes work for us that you cannot begin to imagine.

275

We are after all, a small minority, even though we can exert unusual powers. This keeps us continually busy trying to relieve the situation, even though so few understand what is really wrong.

Your own work will now soon profit from your satisfactory solution of the mechanical problem, but in the meantime you are far behind schedule, and so not in any position to undertake the preparation of new material. After the New Year, things will be better in that respect, but until then you have all you can do to make up lost ground. So far as your little group here is concerned, you are doing well, all things considered, but you may profit by reminding yourselves more often that you three together are one of our active points of contact with the world, so that even what may seem to be just day to day routine, has deeper values than may appear. You, Frater, are so depleted just now, that it will not do to subject you longer to a strain of communication. Next time we expect you to be in better condition, and we shall then have more to say.

Vale.

FORTY-NINTH COMMUNICATION

Thursday, November 4, 1948 8:00 P.M.

Ave Frater et Sorores.

(H. had asked if They had had anything to do with the election.)

Yes, we helped in the election. Not, by influencing anyone's decision as to how to vote, for we never work that way, but by sending into the Group Mind of the American people the determination to get the facts and act on them without much reference to radio, advertising, editorials or polls. We are, as you know, just as much as ever on the side of the common people, for many of us in this incarnation came from that great source of power. It happens that my body sprang from a more privileged group, as the world counts privilege, but I can assure you that its heredity and early environment were hindrances rather than helps. I always cringe a little when some Theosophist speaks with bated breath of "the Master, the Prince." If I were really the reincarnation of Francis Bacon, or of St. Alban, that would be something else. But the noble line of Rakoczy, except for one great liberator, call for low breath only because one does not commonly speak too loud about unpleasant things!

(H. interpolated here that those ancient Hungarian and Balkan families were not much better than mountain bandits in olden times.)

Exactly! One might as well be proud of descent from Al Capone! The result of the election does not mean however that all will be easy and pleasant. What is ahead, is, as we have said before, not known as yet even to most of us. But it was necessary, if it could be accomplished without coercion, to put a party in power having at least some notion of human rights apart from the selfish interests of a moribund capitalism. Not that the foreign policy, if it can be dignified by that name, of the Democrats is much to the point. You will *see* in the next two years that neither the Marshall Plan, nor the Truman Doctrine, will do much for

World Peace. What is even more important just now is the domestic situation in America. Had that been at the mercy of the reactionaries, they would have had to throw the world into a war to avoid revolution at home, and the policy-makers among them were prepared to do just that, in order to have the excuse of national security to set up a police state. We think we may be able to help the President escape from the presently too strong influence of military advisors, and unless General Marshall changes his mind, there is prospect of having a civilian at the head of the State Department.

What needs all the influence you, and other like-minded people can bring to bear, is: whatever will strengthen the U.N. That is our own project, and has been since before the day of Columbus.

(H. asks, "Will Russia feel less worried about us now that the Republican reactionaries were beaten at the polls?")

No. Because Russia has as little faith in Democrats as in Republicans. What will be one result is that Stalin, who is not by any means a muddy thinker, will very well understand that America is not going Fascist, and that American labor and farmers really exert power. It will be hard to overcome Marxist prejudice, for Stalin is essentially the High Priest of a religion, and all religions have a common weakness: their adherents fear everybody who does not agree with them. Stalin and the Russian Marxists are no exception. What is a mistake is to suppose that all Russians are of the same opinion. Most Russians are close to fanaticism in their love of Russia, and while they fear the U.S.A. they will go on being suspicious. Of course the Russian government is Marxist, and this emphasizes both the fear and the suspicion, with results that have already been obvious. The sad thing is that reactionaries and cynical self-seekers in this country have been able to arouse corresponding fears of Russia and its economic theories in America. The witch-hunting is not ended unfortunately, and it is a plain statement of fact to say that we are more gravely concerned about fear and suspicion in the American mind, than about almost any other element of the present situation.

If the U.S. can wake up to its real opportunity to establish better conditions for minority groups, much will be done by that alone to overcome Russian suspicion; and like suspicions elsewhere in the world, where men, just trying the wings of freedom, are wondering about the discrepancies between American words and American actions... It may surprise you to be told that the greater part of the work of the Lodge is concentrated on America rather than on Europe or the Orient.

(A. wondered why, and H. said, "We have a job to do.")

Yes. It is American destiny to lead, and she can do this because there are more favorable conditions here than anywhere else to establish a truly enlightened public opinion, unhampered by the artificial jealousies and hates of Europe and Asia.

So this is why we have postponed our excursion into the Qabalah. That's all very useful and interesting, but you nor your students need it now. Nearly so much as you need to put all your spiritual force behind the idea of One World, in which America, by deeds, as well as words, shows that the way to freedom is wide open for all who are willing to walk in it. For this you have had more than adequate training, and to do your part in this is now a matter of greatest importance.

Vale.

HISTORICAL NOTE

The U.N. voted Israel a state on November 29, 1947. The British left Israel on May 14, 1948.

War broke out in the Mid-East on May 15, 1948. Cease fire on June 11, 1948 One week of fighting broke out again.

Fighting ended January 7, 1949.

A peace treaty was signed with Egypt on February 24, 1949, with Lebanon on May 23, 1949, with Jordan on April 3, 1949, with Syria on July 20, 1949.

These are Ann Davies' notes, apparently compiled from the L.A. Public Library by telephone. They are in reference to the Master R. 's comments in the latter Communications about the world situation, and the Middle East in particular (Comm. #45). It would appear that his work in this area was the main reason that the Communications were discontinued.

Appendix III:
The Grade Structure of the Order

Third Order:

Second Order:
7=4 Adeptus Exemptus
6=5 Adptus Major
5=6 Adeptus Minor

First Order:
4=7 Philosophus
3=8 Practicus
2=9 Theoricus
1=10 Zelator
0=0 Neophyte

.

Appendix IV:
The Fruits of Adeptship:

No clearer statement of the position of the Chiefs of the R.O. of A.O. could well be made. It says the work of the Order leads straight to adeptship. With this in mind, those who wish to form some notion of just what kind of adeptship it leads to, should consider the following:

During the winter of 1922-1923, the Chiefs of A-TOUM Temple, No. 20, Los Angeles, California, announced that they had received from London some new lessons on the Qabalah. From these, they said, they were permitted to select certain more or less exoteric matter, which they would give in a series of public talks. Members of A-TOUM Temple were urged to bring prospective Candidates to these public meetings, so that the taste of Qabalistic doctrine there given might arouse an appetite for further knowledge, and thus lead to an increase in the membership of the Temple. The lessons were not supposed to be part of the A.O. curriculum; but it was intimated that they were written by the G.H. Head of the Order, Soror Vestigia Nulla Restorum. Thus they were invested with the prestige of high Rosicrucian authorship. Such was the claim. The facts are as follows:

Six copies of these lessons are in my possession. All but one contain extensive plagiarism-not from any ancient source, but from books by modem writers. The books are listed below, and the numbers in parenthesis indicate the number of thefts from each:

a. "Tarot of the Bohemians", by Papus (3)
b. "Numbers; Their Meaning and Magic", by Isidore Kozminsky (4)
c. "Pictorial Key to the Tarot," A. E. Waite (1)
d. "Introduction to the Study of the Tarot," Paul F. Case (1)
e. "Hidden Way Across the Threshold", J. C. Street (2)

These plagiarisms are not small speculations. In some instances whole paragraphs have been stolen without the alteration of a single word. The thefts from Doctor Kozminsky are thinly disguised, perhaps because he is (or was, at last accounts, a V. H. Frater of the A.O.).

Practically all matter having a direct bearing on the Qabalah is from books of Papus and Case. A whole lesson, dated Dec. 28, 1922, is from Street's "Hidden Way." It is copied without change from pages 46 to 49, beginning at the 5th paragraph on page 46, and ending with the last paragraph on page 49. The 3rd and 4th paragraphs on page 48 were not copied into the lesson.

Judging from the amount of material stolen from his book, the compiler of these lessons regards Street as a great Qabalist. He was really a Spiritualist. The "Hidden Way" is an anti-Theosophical volume, written to combat the work of Madame Blavatsky. It is a hotch-podge of quotations, thrown together helter-skelter, which betrays the ignorance of its compiler on every page. Street's claims to consideration as a Qabalist may be judged from the following quotations:

On page 200 he defines Sephiroth as "Elementals of the Astral World," declares that they "are both finite and infinite," and then says, "They are Harmonies Divine, Creative Wisdom and Conceiving Intellect." In other words, he teaches that "Creative Wisdom and Conceiving Intellect" are "Astral Elementals," and that these "finite and infinite" existences are "Sephiroth."

On page 99 he mentions "the ancient Sanskrit of the Jews." One need not be an occultist to know that Jews never had Sanskrit, either ancient or modern.

From such an (!), authority whose book betrays him as a blatant pretender, unable to write correct English, the Head of the R.O. of A.O. steals a whole lesson of what she is pleased to call Qabalah. That is, the statements of the Chiefs of the A-TOUM Temple point to the G. H. Soror V. N. R. as being not only a plagiarist, but a very silly and bungling one. If the Chiefs of A-TOUM did not get their "Qabalah" lessons from London, but compiled them themselves, then they have lied about V.N.R., and are guilty not only of literary larceny, but of dragging the good name of the Head of the Order into the mire.

In three instances, these thefts are from living writers, of whom two were once members of the A.O., while the other (Kozminsky) was at last reports head of an Australian Temple. He from whom the greatest number of paragraphs has been purloined is one whose studies of Rosicrucian sources made him so dangerous to the A.O. that V.N.R. expelled him. She did so because the Imperatrix of the Thoth-Hermes Temple informed her that Frater Perseverantia (Paul Case) doubted the claims of the A.O. Her letter of excommunication states explicitly that Fra. Perseverantia's name is erased from the rolls of "my (!) Order" because he has expressed doubt-not for any other cause. Yet the Chiefs of Thoth-Hermes have permitted, if they have not encouraged, the circulation of false reports as to the reasons for that expulsion. While the Chiefs of A-Toum commit, or connive at, a clumsy theft of Perseverantia's Qabalistic knowledge, the Chiefs of Thoth-Hermes permit their members to believe frightful tales about his "black magic" and his exposure of A.O. secrets. One set of Chiefs robs, and the other set slanders or permits to be slandered, a man whose Rosicrucian "crime" was the honest expression of doubt.

Again, the V.H. Soror Non Mihi Solum has mis-stated facts in regard to the disposition of Second Order books formerly belonging to her brother. She says, "At his death , through an absolutely blameless mistake, all his work-all the MSS of the Second Order, always so carefully guarded by him-were sent by his executors to our then Cancellarius, a man who, I truly believe, knew less about the work and meaning of it than any member now present. Not realizing, not understanding either rules or dangers, he permitted all his work to become practically public to members of the Second Order, regardless of their Grades! To this fact I attribute all our recent troubles."

Soror N.M.S. speaks what is false. She knows it is false, and so does every Second Order member. The books were not sent to the Cancellarius through any mistake of her brother's executors. They were sent to the Cancellarius because the rules of the A.O. made him the custodian of ALL books left after the death of any member. The mistakes if any, in giving out the books, were not made by the Cancellarius. The only MSS which any member of the Second Order had access to were such as belonged to Grades which all then in the Second Order had attained-with just two exceptions. These two MSS were given to Fra. Perseverantia by the Imperatrix's brother himself, before he left for California, so that Fra. Perseverantia might use the knowledge they contained to assist him in his work as SubPraemonstrator.

The V. H. Soror strives to create the impression that misuse of magical formulas in these MSS caused the trouble. To do so, she has to slander a man who stood by her when his closest friends had given up the A.O. in disgust. At the period she mentions, he had done more work, and had studied more Second Order texts than she. At that time, in fact, no Second Order member knew less of the theory and practice of the A.O. work than Soror Non Mihi Solum. Without cramming she could not have passed some of the First Order tests.

Her fantastic interpretation of the A.O. troubles is merely amusing; but were there any truth in it, the blame must rest with S.R.M.D. and V.N.R. Not until V. H. Soror Nunc et Semper wrote to Sub Spe for a list, did Thoth-Hermes, the oldest Temple in America, have any definite information as to what MSS were in the Second Order curriculum, the sequence in which they were to be studied, or what examinations were to be taken by Second Order members. Michael Whitty died without ever knowing though he had asked S.R.M.D. and V.N.R. for this information, over and over again. That the Chiefs of Thoth-Hermes have it now is due solely to Nunc et Semper's determination to have some semblance of system in the work.

Soror N.M.S. asserts that the A.O. curriculum is the straightest road to adeptship. The facts recited herein show that either the Head of the A.O., or the Chiefs of A-Toum Temple, are adept at stealing other men's thoughts and words (Perhaps just a little too clumsy to be called "adepts"). Careful study of Soror Non Mihi Solum's words indicates that she is rapidly becoming adept in the perversion of facts, and in the use of suggestion to arouse the emotions of her hearers so that their judgment may be warped by sentiment. This attempt to sway the imagination of her Fratres and Sorores is a true example of "black magic." She says all knowledge is collected in the A.O. curriculum. How does she know? Who but one who consciously possess ALL knowledge can say this truthfully. Is the V.H. Imperatrix ready to claim omniscience, ready to set herself on the throne of the Lord of the Universe? She says the A.O. work is such that a student may become an adept in one lifetime. As a matter of fact, she has never known an adept, is not an adept herself (not even an A.O. "Adept" in the strict sense), and when she states these things is guilty of false pretense by using for a belief the form of words which is proper for nothing other than the declaration of positive knowledge.

Do you aspire to adeptship in plagiarism? Do you accept the "spiritual" guidance of Chiefs who blacken a former Frater's reputation with one hand and steal his ideas and words with the other? Have you sufficient regard for your mental and spiritual health to do a little research work-to read the article on Dr. Dee in Lewis Spence's "Encyclopedia of Occultism," and "A True and Faithful Relation of What Passed between Dr. John Dee and Some Spirits?" You can find both books in the New York Public Library. They prove, up to the hilt, Frater Perseverantia's contention (which has never been answered by the present Head of the Order) that the Tablets of Earth, Air, Water and Fire used in the A.O. Rituals from 1=10 to 4=7 are not of Rosicrucian origin, but were made known to the world through the slaying of a tricky medium (Kelly) who had his ears cut off for counterfeiting. These tablets form the pivot around which the whole practical magic of the A.O. revolves. Through Kelly, Dr. Dee received them from a supposed "angelic" being, who also told Dee that he and Kelly should share their wives.

Your Imperatrix warns you to study nothing but the A.O. curriculum. Why? Because if you do, sooner or later you will find out that you are caught in the meshes of a lying imposter. You have taken an obligation to your own Higher Soul, an obligation more binding than any given to the Chiefs of an Outer Order. Keep it. It is your duty to find out whether I have stated facts in this letter. This is an attack on your Chiefs and on your beliefs. I tell you that you are fighting on the side of the powers of darkness, that your strength and time and energy are being expended to further the destructive forces of the Pit. I tell you that you are being guided by men and women guilty of theft and falsehood. You cannot dismiss this letter with a shrug of disbelief. It is too specific. If you want further details, you can have them. If you want to be led by the nose, you can have that, too. Are you one of those who can be fooled all of the time, or do you stand on your own feet and think for yourself?

Yours sincerely, Perseverantia

I retain my motto, because it still expresses my highest aspiration, and because I know, that having taken it in good faith, and having received initiation in good faith, too, I have through it made contact with the Invisible Order of which the A.O. is a paltry counterfeit.

Appendix V:

A List of Mottos:

1. Perseverantia – Paul Foster Case
2. Resurgam – Ann Davies
3. Sapere Aude – William Wynn Westcott
4. 'S Rioghail Mo Dhream – S.L. MacGregor Mathers
5. Doe Duce Comite Ferro – S.L. MacGregor Mathers
6. Vestigia Nulla Restorum – Moina Mathers
7. Sanctum Regnum – A.E. Waite
8. Deo Non Fortuna – Dion Fortune
9. Gnoscente et Serviente – Michael Whitty
10. Unitas – Elsa Barker
11. Heraclion – Charles Lockwood
12. Pophra – E. Daniell Lockwood
13. Nunc et Semper – Lilli Geise
14. Vota Vita Mea – Howard Underhill
15. Aude Sapere – Elma Dame
16. Honore et Virtute – Dr. T.B. Kenny
17. Non Mihi Solum – Mrs. Gertrude Wise

Appendix VI:
Select Bibliography of Paul Case

Current Curriculum of B.O.T.A.
- Seven Steps in Practical Occultism.
- Introduction to Tarot.
- Tarot Fundamentals.
- Tarot Interpretation.
- The Master Pattern.
- The Tree of Life.
- 32 Paths of Wisdom.
- Sound & Color: A Correlation.
- The Great work: Spiritual Alchemy.
- Esoteric Astrology.
- The Oracle of Tarot.

Included in B.O.T.A. curriculum circa 1969
- The Magical Language

Published by the Fraternity of the Hidden Light
- Occult Fundamentals & Spiritual Unfoldment (Formally Sections A&B)
  Published 2007
- Secrets of Meditation & Magic: (Formally Sections C&D)
  Published 2008

Other Courses:
- The Extension of the First Year Course.

Books:
- The Kybalion. (By three Initiates) (1912)
- An Introduction to the Study of the Tarot. (1920)
- A Brief Analysis of the Tarot. (1927)
- Tarot: Key to the Wisdom of the Ages. (1947)
- The Rosicrucian Order. (circa. 1927)
- The Book of Tokens.
- Daniel: Master of Magicians. (circa 1935)
- The Masonic Letter "G". (circa 1935)
- The Great Seal of the United States.
- The True & Invisible Rosicrucian Order. (Editions: 1927; 1928; 1933; 1981)
- The Name of Names.

289

Periodicals:
- "Tarot," in *"The Word."* (1916).
- "Article on Tarot in *"AZOTH"* (1918).
- Various Articles in *"AZOTH,"* under various pseudonyms.
- Articles in *"Wheel of Life."*

Unpublished:
- The Life Power.
- The Flaming Cube of the Chaldees.
- The Cube of Space.

Appendix VII: Paul Case as a Priest

Appendix VIII: Letters to Israel Regardie

2380 Monterey Road San Marino, Cal. January 15, 1933

Care Frater:

Thank you for putting me in touch with Miss Hughes. She has sent me a very interesting and understanding letter, to which I have answered at some length. I concede the value of your testimony that no harm has come to yourself, or to members of the English Temples you are familiar with, through the use of the Enochian material. Yet I might say that I still believe the Enochian stuff perhaps more subtly harmful than appears even from such experiments. If the Order's method of evoking the elementals were purely Enochian, then I should have nothing to say. But since it is a mixture of the Enochian language and tablets with other, and probably older, materials, it seems not unlikely to me that such success as attends the use of the rituals is due rather to the real effectiveness of the various pentagrams, etc., than to anything else.

At any rate, I have found by experiments carried out now for more than seven years, that the elementals can be invoked precisely as well without the Enochian tablets or names. Instead of the latter, we have used Hebrew divine and angelic names, with unusually good results.

You may be very sure that my objections are not to ceremonial. It is only that I have had so much experience of the subtle dangers of corrupt ceremonial, that I prefer to be what seems to me on the safe side by eliminating from the rituals something that is certainly suspect as coming from a dubious source, by no means clearly connected with "Rosicrucianism." Evidently Miss Hughes has some doubts similar to mine, for she writes me that she would be glad to have some assurance that the "Enochian language" is really a language at all!

Of course, too, I know that one does not swallow the Qabalah whole. My Warsaw edition of the Sepher Yetzirah, with comment by Saadia Gayon and others, is sufficiently full of grotesqueries. Yet it has a kernel of real value, as have even some parts of the works you mention. If I could find anything beyond the subconscious and complex elaboration of a dubious, if not false, premise in the Enochian magical methods, perhaps I would use them too. But after about thirty-three years of research and experiment, I begin to be somewhat wary.

As to Tattvas, it is true enough that the Order work with them is not from "Nature's Finer Forces." I don't know who worked out that scheme, which is rather less effective than some of the Tantrik practices it closely resembles. But what has it to do with Qabalah, or with anything announced in the "Fama" or "Confession" as Rosicrucian philosophy or practice? Again, like the Enochian system, it seems to me to have been lugged in by the heels. And I have had enough experience of the inventiveness of charlatans to find it easier to believe that Mathers invented the Tattva technique, or adapted it from some obscure Hindu treatise, than to suppose it to be something transmitted from the Third Order. Even Spencer Lewis has managed to work out some surprisingly plausible formulas; but the presence of those formulas in his system does not convince me he is the "only true channel" of Rosicrucian instruction in America.

The Scottish Rite Library in Washington has some interesting early Rosicruciana written by Kenneth Mackenzie. Some years ago, in searching through the material, I got on the track of the hints that led me to believe that our Order rituals must be in some sense an adaptation or expansion of rituals used by some society in the days of Lytton, Levi, Hockley and Spedalieri. More recently, in the library of the Massachusetts Grand Lodge, I came upon a French ritual of the 33 degree, which contains not a little material closely resembling some of the magical work studied by Z.A.M. members.

Roughly, what I think of the G.D., as it developed in the hands of Woodman, Westcott and Mathers, is that it was based on earlier rituals (or outlines of rituals) which were probably dug up somewhere by that indefatigable library-hound, Mathers. I fully believe that the "Tree of Life" outline is workable, and that the Grade scheme must adhere to it. I know that the 0=0 and Vault rituals are magically effective. So are the opening and closing ceremonies of the Grades from 1=10 to 4=7, inclusive (with or without the Enochian additions.)

It has been my experience that whatever the Third Order may be, it sometimes operates in what to us may seem to be very devious ways—using what tools present themselves, whether or not those tools be ideal. Thus my feeling about the Order as it stands is that it is certainly in the line of the ancient tradition, but that it also is cluttered up with a lot of material which may, some of it, be well enough, but which does not really belong in the Order system.

As for the Knowledge Lectures, they are of various worth. Those on astrology are probably the worst presentation of that abused art that I have ever encountered. I have never yet known anyone to make even respectable progress in astrology from studying the Order lectures. Invariable they have had to use supplementary work; and in more than one place the lectures are positively confusing.

The text on Geomancy is good, but is almost a word for word crib of one in my possession, written about 1830. This never was printed, so far as I know; but I learned all my geomancy from it, years before I heard of the Order.

Yet I concede your point that one who enters the Order prepared to work will find there a lot of material that is not easily found outside. The Order does teach a coherent system in the main, and deserves to be perpetuated on that account. But it does not teach a system which has been restricted to circles of obligated initiates, and in the variant of the G.D. which was active in America under the direction of S.R.M.D. and V.N.R. precisely that claim was not only implied, but was also directly stated. Thus I am glad to find in Miss Hughes' letter not a little evidence that she and her fellow Chiefs put the emphasis rather on the work itself than upon any notion of "apostolic succession" from the "original" Rosicrucian Fraternity.

A special interest in the very things that are the backbone of the Order system had made me unusually familiar with most of the material long before I entered it. Circumstances enabled me to make a good livelihood by working about three hours daily; and most of my spare time was spent in the excellent libraries of New York and Chicago, where there is a wealth of material for the research worker in this field. Perhaps the fact that I was actually born in a public library (or, at least, in the house where it was located) helped me to get on the track of the essential material comparatively early in life. I am sure, too, that I had direct help from the Third Order, though when that help was received I did not identify where it came from.

At all events, with the exception of some more or less speculative material in the Flying Rolls, the technique of the Tattvas, and the actual ceremonials of consecration of implements, together with the ritual of the Pentagram and Hexagram, I found nothing in the Order texts that had not been long in print. Which is, of course, no criticism of the value of the Order's curriculum, but merely an evidence that in obligating its members, those who were responsible for the obligation permitted it to be assumed that the bulk of the Order's knowledge could be gained nowhere else. And I contend that no good can come of any sort of trading in the probable ignorance of another. Much better would be the frank admission that the curriculum of the Order is an eclectic combination of knowledge and practices which have been found to be valuable. And precisely that admission is what our present variant of the old pattern does make to all its new members.

Believing, then, that the present European form of the G.D., as you know it, is undoubtedly preserving much that is worthwhile, and that in its higher grades there are those who have established, as we have in America, real contact with the Third Order, I am as strong for "orthodoxy" as any one. But I submit that "orthodoxy" simply means "correct teaching" and that the burden of my criticism is that MacGregor (and nobody else) introduced alien elements into the stream which seems to have come to us through Mackenzie, Levi and their contemporaries. In eliminating the Enochian elements, we in America have lost nothing of practical effectiveness. And from what Miss Hughes says, I believe it likely that there have been some reforms in the grade rituals below 5=6, as you work them.

At any rate, it is good to know that on both sides of the Atlantic there are serious workers who are following out the pattern of the Tree of Life. And I certainly hope we can work out some way in which to co-ordinate our efforts.

Yours fraternally, Perseverantia

2401 Hanscom Drive South Pasadena, Cal. August 10th, 1933.

Israel Regardie, Esq., American Express Co., 6, Haymarket,
London, S. W. 1.

Dear Sir and Brother:

Your prompt response to my letter came as a welcome surprise when I returned from a three-day retreat into the dunes at Oceano, about 200 miles north of this place. I hasten to answer because I see that my somewhat hastily written screed led you into a not unnatural misinterpretation of that part of my letter which had to do with Dam-Car.
not without significance that in some old Hindu representations of Agni that god is shown as a lamb carrying a notched banner, on which is blazoned a swastika. This symbol is the same as the familiar Agnus Dei of the Roman church, and some hint that the G.D. ritual-sources included this knowledge is to be found in the passages dealing with Abiegnus.
It is curious, too, that the letters K and R, or at any rate the sounds now indicated by these letters, begin the name Krishna, compose the Egyptian name for Horus (hieroglyphically "put in Egyptian symbols for Horus here"), are shown again in the Chi-Ro, and are the first two sounds in the name ChVRM, Hiram, according to one spelling—the one used in the Biblical reference whence the 3rd degree allegory is drawn.

The practical point, which is certainly susceptible to verification, is that initiation is in some sense a chemical process, involving subtle changes in the bloodstream of the initiate.

Yoga breathing, for example, has a tendency to raise the carbon monoxide content of the blood, just as does the inhalation of tobacco smoke. Patanjali is careful to tell us that the Siddhis may be brought into manifestation by chemical means, by which he intends to indicate the use of certain drugs. (To be sure the reaction from these drugs makes them unsatisfactory for the purpose of genuine unfoldment; it being, so to say, too high a price to pay for the Siddhis). But it seems to me very clear that all practices leading to this evolution of our latent powers must include the chemical changes I have referred to. Hence Brother C.R. meets the Wise Men

296

in the temple of the Blood of the Lamb—or, in plain language, one establishes rapport with the Chiefs of the Invisible Order because of subtle physiological changes in one's own body, and particularly in the chemical state of the blood-stream. Yoga practice brings about these changes. So does ceremonial magic. So do some kinds of ascetic practice. So do drugs. But I agree with you that for the right sort of temperament there is no method more suitable than ceremonial magic. And here I am, as you are, dealing with the results of prolonged experiment. The Qabalistic interpretation of C.R. and of Dam-Car is but the recognition of a formula which sums up an experience. The more so because the Temple is in Arabia, which place-name means "desert," or "sterile," and so corresponds exactly to the temporary state of Brahmacharya which is indispensable to success in this kind of practice, as it is, in lesser measure, to success in say, boxing or foot-racing. But temporary only, observe, hence the Fama says that C.R. bargained with the Arabians for a specific sum. And this, too, after he had obliged to tarry in Damascus ("work") by reason of the feebleness of his body. Notwithstanding which feebleness he gained favor with the Turks by reason of his skill in physic. Consider that the Turks belong to a wave of development in the human organism preceding that to which we belong—the Mongolian powers of physical recuperation are probably known to you—and this becomes plain enough. After the transmutation of "Brother P.A.L." at Cyprus (birth-place of Venus, and easternmost island in the Mediterranean Sea) C.R. continues his journey, stops at Damascus, hears of the Wise Men, and then abandons his quest for "the abode of peace" (Jerusalem). As a result of his training at Dam-Car he translates the Liber Mundi into Latin, the language of science. (Compare Boehme's declaration that in his brief first period of illumination the book of nature was opened to him). Then he goes down into Egypt to study plants and animals. Thence to Fez, the intellectual center of that period, where he found the Qabalah mixed with the errors of their religion—just as the Reception has always been distorted by mere intellectuality.

The whole thing adapts itself perfectly to the actual experience one goes through. But it offers no comfort whatever to Christian orthodoxy, or to Christian heterodoxy, for that matter.

As to the circumstances which led to my rejection of the historic pretensions of the G.D., they are, in brief, as follows:

297

1. I became a member of Thoth-Hermes Temple (established, I believe, in the late nineties by S.R.M.D., who conferred the honorary degree of 7=4 upon a Mrs. Lockwood, then an associate of W.Q. Judge. She went to Paris to get her contact with S.R.M.D., and Thoth-Hermes languished along as a little group of serious thinkers until Michael Whitty came into it.) My initiation followed the publication of my Tarot articles in THE WORD and AZOTH, in both of which magazines I gave the correct attribution of the major trumps to the Hebrew alphabet. This I had arrived at by what then seemed to me to be independent research, before anything was published about it in the Equinox, or elsewhere. Since then I have found out, of course, that my research was by no means so "independent" as I supposed.

2. A quarrel among the chiefs of Thoth-Hermes led to the withdrawal of Mrs. Lockwood, the then Praemonstrator and her husband, who was Imperator. S.R.M.D. being now dead, V.N.R. appointed Whitty's sister as Imperatrix Howard Underhill (an excellent astrologer) as Cancellarius, and Whitty as Praemonstrator, with myself as Sub-Praemonstrator. This was early in 1918. Whitty's health failed as a direct result of magical practices based on Order formulae, but sadly deficient in adequate protection, and at his death I became Praemonstrator

3. N.R., supposedly 7=4 in fact, then began to display extraordinary misunderstanding of the American situation. She encouraged a Frater in Chicago to initiate anybody possessed of $10 (by mail), and soon the country was flooded with Neophytes who had never seen the inside of a Temple. She also muddled a situation which arose in Thoth-Hermes so badly that certain of us who were heart and soul devoted to the welfare of the Order, and had then no doubts as to its authenticity, became convinced that she, at least, was no representative of the Secret Chiefs, nor possessed even the lesser clairvoyance which should have enabled her to straighten out the situation.

4. Then, for the first time, I began to examine the evidences we had as to the claims of the G.D. Brodie-Innes made solemn asseverations that he had verified them, but offered nothing in the way of evidence. And just at this juncture I began to examine the rituals and knowledge-lectures, etc. that were supposed to be in the direct line of historical descent from

the original Foundation. I found nothing that was not in print prior to the establishment of the G.D., except certain negligible contributions to the Flying Rolls, and the material on the Tattvas.

But the Tattva instruction was so evidently pirated without the slightest acknowledgement from Rama Prasad's Nature's Finer Forces that Brodie-Innes himself recognized the necessity of a revision of the text. The rituals had two "high spots," as we say in America. The first was the Neophyte ceremony, the second the Vault ceremony. The others were, as A.C. has remarked, turgidly written parades of the occult information possessed by S.R.M.D., and written in a style so peculiarly his own that nobody could mistake it.

5.The magical ceremonials, aside from the pseudo-Egyptian interpretation of the two rituals just mentioned, revolved largely around Dee's and Kelly's tablets. Now, I am far from denying that one gets results of a kind by the use of these tablets. Nor would I go so far as to say that the Enochian language is to be disregarded by any student of magic. On the other hand, it is not beyond the power of man to invent a coherent language. I did that very thing as a boy. On a grander scale we have Volapuk, Esperanto, and Id o. To say nothing of the language of Mars, which you may find in that interesting volume "From India to the Planet Mars," by Flournoy.

My criticism of this part of the G.D. work is: (First) that it emanated so largely from Kelly; (Second) That the tablets are part of a rigmarole by which Kelly persuaded Dee that they two were to be the puppet-masters of a new European political order which should supersede the kingdoms then reigning; (Third) That the same angel who dictated the Tablets also required that Kelly and Dee should have all things in common, including their wives; (Fourth) That the whole project came to the same ignominious end that is to be expected of human undertakings based upon the promises of spirits; (Fifth) That there is no good reason to suppose that Kelly and Dee, or their enterprise, to say nothing of their magic, correspond to anything Rosicrucian; (Sixth, and most important) That I have personal knowledge of more than twenty-five instances where the performance of magical operations based on Order formulae led to serious disintegrations of mind or body. From this last I have been preserved by the fact that my elevation to the Office of Praemonstrator came just before my advancement to the office of Hierophant, so that I never performed the Hierophant's part of the rituals. And these investigations I have just mentioned came to pass just before I had completed preparations for the actual use of the formulas available to the 5 = 6 Grade. Perhaps the most conspicuous example of the unfortunate consequences of the use of these formulas is A.C. himself; but there are plenty of others that I know personally whose personal shipwreck has been just as complete, even though their smaller tonnage, so to say, makes the loss seem less deplorable than the disintegration of that great genius whom I admire and love just as much as you do, though my personal contact with him has been of the slightest. Judging from your Tree of Life, you will be ready to break several lances with me on this last criticism. Let me say again, then, that I do not question at all the magical efficacy of some of the formulas. S.R.M.D. knew a lot about magic (more than he did about Qabalah, it seems to me), but there was a twist in his make-up that made him

a most dangerous guide, as many have found to their cost. The whole Enochian procedure is indubitably potent. So are some of the practices of Obeah, to which I have given long study, ever since I spent my childhood winters in the British West Indies.

So, too, are mescal buttons, and hashish, and opium, and even Scotch whiskey. But even as the Chinese in Lamb's essay had to learn sooner or later that it is not necessary to burn down a house to roast a pig, so, I fear, will those who rely on G.D. formulas for magic learn to their cost, perhaps too late, that there is far more to magic than getting results.

6. It is perfectly true that the Vault ritual "does something" to those who are ready for it when they receive it. It did to me, and to several others of my acquaintance. I believe that the potency of this ritual and the effectiveness of the Neophyte initiation are explicable on the theory that S.R.M.D. came into possession of certain rituals that probably emanated from the circle of which Kenneth Mackenzie and Eliphas Levi were members. It is part of my definitely verified

knowledge that the Tarot material in the G.D. is a partial representation of work done by Mackenzie, and left in Mss. At his death. But all this has nothing whatever to do with the G.D.'s explicit claim that it has warrants from the "original Rosicrucian Order" established by an actual person whose mystical name was Christian Rosenkreutz. That there is an Invisible Rosicrucian Order I am perfectly sure. That it inspired the Fama and Confessio I fully believe. That there have been societies working on the R.C. pattern, which is that of the Tree of Life, I also doubt not at all.

But that the G.D., which V.N.R., before her death, was accustomed to call "my order," is in the authorized line of descent from such a society established in any period around the 1400's or 1500's I most seriously doubt. After all, a tree is known by its fruits. Also by its roots.

And one of the tap-roots of the G.D. historical claim is the cipher manuscript from which the rituals were composed. Waite, in his big book on the Order, published a photograph of a page of that Ms. It is fairly easy to decipher, and it contains the anachronism pointed out in his comment. It refers to the "Egyptian Funerary Ritual" when the fact is that the Book of the Dead is not only not that, but was not known at all by that title at the period when the cipher was supposed to be written.

"Evidence of continuity which is practically incontrovertible" I have, and on the grounds you mention. But the continuity is of a stream of inner relationship. Even when one enters an organization built on false pretense, he must encounter some truth. And those who have been in the Vault have made their contact with the True and Invisible Order, not because of the historical claims of S.R.M.D. with reference to the G.D., but because there are actually true formulas among the hotch-potch of good and bad and indifferent which one finds •in the "esoteric" literature of the G.D. Even that ridiculous Rosicrucian impostor, Spencer Lewis, who heads the A.M.O.R.C., cannot avoid getting some good stuff into his lessons, and I have known two or three persons who actually made their first contact with the real thing through his Order. What I object to in the G.D. is the subtle mixture of really poisonous material with so much that is of value. And to get rid of the poison has been my principal undertaking form more than ten years.

The consequence has been that I have been obliged, as you suspect, to formulate the rituals anew. But there is no pretense to the sort of historical continuity that is offered by Lewis, or Plummer, or Clymer, or the G.D., or any other "true Rosicrucian Order." Neither is there any blind reliance upon invisible Chiefs in the astral plane or other "higher worlds." But one who addresses himself to the work does find that, as in the Fama, one who tarries in Damascus long enough to master the infirmities of his body does hear of the Wise Men at Dam-Car. An in due course he makes his firsthand contact with those Wise Men, has his eyes opened, and makes his own personal translation from the book M. After which he follows out, step by step, the course marked in the Fama, reproducing in his own experience the incidents of that allegory.

As to Fohat, that was a "feeler." I share your feeling about H.P.B. as a Cabalist, and your anathema against Skinner is the voicing of my own thought. Nevertheless, if there is anything Tibetan called "Fohat" (which I sometimes doubt, as I doubt everything from H.P.B.) It is too much like Shakti not to belong to Teth and Key 8.

And of course Shakti has her place in Binah. Yet precisely that, it seems to me, makes Shakti belong also in the 19th path. For if there be one thing that Qabalah seems to reiterate, it is this: "Never forget, you who aspire to the Reception, that all the various categories are but aspects of the One Thing, seen from different points of view. The whole Tree is in any Sephirah. Equally is the whole Tree present in any single path.

Poor Frater Achad! He tried to interest me in the "purple papers," and did so to the extent that I traced them to one source in Washington, D.C., although that, naturally, was only a relay-station, and the persons active in it knew almost nothing of their actual superiors. I have a notion as to what is really behind the scenes, for this is not the only; thing of the sort I have encountered. The idea seems always to keep the member so busy with nonessentials and with reading that he does little or no work. Just crams himself with words, or busies himself with distributing papers—for which service in extracting generous contributions from the undiscriminating he receives as recompense a high-sounding Sanskrit title!

One of my occasional correspondents writes me that he has been in touch with you-Sidney French, of New York City. He is really trying to learn something, and do something with what he learns. I am glad to hear that you are in communication.

As to my books, there are only three—An Introduction to the Study of the Tarot, which is a reprint of twelve papers published in AZOTH (and a dreadfully inadequate performance); An Analysis of the Tarot (based on Waite's Keys, and pretty bad); and The True and Invisible Rosicrucian Order. The last is now out-of-print. It was done on the mimeograph, and then bound in a small edition. I intend getting out a large edition in the near future, done, probably, in the same way. Most of my work is in the form of correspondence lessons, and most of the lessons are subscribed to by persons whom I encounter by the peculiar American device of giving public lectures and then forming private classes. It is one of the most loathsome of the products of American civilization, and I am so thoroughly fed up with it that I am now beginning to experiment with another method of getting in touch with students who will really work.

As this method will involve the rearrangement of the whole curriculum, all of this revolving around the Tarot and the Tree of Life, it seems unlikely that I shall get a real Tarot book written for some time to come. Our problems in this country are peculiar, and have to be met in the way that solves them, irrespective of personal preference for more stately ways of procedure. But I'm having a good time doing the only thing that seems to be worth doing. And though one has to blow away a lot of chaff, there do remain some grains of real wheat in the persons of determined workers who sooner or later "make the grade."

Your Brother in L.V.X.,

Perseverantia (signature)

5=6

Index

307

A Special Invitation

The Fraternity of the Hidden Light, also known as the **Fraternitas L.V.X. Occulta,** is an initiatic, teaching and healing Order of the Western Mystery Tradition. We are dedicated to the practical study of the Arcane Sciences.

Entry into the Fraternity is by invitation only, after the completion of preliminary studies. Membership is opened to all sincere seekers without regard to age, gender, sexual orientation, ethnicity or religion. Examples of areas of study are: History of the Western Tradition, Symbolism of the Sacred Tarot, The Hermetic Qabalah, Esoteric Psychology, and Theurgy.

Sincere aspirants may request further information by writing to:

The Director of Probationers
The Fraternity of the Hidden Light
P.O. Box 836432
Richardson, TX 75083-6432
U.S.A.

Or by visiting our web site:

lvx.org

Lightning Source UK Ltd.
Milton Keynes UK
UKHW010656021220
374498UK00001B/56